Dangerous Injustice

RealClear
Publishing

www.amplifypublishinggroup.com

Dangerous Injustice: How Democrats Weaponized the DOJ to Protect Biden and Persecute Trump

For more information, please contact:
RealClear Publishing, an imprint of Amplify Publishing Group
620 Herndon Parkway, Suite 220
Herndon, VA 20170
info@amplifypublishing.com

ISBN-13: 979-8-89138-503-0

Printed in the United States

To my spiritual advisors,
Clarkus Maximus, Cruzan6, #31,
Sunny and Company,
and my favorite uncle, Paul.

Dangerous Injustice

How Democrats Weaponized the DOJ to Protect Biden and Persecute Trump

Joseph B. Sweeney

RealClear Publishing

CONTENTS

PART III

Trumping Up Espionage Charges

PART IV

A Uniform Vigilance

INTRODUCTION

Washington's Warnings

Published in 1796, George Washington's "Farewell Address to the People of the United States" was a twenty-six-page love letter to the young nation, from the man who, in so many ways, had helped birth it and raise it through adolescence. All but forgotten today, Washington's Farewell is little more than a footnote in the history books, cited mostly for Washington's warning to avoid foreign entanglements and wars. But Washington's Farewell also prophetically warned of two other potentially fatal threats to the nation: regional factions and political party passions.

"Factions" was Washington's term for strong regional interests that he feared could prevail over, and destroy, national unity. The first president implored the different regions of the fledgling country to focus on their common bonds of nationhood. "The name of American, which belongs to you, in your national capacity, must always exalt the just pride of patriotism more than any appellation derived from local discriminations." Washington lectured the burgeoning nation that its liberty was inextricably intertwined with national union. "The unity of government which constitutes you one people" he emphasized, "is a main pillar in the edifice of your real independence."

Washington's fateful warning against the danger of factions, unfortunately, went unheeded. As northern states came to rightly view slavery as a stain on the nation, wanting it outlawed, southern states, which benefited economically from the evil practice, opposed the North's efforts. Instead of seeking a nationwide solution to end slavery, the two factions increasingly vilified and alienated each other, leading to civil war. More American soldiers died in that war than all other American wars combined.

As for the other danger raised in his Farewell Address—political party passions—the Founding Father had especially strong admonitions. "Let me now . . . warn you in the most solemn manner against the baneful effects of the spirit of party." While conceding that political passion was a "fire not to be quenched," Washington also sternly warned that it "demands a uniform vigilance to prevent it bursting into a flame, lest instead of warming it should consume." Washington beseeched his fellow citizens to fortify themselves against their darker angels. "You cannot shield yourselves too much against the jealousies and heart burnings" from the basest emotions raised by party bickering, which "tend to render alien to each other those who ought to be bound together by fraternal affection." After diagnosing this potentially fatal disease, Washington prescribed the cure: "the common and continual mischiefs of the spirit of party are sufficient to make it the interest and the duty of a wise people to discourage and restrain it." That prescription is still valid today. But We the Patients have not been following doctor's orders. Party-driven dissensions have come to define the country, and instead of discouraging or restraining, we have been amplifying them. Having failed to shield our hearts and minds, we are eroding the fraternal affection we should naturally have for each other, fostering condescending and irrational hatreds, destroying friendships, marriages, familial attachments, and neighborly bonds.

Worse yet, these two potentially fatal diseases Washington identified—factions and political party passions—have, to some extent, merged. In Washington's era, factions were defined by geographic boundaries. Today, they are often defined by population density. Big cities versus rural areas. And big cities tend to be dominated by one political party, while the rural areas are mostly dominated by the other. Faction and party passions—each potentially lethal standing alone—have largely melded, compounding their deadliness.

Danger from this merger is further intensified by the metamorphosis of modern-day American politics into the new opiate of the masses. Spiritual certitude, a necessary and salutary component of religious faith, has spread into politics, where it is most unhealthy. Party leaders are now worshiped like Messianic figures, and criticizing someone's political party—even challenging their party's position on any issue—is now akin to attacking religious belief. As each party has come to view itself as righteous and good, and the opposing party as corrupt and evil, battle lines are drawn along holy and unholy. Civil debate and compromise are among the casualties when the options are narrowed to victory for one side and defeat for the other, or protracted war. Inability to work together leaves only brute force, winner-take-all politics, with all the accompanying grudges and vengeful feelings. Exactly what our first president, long ago, cautioned against: "The alternate domination of one faction over another, sharpened by the spirit of revenge natural to party dissension."

Party passions in Washington's time were at least constrained by the relatively primitive means to fan the flames: newspapers, pamphlets, town square speeches. Even then—even when party passions were consigned to the printing press and vocal cords—Washington feared the unrestrained spirit of party. Today, technology permits us to mainline party histrionics and hysterias, at will, in real time. Shielding ourselves from the "baneful effects of the spirit of party" is nearly impossible, and we have not displayed the fortitude to resist injecting divisive, drug-of-choice news streams directly into our systems.

Voltaire once wrote that "whoever can make you believe absurdities can make you commit atrocities." The witty and insightful French philosopher based his observation on the rationale that once "one faculty of your soul has been dominated, other faculties will follow as well." Human nature has not changed, and nowhere is this more evident than in modern-day American politics, which has caused people to believe an abundance of absurdities. The word "woman" cannot be defined. There are more than two sexes. Walls don't work. COVID-19 could not have originated in a lab. Hunter Biden's laptop was not Hunter Biden's laptop. Trump wants you to inject bleach into your veins. Parents opposed to sex education for third graders are domestic terrorists. Donald Trump is an existential threat to democracy who will end the Republic, and he must be stopped at all costs. Joe Biden is the sharpest guy in the room—he just had a bad night, a cold, and was *overprepared*.

Those who were made to believe in these absurdities—and many more—would have no problem committing, or at least fully supporting, the atrocities of injustice that were sure to follow.

Perhaps it was inevitable that, as you will soon see, the nation would devolve to a point where a reigning political party, on the thinnest of legal veneers, would brazenly usurp the justice system to eliminate a political rival. Perhaps it was inevitable that the Democratic party's vilification and attempted political assassinations of Donald Trump would create an atmosphere that would lead to an actual assassination attempt, which occurred while this book was going to print. For years President Biden and the Democratic party whipped up political rage amongst their ranks by repeatedly labeling Trump as "Hitler," "a demagogue," and an "existential threat to democracy" who would destroy America's freedoms and our Republic. As Voltaire wisely noted so many years ago, once "one faculty of your soul has been dominated, other faculties will follow as well." And so perhaps it was inevitable that emotionally and mentally vulnerable people would become so dominated by the rageful rhetoric their political party relentlessly hammered into them—"Trump is

Hitler!"—that the loss of other faculties would follow, permitting a belief that murder is acceptable, and even salutary.

If we are to survive as a nation, we must heed Washington's urgings to vigilance and restraint and start weening ourselves off the daily helpings of alienations. For if we do not, the hunger pangs driven by party politics will devour our few remaining bonds of fraternal affection. We must return to a culture of greater civility and tolerance, a culture where in challenging times, fairness and justice prevail over the tyranny of those who have smugly convinced themselves that their ends justify their means. But as you will soon see, in disturbing detail, there is much damage to be undone, the most prevalent being the weaponization of the government, particularly the justice system, against a political rival.

CHAPTER 1

American Stasi

Examples of the Democratic Party's corruption of the American justice system for political means can be traced back to at least former President Donald Trump's 2016 presidential campaign. Continuing and escalating throughout Trump's presidency, and after, the aggressive weaponization of federal law enforcement against Trump reached the unimaginable when on August 8, 2022, thirty Federal Bureau of Investigation (FBI) agents, armed and authorized to use deadly force, raided the home of the former president of the United States. As Americans were witnessing this ignoble first in their nation's history, FBI agents were searching every inch of Donald Trump's home, seizing every single document from Trump's presidency. They even took his passport.

Before the raid, most Americans assumed that such an event could only happen in a third-world country, police state, or nation ruled by an oppressive regime. And they were right. They just didn't realize their country had become the latter two.

Sitting President Joe Biden's administration subsequently filed two criminal indictments against Biden's strongest political rival: one for interfering with the 2020 presidential election and another for violating the Espionage Act by mishandling classified information. These indictments were also firsts in American history, for no former president had ever faced federal indictment, let alone by an administration of the opposing political party. And no presidential administration had ever prosecuted the presumed challenger to the incumbent in the upcoming presidential election.

Ironically, while the Biden administration was prosecuting Trump for retaining classified documents from his presidency, it learned that Biden had also retained classified documents from his time as a senator and vice president. After covering up Biden's malfeasance for months, his administration was eventually forced to acknowledge the discovery—but they still hid the details of Biden's illicit conduct from the public.

Now, both the current and former presidents were being investigated for potential Espionage Act violations. But as I will show, these highly political investigations were handled *very* differently.

To understand the extent to which political party affiliation determined the conduct of these investigations, you need to understand the cases against Biden and Trump, and to understand the cases, you need to understand how national defense information is classified and protected. As a former Central Intelligence Agency (CIA) lawyer, I spent decades working with classified information—and supporting investigations and prosecutions of the mishandling and theft thereof. Therefore, I'm particularly well suited to provide this needed context.

As with many legal matters, precedent is important—which is why I'll review the few historical cases (most of which I worked on) where senior government officials were caught mishandling classified information. These cases involved fairly arcane laws and legal doctrines, but I have done my best to explain them in a manner that anyone can understand. All the cases where high-ranking officials mishandled classified information are, not surprisingly, saturated with politics. Every action and every inaction in these cases has a political undercurrent, crosscurrent, undertow, or outright tidal wave, and one cannot honestly analyze the cases without examining the politics. So be forewarned: the political autopsies you will witness, especially in Trump's case, are graphic and disturbing.

After absorbing all this background, the stark disparities and political biases between the historical precedents and Trump's case—and between Biden's and Trump's cases—will be shockingly clear. As will the necessity for a spectrum of reforms. Along those lines, I will share some thoughts on how we can improve the nation's political climate and offer blueprints for structural reforms to help prevent any future president or political party from ever again usurping the American justice system to persecute political opponents and retain power.

So, prepare yourself. You are going to see, through the eyes of an insider, your government at its worst. You are going to see how a political party turned American law enforcement into nothing less than the American Stasi.

PART I

Matters of National Security

CHAPTER 2

Classifying & Protecting

Presidential Executive Orders: From Cradle to Grave

Every president since Franklin Delano Roosevelt has, through presidential executive order, mandated a system for safeguarding national security information through classification.

Executive orders are not the law of the land, as they do not pass through the constitutionally required legislative process for enacting federal law, but they are a form of federal law, as they establish law and policy within and for the executive branch of the U.S. government. Basically, executive orders assist the executive in governing itself.

The U.S. Supreme Court has examined and upheld the legality of executive orders classifying information. In doing so, the court acknowledged that the legal bedrock for classified information is executive power: "The President, after all, is the Commander in Chief of the Army and Navy," and the "authority to classify and control access to information bearing on national security . . . flows primarily from this constitutional investment of power in the President, and exists quite apart from any explicit congressional grant."[1] It is a basic but important fact: classified information belongs to the executive branch and, specifically, the president of the United States. The judicial branch does not create or control classified information. Congress does not create or control classified information.

The president owns classified information from cradle to grave and every step in between.

Most laws have exceptions, and no branch of our government is completely autonomous even within its own sphere. Checks and balances, incorporated into every aspect of the U.S. Constitution, are much more pervasive, nuanced, and intricate than most realize, as the framers believed that absolute power, anywhere, would be abused (and history has proven them wise). Much of our constitution is really designed to curb human behavior and the tyranny of the majority, which the framers experienced firsthand under the Articles of Confederation that preceded the Constitution. So, no one branch of government reigns supreme, even within its own domain, and I emphasize this to acknowledge that there are exceptions—minor ones—into the president's domain of classified information, and I will discuss some of them at appropriate times. But they are minor, and they do not negate the basic truth that classified information is born, raised, and buried within the executive branch.

To protect the classified information it creates, the executive has promulgated many restrictive rules and procedures for marking, compartmenting, storing, transporting, discussing, accessing, destroying, and declassifying.

Under the current executive order governing classified information (Executive Order 13526, which was issued by President Barack Obama and took effect in 2010), to be eligible for classification information must fall within one of eight specific categories. These categories are predictable, including things like military plans, intelligence activities, and foreign relations.

Executive Order 13526 (and every order since 1953) has three levels of classification: CONFIDENTIAL, SECRET, and TOP SECRET. Classification level is determined by degree of likely damage to national security that reasonably could be expected to result from unauthorized disclosure of the information. Information is TOP SECRET if unauthorized disclosure reasonably could be expected to cause "exceptionally grave damage." It is SECRET if "serious damage" is reasonably likely. And it is CONFIDENTIAL if just "damage" is reasonably likely to occur.

For at least the last three decades, executive orders have created two categories of officials authorized to classify information: *original classifiers* and *derivative classifiers.* Original classifiers include the president, vice president, and agency heads and officials designated by the president. Agency heads are also permitted to delegate, in writing, original classification authority to a small number of agency officers. Given the small number of original classifiers, over 99 percent of executive branch officers classify information as derivative, not original, classifiers. Derivative classifiers classify information pursuant to classification guides created by their agency, and the guides list many categories of information and provide detailed guidance for classifying those categories.

When I first started at the CIA, I stressed over every document I drafted, diligently thumbing through the CIA classification guide to ensure that I was not overclassifying or underclassifying whatever I was composing. Even a one-sentence internal email could be a source of consternation. We, of course, had detailed training on how to classify information, but when you are sitting alone in your office and drafting classified documents for the first time, it can be intimidating. After a while, I had the classification guide mostly memorized. The guide was thick, but my duties required me to frequently consult the guide.

I spent over half of my CIA career in the Litigation Division of the CIA Office of General Counsel as line attorney, deputy, acting chief, and, eventually, chief, where one of my primary duties was to draft or supervise the drafting of sworn declarations for original classifiers for filing in federal courts. These declarations explained to federal judges the classification system generally and the specific classified information at issue in the case or controversy before the court. The declarations were often filed under seal because they themselves were classified. As a result of these duties, I am much more familiar with the ins and outs of classification than the typical executive branch employee with a security clearance, even though I was, like most, a derivative classifier.

Many rules pertaining to classified information are contained in agency-internal directives, but the basic requirements are listed right in the executive order, and some are quite detailed. For instance, Executive Order 13526 expressly requires bi-annual training on classification for derivative classifiers and yearly training for original classifiers. Agency directives require higher-level security for more highly classified information, and the most sensitive classified information must be stored in a sensitive compartmented information facility (SCIF).

A SCIF could be just one room or an entire building, and there are detailed requirements for building and maintaining SCIFs. Some classified information is so sensitive that, even when contained in a SCIF, it needs to be stored separately in a safe. In addition to varying storage requirements, different levels of classified information may also need to be disposed of differently. As a new CIA employee, I recall holding a yellow Post-it Note in my hand, and given what was scribbled on it, I was sweating over which garbage bag to throw it into.

At the TOP SECRET level, information is often further compartmented. This may be an oversimplification, but think of compartmented TOP SECRET information as a jigsaw puzzle where each puzzle piece represents a compartment, and you need to be granted access for that compartment before you could see what's on that puzzle piece. If you see "TOP SECET SCI" at the top of a document, that means the information has been further compartmented as sensitive compartmented information (SCI).

The requirements for marking classified documents are voluminous and complicated. There are detailed rules for labeling headers and footers; marking paragraphs; and recording the identity of the classifier, reason for classification, etc. These rules apply to all documents, including handwritten notes. And if someone negligently forgets to add classification markings to a document containing classified information, that does not mean the document is not classified or the sensitive information in the document has been declassified. This is often misunderstood, but failure to properly mark a document containing classified information simply means that the document was not properly marked even though it was, and remains, classified. And if a lower-level executive branch officer mistakenly publicly releases classified information, with markings or without, the executive branch is not somehow bound by the mistake. It will refuse to confirm or deny the accuracy of the mistakenly released information and continue to treat it as classified everywhere else.

Conversations involving classified information can only occur in cleared areas such as SCIFs, and if you are on a phone, a classified conversation must be over a secure line that is approved for the level of classified information you are discussing. As a CIA lawyer, I had different phones on my desk for different types of conversations. A normal phone line, in government speak, is an "unsecure" or "open" line because there is no encryption, and anyone could be listening. As a business practice in the intelligence community, whenever you are speaking on an open line, you assume your adversaries are listening. After years of working with classified information, you learn how to converse on an open line while avoiding sensitive details.

I have had thousands of conversations that went like this: "Remember the guy overseas you wanted me to talk to about that thing? Well, I finally talked to him, and he gave me the details on how he got the information from that other guy—I think the details will be helpful for you, but I can't get into them on this line. Can you get to a secure line?"

Access to classified information is strictly controlled by the executive branch, and the basic requirements for access are dictated in the executive order. To be granted access to classified information, an individual must: (1) have the appropriate security clearance; (2) sign a nondisclosure agreement; and (3) have a need-to-know. Many executive branch employees only have SECRET level clearances, which can be granted after basic background checks and are relatively easy to obtain compared to TOP SECRET clearances. The process for obtaining a TOP SECRET SCI clearance is extensive, and, at my agency, included a background investigation, interview, financial checks, a polygraph test, a physical exam, and a psychological exam.

After taking my applicant psychological test, I was required to meet with an agency psychiatrist. The psychiatrist only had one question for me, and it was something very generic along the lines of a Freudian, "Why didn't you love your mother growing up?" I said there must be a misunderstanding because I had always loved my mother. Then he pointed me to my answer to a question on my exam, and I saw that I had mismarked a multiple-choice box because I was moving too quickly through the test. After I explained the error, we both had a good laugh, I chatted about my mom a bit, and he told me I was free to go.

There was no laughing at my polygraph test. The agency is hypersensitive about protecting details about the test, and for good reason: foreign intelligence services are constantly attempting to penetrate the tempested walls of the CIA, and they would love to know how to prepare their spies for all the tests they would face to gain entry, particularly the polygraph. It is not well known but is a matter of public law that the CIA director has the authority under the Privacy Act to exempt categories of files from being subject to Privacy Act requests. When I was practicing (and I doubt this has changed), the only category of files for which the CIA director had exercised this authority was polygraph records. So, if a current or former CIA employee made a formal request for their polygraph records, the agency would deny the request without even searching, and that response is perfectly legal because the authority for the denial is explicitly granted in the law. All this is a long way of saying that the agency protects polygraph-related information like a momma bear protects her cubs.

Anyway, I was a little wild in high school, and there were some things from that time I really did not want to talk about during my polygraph test, but the damn polygrapher quickly figured out what I really did not want to talk about and was adamant that I tell him everything about the things that I really did not want to talk about. So, the test was very unpleasant. Two days of unpleasant. I saw the polygrapher years later as I was entering the CIA cafeteria to get a sandwich. I skipped lunch.

If you pass all the tests (and trust me, you should just tell them everything right up front, especially the stuff you really don't want to talk about), then you need to sign a nondisclosure agreement that includes lifelong legal obligations. The forms vary, but the CIA form (and probably all intelligence agency forms) requires you to relinquish some First Amendment rights, as it contains an explicit prepublication review clause. That clause requires the signatory to seek and obtain executive branch approval before publishing anything that basically pertains to work performed for the government. This requirement, which has been upheld by the U.S. Supreme Court, is a good example of the sacrifices one must make for the privilege of doing sensitive work for the U.S. government.[2] No one is forced to accept this lifelong obligation. But if you want a job at the CIA, accept it you must.

Even after passing all the tests, signing a nondisclosure agreement, and receiving a high-level security clearance, you don't just automatically get the keys to the kingdom. You still need to have a bona fide need-to-know for specific classified information before you are granted access to it. "Need-to-know" is defined in the executive order as being required to perform or assist in a lawful and authorized governmental function. That means you only get access to specific classified information that you need to perform your job duties.

Although presidents dictate a spectrum of very strict rules pertaining to how executive branch officers create, access, safeguard, and declassify national security information, that does not mean that a president is bound by any of those rules. He is not. Some commentators have claimed that a president, if he declassified information, would need to ensure his staff removed markings, wrote a memo, stamped the documents as declassified, etc. That is flatly false. As uncomfortable as it may be for you to hear this, a president can declassify the most sensitive of information just because he wants to, and in doing so, he is not bound by any standard or procedure. Because he is the president. A president could declassify information orally, or scribble it on a cocktail napkin with a swizzle stick while quaffing dirty martinis. Everyone below the president must follow his orders, but his orders don't bind the Big Guy himself. President Biden could take a box of classified documents home with him to Delaware for the weekend and, without even bothering to declassify them, scatter them across the sand as a giveaway to sunbathers on Rehoboth Beach. He will have committed no crime. Because the classified information legally and uniquely belongs to him, and he can do whatever he bloody well pleases with it.

You may not like that. But you not liking the law does not change it.

As I mentioned earlier, every area of law has exceptions to the general rules, and national security law is no different. There are minor exceptions to the president owning all classified information from birth to burial, and one of those minor exceptions is a federal statute that safeguards a specific category of national security information: nuclear information. While this category is narrow, it creates overlap with the system of classification under presidential executive order, which can be confusing.

"Nuclear information" is protected by the Atomic Energy Act (AEA). Originally passed in 1946, this federal law established an independent federal entity (the Atomic Energy Commission, now defunct) for promoting the use of atomic energy for peaceful purposes consistent with national security and public safety. Complicated and broad ranging, the AEA is a dense federal statute. If you have difficulty sleeping at night, pull up a copy of the AEA. You will be sleeping soundly before you even get to the definition of "byproduct material."

Among many other things, the AEA established a separate classification system to protect a specific category of information: restricted data (RD). The definition of RD has changed since the initial law was passed, but today it includes data concerning the design, manufacture, or utilization of atomic weapons; production of special nuclear material; and use of special nuclear material in the production of energy. When "classified" by the AEA , nuclear information is simply labeled "RD," as the AEA system does not follow the executive order paradigm of CONFIDENTIAL, SECRET, or TOP SECRET. As a practical matter, this distinction is merely technical. RD is also classified under the executive order, as it pertains to "United States Government programs for safeguarding nuclear materials or facilities" and "the development, production, or use of weapons of mass destruction," which are eligible categories for classification under the order. Hence the confusion, given there is obvious overlap between the two systems for classification.

After its passage, the AEA was amended many times, and one amendment added a new category of AEA classified information: formerly restricted data (FRD). FRD is information that was removed from the RD category because it related primarily to the military utilization of atomic weapons and could be "adequately safeguarded in a manner similar to national security information." That standard—"in a manner similar to national security information"—means classification by presidential executive order. So basically, FRD is information that is classified under just one system—executive order—when previously it was classified under two systems.

This background is helpful in our later analyses of Biden's and Trump's cases, as there was much publicity over Trump possessing "nuclear information." Trump's case did not have any RD but did involve one FRD document. Biden's case involved two FRD documents.

Criminal Laws Covering Classified Information

"Unauthorized Removal & Retention"

Only one law criminalizes theft of information classified under presidential executive order. This law, passed in 1994, was originally only a misdemeanor (maximum sentence of one year in jail). As you will soon see, this law was historically the go-to charge for the Department of Justice (DOJ) when a case involved a high-ranking public official who mishandled classified information, given that the charge was only a misdemeanor. In 2018, the law was upgraded to a felony (over one year in jail and maximum sentence of five years), making it a much more serious crime. Highly specific by design, the law only criminalizes a very specific conduct:

> Whoever, being an officer, employee, contractor, or consultant of the United States, and, by virtue of his office, employment, position, or contract, becomes possessed of documents or materials containing classified information of the United States, knowingly removes such documents or materials without authority and with the intent to retain such documents or materials at an unauthorized location.

While not obvious, this "unauthorized removal and retention" law does not apply to elected officials. The Supreme Court has ruled that the term "officers of the United States" does not include elected officials, and that is the only term in the law that might have included such officials.[3] Members of Congress, vice presidents, and presidents are, therefore, not covered by this law, but it does cover a broad range of federal government officials, all the way up to cabinet members.

Under this law, the removal of classified information must have occurred with "the intent to retain . . . at an unauthorized location." That is a very specific intent element, and if someone removed classified information without the intent to retain it, they would not have violated this law. This may seem like a minor issue—and as a practical matter it probably is, as people don't generally knowingly take classified information without the intent to keep it—but in a criminal case, a prosecutor would have to prove this element beyond a reasonable doubt, because it is an element of the crime.

Lastly, this law only pertains to someone with lawful access who "knowingly" removes classified information. If such a person mistakenly takes a classified document home, they have not violated this law. Over the years I worked on countless cases where, after investigation, it was apparent that someone just made an honest mistake. Those cases are handled as security violations. Security violations are routine and would generally result in a form of administrative punishment, ranging from the minor (oral or written reprimand) to the major (revocation or suspension of security clearance and job termination). If the conduct rises to the level of "gross negligence," an individual could also be facing criminal penalties under the espionage statutes.

The Espionage Act

Although only one criminal law specifically protects classified information, there is another law that protects, more broadly, and potentially much more severely, national defense information (NDI): the Espionage Act. The Espionage Act does not use the term "classified information," because the law was written in the World War I era before presidents started classifying information. Nowadays, NDI is classified by executive order, so as a practical matter, NDI equates to classified information. DOJ has always taken the position—and for good reason—that when it comes to the Espionage Act, if information is not classified, it is not NDI.

While as a practical matter, classified information and NDI are synonymous, as a technical matter, there is an important difference for a prosecutor. Since the Espionage Act only protects NDI, it is not enough for a prosecutor to just show that information was marked classified. Classification is evidence that the executive branch considered specific information to be NDI, not that it *is* NDI, so if a case goes to trial, a prosecutor must still prove that the information at issue is national-defense related. A delicate task, and one which I have extensive experience supporting.

Thus far, I have purposefully avoided using extensive legal citations and legal terms, as they can be confusing and distracting to non-lawyers, and I am not trying to write a legal brief or law review article. But I will include just a bit here, as it is helpful to understand an important line of demarcation in the Espionage Act. While the Espionage Act criminalizes a broad range of conduct, there is an important distinction between conduct covered by the act's two key sections—793 and 794. Think of a prosecution under Section 793 as "espionage light" and a prosecution under Section 794 as "espionage heavy."

Section 793 covers a broad range of illicit activities—from merely attempting to gather NDI, to gathering it, to trying to obtain it, to obtaining it. These crimes include an intent element whereby the individual must have engaged in the conduct "with intent or reason to believe that the information is to be used to the injury of the United States, or to the advantage of any foreign nation." So, it is not a crime to have just engaged in the conduct: the conduct must have been committed with at least a reason to believe that the information would be used to harm the U.S. or aid a foreign country. Proving this specific intent may or may not be difficult, depending upon the evidence in a case, but it is nonetheless a prosecutor's burden to prove this element of the crime beyond a reasonable doubt.

Section 793 also makes it a crime for anyone with either lawful or unauthorized possession of NDI to attempt to transmit or to transmit it to any person not entitled to receive it, or to willfully retain it and fail to deliver it on demand to an officer or employee of the United States entitled to receive it. The intent element for these crimes is different, as it does not require the intent or reason to believe that the NDI is "to be used to the injury of the United States, or to the advantage of any foreign nation." Instead, there is a much lower intent standard: that "the possessor has reason to believe [it] could be used to the injury of the United States or to the advantage of any foreign nation." This means that, for these crimes, the intent element is "could be used" not "to be used." The "could be used" must still be proven beyond a reasonable doubt, but it is a much lower burden for the government.

Lastly, 793 also criminalizes gross negligence in handling NDI. When someone "entrusted with or having lawful possession or control" of NDI "through gross negligence permits the same to be removed from its proper place of custody . . . or to be lost, stolen . . . or destroyed," they have committed a crime. This crime has no specific intent element because gross negligence—a conscious and voluntary disregard of the need to use reasonable care—does not require intent. Gross negligence is more egregious than ordinary negligence (a mere failure to exercise reasonable care). This part of Section 793 also makes it a crime if someone with lawful possession of NDI knows it has been illegally removed from its proper place of custody, lost, stolen, or destroyed, and fails to promptly report it. The maximum sentence for all Section 793 crimes is ten years in prison. That makes 793 a serious felony, but not as serious as Section 794.

Section 794 criminalizes more egregious conduct—"classic espionage"—such as a foreign spy stealing NDI to give it to a foreign country. Punishment under 794 includes life imprisonment or death. So, a Section 794 charge could get you the modern-day equivalent of the Ethel Rosenberg smoking hairdo, which really put the "P" in permanent.

CHAPTER 3

Espionage Investigations & Prosecutions

Throughout my career, I was honored to support some of our nation's top prosecutors, and I gained great respect for the critical role they play in our justice system.

Prosecutors wield enormous power. They can compel testimony; search your home, computer, car, and cell phone; record your conversations; read your mail; obtain your bank records; track your movements; and, ultimately, take away your freedom and—in extreme cases—your life. That awesome power should be used wisely and judiciously, for a prosecutor's mission is not only to seek justice but to seek justice fairly, without bias and without abusing the nearly unchecked power they wield.

While I was privileged in my work at the CIA to assist prosecutors in their pursuit of justice, my focus was not on the success or failure of their endeavors. My job was to protect, to the greatest extent possible, classified information that was implicated by the criminal case. It was exhilarating to work on high-profile criminal cases where the courtrooms were packed with reporters and the daily dramas were featured in the nightly news and the next day's headlines, but my work was done in the shadows, far away from a podium or camera. I spent more time in a judge's chambers than in an open court, and if I drafted a legal document, it was usually filed under seal. The Spanish have a saying: "There is only one who knows, and that is the one who fights the bull." I never fought the bull. But I helped the matador suit up, and I enjoyed ringside seats to the bullfight.

Prosecutors are accustomed to getting what they want, and if they can't get it voluntarily, they can compel it from just about anyone. However, when a criminal case involves classified information—and all espionage prosecutions will—prosecutors must seek permission to use the classified information from the owning entity within the executive branch (in government speak "the equity owner"). When the equity owner is in the intelligence community, quite a bit of negotiation can be involved. Intelligence officers are also accustomed to getting what they want, at least when it comes to protecting their classified information, and they often do not take kindly to their sensitive information being put at risk because of a criminal prosecution. I often found myself acting as a high-stakes mediator between one party aggressively wanting to use information and another party opposed to that information being used. Prosecutors would educate me on why classified information was necessary for their case, and intelligence officers would educate me on the sensitivities of that information and the likely damage from its disclosure. Often, neither party got everything they wanted, but they both got a resolution that they could live with.

After decades walking the strained line between seeking justice and protecting national security, I developed exceptional instincts to balance the inherent tension between those two often conflicting government missions. Criminal cases can impact CIA equities in many ways, and different types of criminal cases required different balancing strategies. The most difficult criminal cases were the ones where all my efforts were focused on keeping the initials "CIA" off the public record, because the CIA's mere involvement was itself a classified fact that needed to be protected. The most exciting cases, by far, were the espionage prosecutions. Those cases involved sensitivities that needed continual protection from public disclosure, but the CIA's presence was generally acknowledged. This permitted me, to a small extent, to step out of the shadows, and the work was particularly exciting, as it was at the core of the spy business.

True Believers

Espionage prosecutions, like all criminal cases, may be resolved through plea agreements and often are, but occasionally a plea cannot be worked out and a case goes to trial. And by chance, the first espionage prosecution I worked on (in the late 1990s) went to trial. I was relatively new to the CIA General Counsel's Office Litigation Division, and more experienced attorneys in the division were carrying full caseloads. So, new cases were going to the new guy. At the time, I did not realize how lucky I was, for many reasons, but I later learned that there had not been any espionage trials in many years. There were espionage prosecutions—major ones—but they had been resolved through plea agreements.

The defendants were Theresa Squillacote, her husband Kurt Stand, and a college friend of theirs, James Clark. All were Cold War–era spies for East German Intelligence (the Stasi). Kurt Stand had been recruited by his father, Maximillian Stand (an old-school Communist) when in college, and the younger Stand then recruited Squillacote and Clark.

Foreign intelligence services know how to spot and exploit human weaknesses. They look for U.S. citizens with vulnerabilities (primarily financial) who either have security clearances and are already "in access" to classified information, or they look for whom they can recruit and then direct into jobs to gain access. Squillacote, Stand, and Clark were the latter, and their weakness was apparently the folly of youth in believing in a governmental system historically proven to be so disastrous that it could only survive through fear, denying basic freedoms, and dictatorship.

In every other espionage case I worked, over many years to come, the motivation was always clear: money. But this was not the case with Squillacote, Stand, and Clark. They were True Believers in Communism, and they did not seek financial reward. Their reward was to assist Communism in bringing down the United States of America.

Squillacote managed to get a job with a security clearance at the Pentagon, so she was the real player. Clark had also obtained a Department of Defense (DOD) job with a security clearance, but it was only as a civilian in a U.S. Army Environmental Division. Stand never obtained a government job. His focus was recruiting, so he went to work for a labor union, which was likely viewed as a target-rich environment for potential recruits.

After East Germany collapsed and the wall fell, the spymaster for the trio, a legendary East German spy named Lothar Ziemer, went to work for the KGB. Ziemer maintained contact with all three in his new capacity, and all three traveled to Germany during this time frame to meet with Ziemer.

In 1992, Ziemer was arrested by the German government for his KGB-related spying activities. It was only after Ziemer's arrest that the trio began openly discussing with each other the details of their covert activities. Spies are trained to compartmentalize information, so while each of the three knew the others were working for the Stasi, the details of their activities were only known by their handler, Ziemer. Ziemer's arrest was the catalyst for them to discuss details amongst themselves, to include making plans for protecting themselves from discovery given Ziemer's arrest. Even though they were concerned for their safety, the trio also discussed possible avenues for staying active for the Communist cause, such as offering their services to Cuba, North Vietnam, or South Africa's Communist Party. Squillacote even went so far as to travel to Amsterdam to meet with a man named David Truong, a North Vietnamese spy, who had been convicted of espionage by the United States in the late 1970s.

Unbeknownst to the trio, after East Germany collapsed, the U.S. government had surreptitiously acquired some of the Stasi's internal files. The East Germans being, well, German, kept meticulous records, and the Stasi files obtained by the United States contained exquisite detail showing that Squillacote, Stand, and Clark had been Communist spies. Some of the Stasi files on the trio even bore Ziemer's signature. The full backstory was like something out of a Hollywood movie: Squillacote was having an affair with her handler, Ziemer, and Squillacote even had a wooden leg that the FBI suspected she used as a concealment device to steal classified documents from the Pentagon.

The Stasi files showed that East Germany had paid for the trio to travel to many countries, including Mexico and Germany, to receive training on countersurveillance, covert communications (including shortwave radio), and removing classification markings from documents. At the Stasi's suggestion, Squillacote went to law school and then worked for the National Labor Relations Board (NLRB), where her father had worked. She obtained a detail assignment to the House Armed Services Committee and from there obtained the job as a DOD lawyer. During her tenure as a federal employee, she attempted to expand her access to classified information by applying to more sensitive government jobs, to include positions in the CIA General Counsel's Office and the National Security Agency (NSA).

Given the FBI knew the trio had been spies for East Germany, it had been targeting them for a lengthy period. By the time they were arrested, the FBI had almost two years' worth of wiretaps on their home phone, having obtained warrants for electronic surveillance through the Foreign Intelligence Surveillance Act (FISA). FISA is a federal statute that created a special federal court, the Foreign Intelligence Surveillance Court (FISC), that sits in secret, and, among other things, issues warrants in matters of national security where there is probable cause to believe the target is the agent of a foreign power. The phone taps were not yielding enough to support an arrest, so the FBI decided to run a "false flag" operation against Squillacote. A "false flag" is when an FBI agent approaches a target pretending to be a foreign intelligence officer to see if the target will make incriminating statements or engage in incriminating conduct.

False flag operations are risky because they can spook a target who might not otherwise have known that they were being watched, but the Squillacote false flag was brilliantly conceived and executed by the FBI Counterintelligence Section. As part of Squillacote's efforts to establish new Communist contacts after Ziemer's arrest, she sent a letter to a man named Ronnie Kasrils, who was a Communist party official in South Africa and a member of the South African government. Squillacote used her spy craft training to establish a P.O. box under a false identity ("Lisa Martin"), which she then used to send a lengthy letter to Kasrils. The FBI had been surveilling Squillacote, so they were aware of the letter. The FBI then sent Squillacote a Christmas card, followed by a letter, both of which purported to be from Kasrils. The letter to Squillacote ("Lisa Martin") praised her for wanting to join the cause and suggested that someone special would be reaching out to her. When "someone special" reached out to her, it was not the type of "special" she expected. It was an FBI counterintelligence officer.

Listening to the surveillance recordings of Squillacote from this time frame was unnerving. She was jubilant and gleeful at having made a new connection to resume helping topple the United States of America. In one of the phone conversations, she bragged about having established her new contact: "I did it, I did it, I did it!" In another she was laughing uncontrollably at her success, "HeeHeeHeeHeeHeeHee" until she was out of breath. In yet another, she bragged that she had "violated 18 lots and lots" (a reference to Title 18 of the U.S. Code, which is where criminal laws are codified). One of the junior FBI officers had the task of playing these recordings at trial. I started calling him "The Mixmaster" and suggested that he set up a series of turntables, wear earphones around his neck, and put the recordings on vinyl so he could DJ club style: "I did it, I did it!—*whicky whicky*—"Lots and Lots"—*whicky whicky*—"HeeHeeHee!"

Squillacote fell so hard for the false flag she provided classified documents to the FBI agent early in the developing relationship without even being asked. The trio were all arrested shortly thereafter and charged under Section 794 of the Espionage Act. Espionage heavy.

Of the documents Squillacote provided, the most sensitive was a SECRET CIA document called a "finished intelligence product." It was a lengthy, detailed compendium assessing everything U.S. intelligence knew about the worldwide illegal arms trade in the mid 1990s. The document was categorized as "Restricted Dissemination," so it was more sensitive than a typical SECRET document. For the prosecutor, it was Olympic gold, as it was packed with national defense information (NDI). For me, it was an Olympic nightmare, as I had to orchestrate within the CIA the plan for use of this lengthy classified document as evidence at trial. For the first time in my career, I had to assist a prosecutor in establishing NDI while protecting as much of the classified information as possible—and there was a lot of it—from public disclosure.

The Right Tool–and the Right Man–for the Job

My grandfather was a tailor and was very good with his hands. My father was just the opposite: he could barely start a lawnmower. That meant my grandfather was frequently at our house fixing clogged drains, loose doorknobs, leaky faucets, etc. Papa Joe would show up with a large bag of tools that he had selected to cover a broad range of potential needs for the task at hand, and I would watch him and assist in small ways. He was a craftsman, and he worked methodically and efficiently. The bulk of the time it took him to fix something was usually spent sizing up the task and selecting the specific tools he was going to use. As he was deliberating and rummaging through his tools, he would always say to me, "You have to have the right tool for the job, kid." Those words have stuck with me throughout life, and their application has gone far beyond fixing drains and doorknobs.

When classified information is implicated in a criminal prosecution, the right tool for the job is the Classified Information Procedures Act (CIPA) (pronounced *seepa*). CIPA is a federal statute that governs the use of classified information in all federal criminal cases. The statute was passed in 1980 to combat the growing practice of "graymail," whereby criminal defendants would threaten to disclose classified information if the case against them was not dismissed. Federal laws are sometimes lengthy, complicated, and byzantine. Not CIPA. The law is a model of statutory clarity. It is brief, practical, and easy to understand. CIPA establishes a series of procedural mechanisms for protecting classified information, to the extent possible, at every stage of a criminal case, while permitting the information to be used (with court-approved alterations) by both defendants and prosecutors.

Technically, CIPA is a procedural statute, but the result of invoking the procedures can have huge substantive impact on a case. For instance, one benefit CIPA provides to the government is that the government can seek court approval to summarize relevant classified information that is going to be provided to a defendant, or to substitute something that is of less sensitivity but would permit the defendant "substantially the same ability" to make his or her defense. So, there may be 500 classified documents that would normally be provided to a defendant, but if the reason they all need to be provided is because they prove or indicate something that can be easily summarized in a paragraph, then the government can seek court approval to summarize the 500 documents into a paragraph. And that paragraph may be unclassified or at least classified at a lower level. This is but one example of the minor miracles that can be achieved using CIPA.

For the prosecution of Squillacote, Stand, and Clark, the task at hand was to protect as much classified information as possible in the lengthy SECRET CIA finished intelligence product that Squillacote had stolen, while still permitting the document to be used as evidence at trial. CIPA was the right tool for the job, but a tool is only as good as the person wielding it. Here, again, I was incredibly fortunate. For the tool was in the hands of Randy Bellows, the senior litigation counsel (SLC) for the Eastern District of Virginia (EDVA).

Most prosecutors have a title of assistant U.S. attorney (AUSA), but Randy's title was SLC, given his long tenure and experience. Randy was the personification of the perfect prosecutor. He treated everyone with kindness, respect, and dignity. He was quiet, careful, thoughtful, and deliberate. His legal mind functioned quickly and instinctively, like a chess master, but his dialogue was always slow and deliberate because he was cautiously choosing every word. Randy's only apparent vice was that he drank a nearly defunct soda (I think it was TaB) and was hooked on sunflower seeds, the debris of which was often scattered across his desk. The FBI agents and I would kid that Randy had probably stocked his cellar with TaB, and that maybe he imported it from some obscure Eastern European country with the only remaining TaB factory.

Randy had an unassuming appearance that was a cross between mad scientist and absent-minded professor, but under that veneer was a fierce litigator. He had such a kind face and gentle demeanor that if you did not know him, you might well underestimate him, and if you made that mistake opposing him in court, it would be a mistake you would not repeat. In short, Randy was a truly wonderful man and a model prosecutor, and I learned a great deal just by having the privilege of watching him work.

Given the classified information implicated in the case (and I can at least divulge that there were many other classified matters in the case that remain classified, and I cannot discuss them), Randy and I often needed to speak on a secure telephone line. This was no problem for me, as I had a secure line within arm's reach, but Randy had to leave his office and go down a long corridor, as at the time the EDVA U.S. Attorney's Office only had one secure line. So, I would call Randy on his unsecure office phone and ask him to go to the secure phone down the hall. Randy never complained, despite this being a disruption for him and a departure from his normal business, and this is just one small example of his professionalism in working with an agency that complicated his work at every step. Throughout my career, I worked with many prosecutors from across the nation, and I can tell you that not all were so gracious.

At Randy's request, I shepherded a declassification project to bring the CIA finished intelligence product down to the unclassified level.

Basically, we blacked out or "redacted" all the classified information. With the assistance of CIA analysts, original classifiers, and others in the intelligence community, we conducted a line-by-line review of the entire document, debating every single word while holding a redacting pen. There was much debate, many meetings, many versions, and the final product looked like a half-completed jigsaw puzzle. At trial, the original document Squillacote provided to the undercover FBI agent was immediately placed under seal after being admitted into evidence, and the redacted, unclassified version, with pre-approval from the court (using CIPA), was placed on the public record in its place.

Defendants in a criminal trial have the right to see all the evidence being used against them, so they can properly defend themselves. That right extends to all criminal defendants, even ones who are accused spies. A jury in a criminal trial has a duty to examine all the evidence so they can determine guilt or innocence. That duty extends to all evidence, even the pieces that are classified. That meant we needed a plan for showing the actual stolen SECRET CIA document, unredacted and classified, to both the defendants and the jury. Now, on the one hand, you really don't want to be giving two accused spies access to a lengthy classified document (in an open courtroom, no less). But on the other hand, they had already stolen the damn thing, so it was not like we were showing them something they had never seen before. Even though necessary, this action still had to be approved by the equity owners (and there were many), which was a bureaucratic challenge that I had to herd through the intelligence community, along with the jury issue.

Jurors are not required to possess security clearances, even when they are being given access to classified information. Remember the extensive vetting for access to classified information? All waived for jurors. No background checks, no polygraphs, no security clearances, no nondisclosure agreements (NDAs). Jurors get instructions about protecting classified information, but that is it. The policy reasons supporting this exception are sound: you can't force jurors to undergo the security state version of a colonoscopy just so they can perform a function that the law requires of them. Also, the government does not want to send the message to jurors that they can't be trusted. But the plan to permit uncleared jurors to be granted access to classified information still had to be approved by the equity owners, and it was, albeit reluctantly.

You know how a dog will cock its head sideways when trying to understand what you are telling it? That was the reaction I got from intelligence officers when I explained how jurors could be provided access to classified information without any vetting, without signing NDAs, and without security clearances. No one liked it, but they at least understood the reasoning and agreed to the unusual access.

At the appropriate time in the trial, the marshals opened the doors to the courtroom and a DOJ court security officer (now called "classified information security officers," or CISOs) wheeled a cart into the courtroom. The cart contained black binders with cover pages stamped SECRET in bright red. Each juror, the judge, the defense counsel, defendants, and the prosecutors received a binder containing the unredacted classified documents being used as evidence. This was in open court, not a sensitive compartmented information facility (SCIF), and most of the people holding binders did not even have security clearances. These are but some of the compromises that must be made when the pursuit of justice collides with protecting national security.

While this practical approach permitted the classified document to be used as evidence in a manner that comported with the defendants' rights and the jurors' need to see all the evidence, the biggest issue for the prosecution remained: establishing that the classified information at issue was national defense information (NDI). Given the finished intelligence product was a CIA document, Randy needed a CIA witness to establish that the document contained NDI. The intelligence compendium was so long that Randy agreed to select about a half dozen paragraphs from the document for which he would elicit the critical testimony.

I never pressed Randy as to how he had chosen the half dozen items he would use to establish that Squillacote had stolen NDI, and he never shared his methodology with me. But it appeared that he chose some of the more sensitive items and ones that laypersons could understand. Smart choices. But I was skeptical whether we could provide sufficient evidence on the public record for DOJ to meet its legal burden without causing harm to national security. Although I was unsure, Randy was an experienced trial attorney, and he was confident he could elicit the testimony he needed without damaging national security. To walk that line, he proposed using CIPA protections and what was technically a request to partially close the courtroom. This approach was called "the silent witness rule."

CIA on the Stand: The Silent Witness Speaks

Putting a CIA officer on the witness stand is always a last resort. Even as a relatively new attorney, I realized this was the riskiest part of the plan, and throughout my career it was something I always tried very hard to avoid. Many CIA officers are undercover, which means their mere association with the CIA is a classified fact, and if an undercover officer must testify, the government has to do legal backflips to get court permission for the officer to testify under an alias and either in a light disguise with no sketch artist present, or behind a screen, or in a cleared courtroom. Such requests go against the grain of how our judicial system generally works, and judges are often uncomfortable with these requests, even though they are necessary. More importantly, witnesses being human, they could get nervous and mistakenly divulge classified information on the witness stand. I called such slips of the tongue "getting blood on the record." This is not a minor concern, as even though direct testimony by a prosecutor can be anticipated, the cross-examination could entail unanticipated questions and witnesses could get flustered and mistakenly disclose classified information in open court.

I won't say which case it was, but I was involved in an espionage trial years later where a government witness slipped and disclosed classified information on the first day of trial. At the time, I was serving as the lawyer for an operational component of the CIA, and the component's equities were implicated in the prosecution, so I was working on certain aspects of the case. The full story is complicated, interesting, and educational, but I will leave it for another day. Without getting into what and how, we got blood on the record the very first day of trial, and by the time I got to work the next day, I had a screaming message from a CIA station chief overseas. Quite displeased, the chief was bearing the brunt of the inadvertent disclosure, which had not gone unnoticed by some of our allies halfway around the globe and was already causing damage that the chief had to mitigate.

So, it happens. And when it happens, the damage is real and the government must decide whether to just ignore the blood on the record or attempt some aggressive measure such as having the transcript redacted, which could backfire by highlighting something that no one noticed in the first place. Also, the criminal cases with CIA witnesses tend to be high-profile cases that are well attended by journalists, and journalists may be taking detailed notes themselves, and they easily pinpoint whatever the government redacted from the transcript. These are but some of the reasons it was always my preference to have the CIA provide testimonial evidence via signed and sworn declarations. No cross-examination. No slip of the tongue. No risk of blood on the record.

But when it comes to establishing NDI, a prosecutor needs a live witness because a criminal defendant must have the ability to cross-examine whoever is providing this critical testimony. And so it was with Squillacote. Not only would a CIA officer need to testify, but that officer would be providing some of the most critical testimony of the trial.

Enter William H. "Bill" McNair. Bill McNair was one of the few original classifiers at the CIA. His title was information review officer (IRO), Directorate for Operations. The Directorate for Operations (DO) is the core of the CIA—it is the directorate for the spies. Much of the CIA exists to provide logistical and technical support and training for DO officers and to process the fruits of the core work of the DO, which is stealing secrets. Bill was the last man standing between DO secrets and public disclosure. Any declassification and public release of DO information had to be approved by Bill. Be it a proposed release for a Freedom of Information Act (FOIA) or Privacy Act request; a civil litigation; a criminal prosecution; or a draft manuscript, resume, or op-ed submitted for prepublication review by a current or former agency officer—all roads led to Bill McNair for approval. Or denial. Bill's nickname inside the CIA was "Doctor No." You can guess why.

Bill McNair was born and raised in Georgia. His family were peanut farmers, and he introduced me to a lifelong love—boiled peanuts—which I can still eat by the bag. A portly Southern gentleman with a slight southern drawl, Bill had a calming demeanor and a personality that could fill a room, quietly, without dominating it. The only thing below average about Bill was his height. While I generally avoid using the true names of CIA officers, Bill passed away several years ago, and his name is already on the public record in hundreds of sworn declarations. I also knew him well and think he would enjoy a little posthumous limelight, which I am happy to provide.

For someone who kept all the secrets, Bill loved to talk. He was a conversationalist extraordinaire. Unless I had nothing scheduled for the next ninety minutes, I never broke the plane of his office door. At his celebration of life, an old friend gave a eulogy and talked about how he first met Bill at a public pool. Bill loved kids and had been talking for some time (as was his nature) with the man's grandchild, and when the young child eventually introduced Bill to her grandpa, she said, "This is the man *with all the words*." I laughed until I cried. And I still cry every time I tell that story.

Bill's supreme gift of gab was rivaled by his relentless and mischievous sense of humor, which was always (at least usually) appreciated in a stressful business. I remember when I was a relatively new attorney and had drafted a lengthy TOP SECRET declaration for Bill to sign for a federal court case. There was often some back-and-forth debating language, and Bill would add additional explanations while patiently and tactfully explaining to me all the things I had not yet learned about the intelligence profession, which were many. But on this occasion Bill said nothing. It was odd and unsettling. He looked at the cover page and saw that it was TOP SECRET; lifted the document to his ear; fanned the pages quickly with his thumb; and then quietly set the document down. Bill then looked at me quizzically and said, "I don't know, Joe—it only sounds SECRET to me."

For one particularly sensitive prosecution that required Bill to testify—and I wish I could tell you more, but I can't—Bill was provided with a disguise by the CIA disguise shop. You will have to let your imagination fill in the blanks, but imagine Colonel Sanders meets the Count of Monte Cristo. I could not recognize him when he wore the disguise, and Bill being Bill, he could not resist taking his disguise on a test run around CIA headquarters. He was belly laughing as he recounted to me how he was riding up a CIA headquarters elevator standing next to an old friend who had no idea he was standing next to Bill.

For many years, Bill patiently and graciously educated me, and generations of CIA attorneys, on the basics (and the finer points) of the spy business and why it was important for us to be protecting certain secrets in civil and criminal litigations. One of the things I learned after thirty-five years in federal service is that you will not be remembered for the great work you did on any particular issue or case. The true legacy you leave—if you leave one at all—will be in the lives you have touched. And that kind of impact is mostly from training subordinates, sometimes peers, and maybe a boss or two. Bill's legacy was a truly lasting one, and I know many of the CIA attorneys he helped train are still working at the agency today.

Over the decades, I had to assist in preparing many CIA officers to testify in federal courts in high-profile civil and criminal litigations. Even though a last resort, it was unfortunately necessary in many cases. The DO officers dreaded it the most. Operations officers prefer to stay under the radar, and—I mean this as a compliment—they are professional thieves and trained liars, so being under oath and required to tell the whole truth, all the truth, and nothing but the truth was akin to showering a vampire in holy water. But not Bill. He loved the challenge, and he never complained about a deposition or open-court testimony. The more important the case, the greater the game Bill would bring. And the Squillacote case was one of his greatest moments in a long, distinguished career.

Given that everyone who mattered would have the actual classified CIA document in a binder right in front of them, testimony could be elicited in a manner that no one without a binder would know the exact details of what the witness was more generally talking about. For instance, the prosecutor could say something to the effect of:

"Mr. McNair, I call your attention to the third paragraph on page twenty-three; could you describe to the jury what sensitive information is in that paragraph and why it is national defense information?"

And Bill would say something like: "Well, this paragraph is describing military equipment that an illegal arms dealer is covertly sending to a country in Africa, some specifics about the equipment, and the manner of transportation." Bill would also add that the paragraph described the sensitive means of intelligence collection used to obtain the intelligence, and that if arms traffickers or rogue nations purchasing the equipment knew that the U.S. government had obtained this information, they could take measures to better protect the secrecy of future shipments, such as changing their modus operandi, dedicating resources to determining how the U.S. government had obtained the sensitive information, and employing countermeasures to degrade or eliminate U.S. intelligence capabilities.

The actual paragraph might have had details along the lines of "a named arms trafficker was moving sixteen Soviet MIG aircraft via rail and had shrouded the planes by removing their wings and placing them in what appear to be cattle cars." Those details would be classified, and would remain classified, but the open-court testimony would be generic enough to avoid publicly disclosing the sensitive details. This approach provides the prosecution enough testimony to establish NDI on the public record without the public hearing the most sensitive details. Hence the name "the silent witness."

Even though the CIA finished intelligence product at issue was classified SECRET and not TOP SECRET, the SECRET category is broad, and some SECRET documents are much more sensitive than others. As Bill put it to me, "Joe, there is SECRET that is just a scoop of plain vanilla, and then there is SECRET with whipped cream, fudge, sprinkles, and a cherry on top." This document was the latter, and I was concerned because Randy had wisely (for his case) compiled a hot fudge sundae. But Bill was as confident as Randy that he could carefully craft his testimony to avoid damaging disclosures while providing sufficient information for DOJ to meet its evidentiary burden.

And it worked. Perfectly. The direct testimony was not difficult for Bill, who was accustomed to having to protect sensitive intelligence sources and methods while simultaneously explaining relevant sensitivities at an unclassified level. But that was just the direct testimony. Cross-examination would be conducted by a very experienced criminal defense attorney, be much more challenging, and a whole lot more memorable.

Defendant James Clark had signed a plea agreement, but plea agreements involve cooperating with the government. Squillacote and Stand, being True Believers, could not stomach having to cooperate with the government they were so dedicated to toppling. So Squillacote and Stand were the only defendants who went to trial, and they had top-tier criminal defense attorneys: Lawrence Robbins for Squillacote and Richard Sauber for Stand. Very experienced, and no doubt expensive, criminal defense attorneys. With an avalanche of incriminating evidence against their clients, especially Squillacote, the defense attorneys certainly had the most difficult jobs in the courtroom. But they did the best they could with what little they had. Robbins, who was a masterful trial lawyer, cross-examined Bill.

Squillacote had obviously stolen classified information and provided it to someone she thought was a Communist spy. That being the case, the best chance she had of being found not guilty was if the information was not technically NDI. The legal standard for NDI is basically that the information relates to national defense, that there be a likelihood of damage from unauthorized disclosure, and that the information be "closely held" by the government. Robbins zeroed in on the "closely held" element when cross-examining Bill and tried to get Bill to acknowledge that the information at issue was not closely held at all, but instead public knowledge. Bill was having none of it, but the exchange between the two was captivating.

The trial had been difficult for the defense, and it seemed that this cross-examination, and specifically this line of questioning, was the best hope for the defendant if she was going to escape a guilty verdict. Robbins was like a high-stakes craps player pushing every chip he had out for a make-or-break final bet. His strategy was to get Bill to admit that the same information that the government was claiming to be classified and "closely held" was actually publicly available and not "closely held" at all. For instance, Robbins would introduce into evidence a professional arms publication like *Jane's Defense Weekly*, and say, "Now Mr. McNair, I call your attention to page twelve, paragraph two. Isn't that the same information that you are saying is classified and national defense information?"

This was a huge problem. If what Robbins was claiming was true, and if Bill acknowledged that it was true in open court, it would have been an official acknowledgement of the classified information that we had gone to great lengths to protect. Bill, of course, knew this, and he gave the perfect answer: "It just doesn't matter." Bill then, at length, explained why it didn't matter. Because even if it was true, there were many independent reasons why the government would have still legitimately classified the information and treated it as "closely held": the government obtained the information through clandestine means; even the smallest deviation in details could give away the intelligence source; timing was a critical element, as maybe the government obtained the information weeks or months before the publication; the publication might have been wrong about some details that the government accurately collected or vice versa; and even if the information was identical, including it in a finished intelligence product showed that the government believed it to be true and important enough to report to senior policymakers within the executive branch. There were other reasons as well, but those were the big ones, and Bill patiently—at first—explained them all.

Robbins was doing his job very well, but all he could do was repeat the same attack for each piece of purported NDI the prosecutor had relied on, and which Bill had covered in as much detail as possible under the silent witness rule. Bill, who was normally unflappable, seemingly became irritated. Finally, with just enough exasperation and irritation in his voice to push back while still being polite and professional, Bill replied somewhat sternly, "Counselor, you're not hearing me: I have been telling you, *it just doesn't matter*!"

Up until this point, the trial judge, Judge Claude Hilton, had been leaning back in his chair, hands folded on his chest, content to let the gladiators hack away. But Bill's reply triggered the judge, who was also now seemingly irritated at a line of questioning that was arguably approaching badgering the witness. Judge Hilton pounced forward from the back of his chair, and rebuked Robbins: "You heard him! He said it just doesn't matter! He is the expert! Move on!" At that moment, every eye in the courtroom was on the judge. Except mine. I was still completely focused on Bill. And right at that moment, as the judge delivered the *coup de grace*, Bill looked directly at me. And winked.

When you know someone well, you can often communicate through facial expression, body language, or a simple look, and I knew instantly what Bill was telling me with his wink: "Don't worry, kid. I got this." Then he immediately took out a handkerchief and dabbed his eye, which I am pretty sure was just for show, in case a juror thought they had seen him wink. Robbins had no choice but to abandon the line of questioning and move on. But the damage was done. Bill's exasperated utterance became like a mantra for the rest of the trial. On re-direct, Randy got Bill to emphasize once again that "it just doesn't matter," and Randy even reiterated Bill's words in his closing argument to the jury.

The government had trained me well to handle pressure. From my plebe year at West Point through six years of service as an Airborne Ranger–qualified infantry officer, I learned to remain calm (or at least to give that appearance) under pressure. And throughout Bill's testimony, I thought I maintained a calm and cool demeanor, even though on the inside I was completely on edge, focused on every word and movement. As Bill stepped down from the witness stand, I finally relaxed. *Mission accomplished*, I thought. At least for me. For now. But there was a lot of trial left, and what was left included one of the most interesting and challenging legal issues in the history of espionage prosecutions.

The Stasi Files

By the time Squillacote and Stand went to trial, I was also carrying a full caseload, so I only attended trial on days when there was testimony or evidentiary matters that I wanted to observe. And there was one specific issue that I had invested considerable efforts in that I did not want to miss, as it involved a unique legal issue that was unprecedented in the annals of espionage prosecutions. This issue was not NDI related, but it is nonetheless worth recounting, as it is a good example of the types of unique evidentiary challenges that can arise in espionage prosecutions, and it is a good example of how much thought and effort can go into something that publicly appears to be ministerial and mundane.

While the East Germans (being German) kept meticulous records, being seasoned spies, they also compartmented those meticulous records to protect the identities of their intelligence sources. For source protection, the Stasi files were separated into "true name cards," "agent data sheets," and "operational files." The agent data sheets contained things like code names and payment details, but there was no personally identifying information. The true name cards contained the personally identifying information. Operational files contained details of specific operations the Stasi was running. To complicate matters, some of the true name cards were on "people of interest" who the Stasi were spying on, so just because there was a true name card on someone, it did not mean they were a Stasi spy. If you were a Stasi spy, there would also be a corresponding agent data sheet in a separate filing system, and to link files in the separate systems, you needed a code number and access to both filing systems, neither of which were digitized (they looked like formal three-by-five cards). While the FBI possessed both the agent data sheets and the true name cards for Squillacote, Stand, and Clark (and they were some of the best evidence in the history of espionage prosecutions), there were three large hurdles preventing the government from using the files as evidence at trial.

The first hurdle was a technical legal matter. The Stasi files were stolen documents. Stolen from a foreign intelligence service. From a country that no longer existed. Using such material as evidence in a U.S. court was legal *terra incognita*. Parties cannot just willy-nilly introduce documents as evidence in a trial. The documents must be, in legal parlance, "authenticated." "Authentication" means that the party proffering the evidence must comply, to a court's satisfaction, with detailed federal procedural rules designed to ensure that documentary evidence is genuine. Sometimes parties will stipulate to authenticity because it is so obvious, and it saves everyone time and energy by not having to call people like document custodians as witnesses. But for such incriminating and unique evidence as the Stasi files, that was not going to happen, and the government had to find a way to comply with authentication rules for SECRET documents that were stolen from the intelligence service of a defunct nation.

The second hurdle was source protection. As a practical matter, the U.S. government needed to continue to protect the source of the files. Whether an intelligence source is a human being or a technical collection, sources are often still providing intelligence and need to be protected from disclosure if they are going to continue to be useful. Even if no longer being used in a specific operation, intelligence sources, if human, still need to be protected for their safety, and if technical, they need to be protected to preserve the secrecy of the technology so it can be used again elsewhere without adversaries developing countermeasures. With the Stasi files, if the government did not disclose how it obtained the files, it might not have been able to get them authenticated, as their origin might be too murky for them to be considered credible enough to be authenticated. While I cannot discuss how the FBI came to possess the files, I can say that law enforcement and intelligence agencies must protect their sources—even at the cost of a prosecutor not being able to use the evidence—which was looking increasingly possible, as it appeared a plea agreement would not be reached.

In addition to the technical legal issues and typical source concerns with the Stasi files, there was another issue that, without being overly dramatic, was of diplomatic magnitude. For the Stasi files were not just stolen German property: the Germans wanted them back.

The Stasi was a foreign intelligence service, but it was also a domestic spy agency, and it aggressively monitored the East German populace. The German people feared the Stasi, and after Germany united, it passed several anti-Stasi laws to prevent anything like the Stasi from ever operating on German soil again. For instance, German laws covering electronic surveillance—even something as simple as a government phone tap—are much narrower and more restrictive than in the United States. Among other things, the German government also created the Gauck Commission, which had the responsibility to gather and catalogue the Stasi files, protect the privacy of German citizens whose names were in the files, and make the files available for review to affected German citizens (somewhat akin to the U.S. Privacy Act). So, the Stasi files were a very sensitive domestic issue for the Germans, which made it difficult for DOJ to ask the German government for assistance authenticating what the Germans rightly considered stolen German property and which they wanted back. Imagine if I asked you to go to the DMV with me to help me register the car I stole from you last week. Now magnify that concern to a level of international diplomacy. That was the dynamic.

As a result of these formidable obstacles, there was a good chance Randy might not be able to use some of the most damning pieces of evidence in the history of espionage prosecutions. As it became increasingly likely that the case was going to trial, Randy's work increased exponentially, and I had comparatively few issues to work on, so I offered to focus on authenticating the Stasi files. I have always enjoyed a challenge, and I took it as my mission to find a way Randy could use the files as evidence. As I was relatively new to the practice of law and had never done trial work, I did what any new lawyer would do: I hit the books.

What I discovered was that the Federal Rules of Criminal Procedure expressly adopt the authentication rules from the Federal Rules of Civil Procedure. And the civil rules had a special rule for authenticating foreign documents. To my extreme delight (because you know how I feel about witnesses), the authentication of a foreign document could be achieved by a sworn declaration from an appropriate foreign government official with an accompanying declaration from a second foreign official swearing that the first official was the appropriate officer to be doing the authentication (and if you think that explanation is convoluted, try reading the actual rule). As the Stasi files were East German documents and East Germany no longer existed, any sworn declaration would also need a statement to the effect that the Republic of Germany was the legal successor to East Germany.

I started a dialogue with the relevant CIA analysts, CIA Counterintelligence Center (CIC) investigators, and operations officers in the Europe Division to see if anyone had any thoughts on a way to approach the German government in such a way that they might be willing to assist the United States in at least this one case. These senior officers all understood the dynamics far better than me, and thankfully, they all were eager to help, which is normally not the case. Let me provide a little background on how the federal bureaucracy normally operates so you can appreciate the unusual situation in which we found ourselves.

First, you should never assume that the executive branch is a monolithic entity. It is absolutely not. Think of it as kingdoms and fiefdoms with overlapping boundaries and varying degrees of connectivity—each with differing missions, sometimes conflicting; different cultures and priorities, often working at cross purposes—all competing with each other for resources and relevance. Amongst these kingdoms and fiefdoms are some strong alliances, shaky alliances, alliances by marriage, open rivalries, and, sometimes, open warfare. Think *Game of Thrones* without the gore and bloodshed but more scheming and political maneuvering. That is the federal bureaucracy. And inside that bureaucracy, two of the largest kingdoms—the intelligence community and the law enforcement community—mostly tolerate each other but often do not get along. I have some truly epic war stories from battles I either watched or fought between these two kingdoms, but they are not central here, so like many other war stories, they will have to wait. But generally, I will say that DOJ's use of classified information in a criminal case is often not supported by the intelligence community.

Classified information can be implicated in two ways in a criminal case: "discovery" and "case-in-chief." If the classified information is discoverable—meaning DOJ has a legal duty to provide the information to a criminal defendant—the intelligence community has little say in the matter but does have some say as to how the classified information is used, as there are available legal procedures the government can invoke to protect the use of classified information within certain parameters. While certain types of information need to be made available to a criminal defendant, classified or not, where classified information is usually implicated in a prosecution is when the government does not have a duty to provide it but rather when a prosecutor wants to use it as evidence to help build his or her case. In government speak, this is called "case-in-chief" material.

The intelligence community, as a general matter, does not want DOJ building a criminal case by using classified information for a case-in-chief. The preference is for DOJ to use classified information for lead purposes only, which means to use it to find evidence that is not classified and to then use that unclassified evidence for the case-in-chief.

As a new CIA attorney, I remember being more than a little shocked when attending a meeting between very senior intelligence community lawyers and equally senior DOJ officials over an issue of whether DOJ could use a specific piece of very incriminating intelligence as evidence in a high-profile criminal prosecution. One of the senior intelligence attorneys glared across the table at a half dozen high-ranking DOJ attorneys—not even trying to hide his contempt—and issued a stern, concise, and unequivocal "no." When the DOJ attorneys attempted to plead their case, he held up his hand, stopping them short, and said, "Our answer is no. We wish the prosecutor the best of luck."

The dynamic was clear: you have your mission, and we have ours, and they are not the same. This was pre-9/11, and 9/11 changed the dynamic to some extent, at least for terrorism-related prosecutions. But as a general matter, the intelligence community has always been, and likely remains, hostile to its classified information being dragged into a criminal case.

But as with everything in life and the law, there are exceptions. And prosecuting a Communist spy who was stealing classified information to help bring down the U.S. government is an exception to the general you-have-your-mission-and-we-have-ours attitude. In a case like Squillacote's, even the most cantankerous of the kingdoms and fiefdoms will lower their defenses to unite against a common enemy.

Given we were all united in trying to find a way to persuade the German government to assist in authenticating the Stasi files, there was a great deal of brainstorming by some brilliant intelligence officers that I greatly appreciated. But no progress was being made, and I was getting worried. Sometimes hard work is just not enough, and you need a little luck, and, here, serendipity intervened. One of the operations officers in the Europe Division told me that by chance a German official who was basically the chief of German counterintelligence was visiting the United States the following week, and that he might be meeting with some U.S. government officials. Given the German official's background, portfolio, and senior position, there was a chance that he might be willing to assist the U.S. government in prosecuting some former East German spies. With the help of the operations officer, I came up with a plan that I briefed to Randy, who was excited by the prospect and, being a far superior attorney, helped me fine-tune a draft affidavit for the senior German official in the event he agreed to assist.

At the end of a meeting between U.S. officials and the German counterintelligence chief, participants were told there was one additional sensitive agenda item, at which time all the U.S. officials left the room, and I was ushered in with the operations officer. I introduced myself, laid out the situation, showed the German official the documents, and explained why we needed his help. He was a tall, thin, stoic man with pure white hair. He was completely focused on the information I was providing to him and said nothing. His face remained blank. When I was done, he asked the operations officer if the phone in the room was an open line and if he could use it. She said, "Yes," and "of course." It was a large conference room, and the phone was at the other end of a long, polished oak table. He went to the phone, pulled a card out of his wallet, dialed, and started speaking barely above a whisper, in German.

Aptitude for language is not in my skill set. I took four years of Spanish but cannot string two coherent sentences together in Spanish, so needless to say, I could not understand a word the German official was speaking. He did not seem upset, but I could not read his demeanor in the slightest and was worried that we had offended him by overreaching with our request. I whispered to the operations officer, "What is happening?" I will never forget the look on her face because her features were also blank, but her eyes were wide and twinkling. She leaned in toward my face, trying to appear nonchalant, and, while barely moving her lips, quickly and quietly whispered, "He is speaking with the president of Germany."

When the German counterintelligence chief got off the phone, he requested a magnifying glass. *Old school*, I thought. He started reviewing the documents, and when the magnifying glass arrived, he thoroughly examined each document, line by line. It was during this examination that he pointed out to me that Lothar Ziemer, the legendary East German spy, had signed some of the documents. He told me he was familiar with the spy's handwriting and recognized the signature, and I quickly arranged for the affidavit to be updated with this helpful tidbit, and a few minor edits. And then he signed it.

The Europe Division operations officer also knew some of the consular officers at the German embassy in D.C. (never underestimate the value of attending Christmas parties) and used those connections to obtain the second affidavit attesting to the authenticity of the counterintelligence chief's signature and the scope of his duties. It probably did not hurt that the president of Germany had apparently approved the request. At trial, the Stasi files were authenticated and admitted into evidence. It was still up to the jury to decide believability, but a judge decides admissibility, and that mission was accomplished in what appeared to be a boring, mundane action. This was still early in the trial, and the defense team fought very hard for their clients, but in the end, the evidence, as presented by a methodical and model prosecutor, won the day.

On the day the jury returned the guilty verdict, I was in Randy's office helping him craft the proposed post-verdict jury instructions. At my request, he added a sentence at the end of the instructions to the effect of, "And please remember that in the course of this trial you were granted access to classified information that, if you disclose to anyone, could lead to you being prosecuted for unauthorized disclosure of classified information."

It was during this brief drafting session that Randy made a comment to me that made me realize that he thought I was a more senior attorney. As I had served as an infantry officer, I knew how to carry myself as a professional, and those traits had led him to assume that he was working with a more seasoned lawyer. I told him that I was a fairly recent law school graduate. Randy leaned back in his chair, his eyes narrowed and then widened with a kind, fatherly warmth as he processed what I had just told him. Then he smirked, leaned forward, and said, "Let me presume to give you some advice, Joe: you present yourself as a much more senior attorney, which is to your benefit—*you should never tell anyone what you just told me*." I appreciated the guidance, which was obviously heartfelt and well intentioned. And I never spoke those words again.

Shortly after my lesson in oversharing, we were back in the courtroom for Judge Hilton's post-verdict jury instructions. Judge Hilton included the last sentence I requested, reminding the jury of its duty to protect classified information and the attendant potential criminal liabilities from violating that duty. After reading the warning, Judge Hilton looked at the jury and said sarcastically, "And on that note, I thank you for your service."

Squillacote was subsequently sentenced to twenty-two years. Stand received seventeen years. Under the terms of his plea agreement, Clark received twelve years and seven months. The defense attorneys filed a massive appeal to the Fourth Circuit Court of Appeals, which, among other things, argued that the Stasi files had not been properly authenticated. The Fourth Circuit rejected all the challenges and upheld the convictions. The published opinion stated that the certifications for the Stasi files had complied "in all respects" with the applicable federal rules and that the district court had "quite properly" ruled for the government in authenticating the documents.

Randy Bellows was already famous before the Squillacote case, as he had prosecuted many high-profile cases in his long and distinguished career. But the Squillacote case extended Randy's bona fides into the national security arena, and following close behind his successful espionage prosecution, Attorney General (AG) Janet Reno appointed Randy to review the badly bungled espionage investigation and prosecution of a man named Wen Ho Lee. After he was appointed to lead the Wen Ho Lee review, Randy called me in my office: "Joe, I want you to know that I am calling you from my secure phone—in my office." He then explained that because he was reporting directly to AG Reno for the Lee review, DOJ had given him his own secure line so that when AG Reno called him, she would not have to wait for Randy to walk down the hallway and call her back. We both got a good chuckle out of him showing off his secure phone like it was a new sports car, and I was happy to hear that the highest levels of DOJ were recognizing Randy's value and treating him commensurately.

Squillacote and Stand were later featured in not one but two segments of the CBS television show *60 Minutes*. One segment was on the Foreign Intelligence Surveillance Court and discussed their case as the couple was subjected to lengthy electronic surveillance by the FBI pursuant to FISA warrants. Another *60 Minutes* segment was fully dedicated to Squillacote and Stand and their prosecution. Mike Wallace, the legendary journalist, interviewed the couple and their defense lawyers Robbins and Sauber, and the segment's theme was that the couple had never spied for anyone but were rather manipulated and entrapped by the FBI. To downplay Squillacote's theft, Wallace described the documents she stole as containing "little of consequence." To downplay the Stasi files on the pair, Wallace indignantly proclaimed that "there wasn't even any assurance that these Stasi files were authentic."

I could not believe what I was hearing. I felt deceived. Violated. The *60 Minutes* segment was a pure propaganda piece with no effort to portray the truth, but considerable effort to portray Squillacote and Stand as innocent victims of an overzealous FBI. In the years to come, I would have over a dozen cases I worked on featured as segments on *60 Minutes*, and in all but one, the *60 Minutes* segment was singularly focused on storytelling, not telling the truth.

As a child, my whole family would look forward to watching *60 Minutes* on Sunday nights. We would all sit on the couch together, mesmerized by the renowned investigative journalists revealing stories of, among other things, government corruption and malfeasance. Seeing my cases on *60 Minutes* was like peeking behind the curtain to glimpse the great Wizard of Oz, and instead finding a devious little man intent on deceiving his audience into believing a fiction he manufactured. Sad. Disappointing. Humiliating. But eye-opening. Once a year or so I will still tune in to watch an episode, but I watch it realizing that it is produced to entertain, not to inform; to push biased narratives, not to report the truth. In a sense, the show really was groundbreaking journalism: it paved the way for what journalism has become.

Working on the Squillacote case as a relatively new CIA attorney, I had no idea that, years later, I would become the legal advisor to the Europe Division in the DO, and years after that, the legal advisor to the CIA CIC. The CIA culture (at least back then) was such that operations officers spent entire careers within the same practice area and, unbeknownst to me, I was making relationships that would serve me well years down the road, especially with the CIC.

Counterespionage: Spying on the Spies

The CIC had a broad portfolio and performed many counterintelligence functions, but the core of CIC was the Counterespionage Group (CEG). CEG conducted investigations of primarily CIA officers and applicants suspected of being double agents. There could be many reasons why an individual would be the subject of a CEG investigation, and many of those reasons would themselves be classified, but Squillacote's was obvious and unclassified, as she had applied to the CIA Office of General Counsel during her DOD career to gain access to more sensitive information. One of the pieces of evidence I assisted Randy to authenticate at trial was

Squillacote's CIA interview record. She did well in her interviews. Thank God we were not hiring.

CIA headquarters is basically a series of vaults within vaults within vaults. It is the security state version of a Russian nesting doll, where each doll has cipher locks, combination dials, passwords, and code words just to get to the next doll. The CEG vault was the only vault at the CIA where on top of all the security measures that every other vault possessed, there was also a telephone by the door. Not an intercom, mind you. An old-timey hard, black, plastic rotary dial telephone that looked like it had been on the wall since the beginning of the Cold War. Or before. If you wanted to speak with anyone inside the CEG vault, you had to dial their desk from the hallway. *Zzzshir. Clunk clunk clunk clunk. Zshir. Clunk clunk*. And so on. After chatting, they would come out to meet you and take you to a secure conference room. Because there was no way any outsiders were getting inside the CEG vault. Not even Ethan Hunt.

CEG officers were a combination of seasoned investigators from across the government, experienced CIA security officers, tenured operations officers who had served covertly all over the world, and retired investigators from across the federal government. Most had unique backgrounds in various areas of counterintelligence. The CIC had only one assigned lawyer to handle all the center's legal work, but that lawyer was always a very senior attorney with experience serving in multiple operational components. Because of the Squillacote case, I was exposed to CEG's work very early in my career, but as closely as I worked with CEG investigators on the case, I was never—ever—permitted inside the CEG vault. So, I spent a lot of time out in a lonely hallway holding a heavy black rotary phone receiver, chatting about some less sensitive action item, or trying to get an investigator to come out of the vault so we could go to a secure conference room. I had not spent so much time holding a rotary phone since dating my high school sweetheart, so at least the hallway experience brought back some fond memories.

It would be many years until I was assigned to be the legal advisor to the CIC. How that came to be is a very funny story, as I was not quite as senior as my predecessors, but it is a story for another day. Once again, I was faced with communicating remotely with the inhabitants of the CEG vault, but at least the phone had been upgraded: green, light plastic, push buttons!

The CIC lawyer, being senior, had a large office in the CIC front office. Big enough for a conference table in addition to a large oak desk, standalone safe, and a sitting area. My predecessor had been content to stay in his office and either answer questions over email or a secure phone or let the CIC officers come to him when they had questions. That was not unusual for how senior lawyers operated. But that was not how I conducted business. If an officer had a question—any officer—regardless of rank, position, or title—I was up out of my chair and on my way to sit with that person and look them in the eye while answering their questions and helping them resolve any issue they were facing.

Body language and facial expressions are important components of communication, and most of the officers I was supporting were a short walk from my office, so I rarely stayed in my chair. This created an issue with CEG. Since I was too senior for them to refuse me access to the vault, and I kept going over to see them, and they could not discuss their work out in the hallway, they had to reluctantly let me in the vault so I could answer their questions.

It took several months, but given that I had become a daily presence in the CEG vault, they finally just gave me vault access so I could let myself into the vault (without using the phone). I purposefully never asked for vault access, because I knew that if I had asked for it, they probably would have targeted me on suspicion of being a Soviet spy. I truly mean this as a compliment—I really do—but counterintelligence officers are the most twisted and paranoid people in the spy business. And that is saying a lot. The fact that I had earned their trust was humbling. I am sure they were still keeping an eye on me, but I knew it was nothing personal because these demented counterintelligence officers were so suspicious, they would have targeted their own grandmothers for asking them at the Thanksgiving table, "How is work?"

Having received the *Good Housekeeping* seal of approval and been granted access to the inner sanctum of counterespionage, I was able to work more closely with all the investigators. In terms of my education as an intelligence officer, it was like going to grad school. While these CEG officers were mostly teaching me their business, after a while I was able to add some value to their work. For example, I realized there was not uniform knowledge across the cadre on the details, legal and bureaucratic, concerning the various forms of intelligence collections that were available to deploy against targets CEG was investigating.

To help, I created a shorthand reference document that would summarize the relevant aspects of the entire range of collection tools that the investigators could possibly use. For every possible way CEG could target someone, I described it in sufficient detail, listed the relevant legal concerns, and explained the necessary legal authorities and bureaucratic approvals that were required to use the collection mechanism or technique. This took me a while, but I condensed it to about a dozen pages or so, because it needed to be a handy desk reference if it was going to be useful.

After a while, whenever I walked through the CEG vault, I saw that the investigators had copies of the reference document out on their desks. Branded with brown rings, scribbled in the margins, highlighted, and dog-eared. From time to time, as laws and policies changed, I would update the reference document, and one day when I was handing out an updated version and one of the investigators thanked me for the update to "the Bible." It was, of course, an exaggeration, but still flattering, and I guess, in a legal-support sense, I was the Guttenberg of CIA counterespionage investigations.

But this was all many years later, and for the Squillacote case, I was still out in the hallway. Working my dialing finger down to a nub.

Eventually, I would serve as the legal advisor to six different operational components within the DO, and as a deputy chief and acting chief in the Litigation Division, all before becoming chief of the Litigation Division. And even though espionage cases rarely go to trial, my CIA litigation career would come full circle to end where it started: supporting an espionage prosecution that went to trial and helping DOJ establish NDI.

The Inept Spy

While the Squillacote case involved establishing NDI at a trial, the issue of whether classified information is NDI can also arise very early in an espionage prosecution. For instance, if DOJ wants a defendant to be held in custody pending trial, it needs court approval, and in an espionage case a court may require some initial showing that the defendant was engaged in espionage before agreeing to hold the defendant pending trial. This happened in one of the last espionage prosecutions that I worked on, where a former covert CIA officer, Kevin Mallory, was caught selling classified information to Chinese intelligence.

Mallory worked as a covert CIA officer in the 1990s, and after leaving the CIA, he bounced around to different national security–related jobs. By 2017, Mallory was financially destitute. He could no longer find work, was months behind on his mortgage, and had about $250,000 in debt beyond his first mortgage. The Chinese intelligence service approached Mallory through his LinkedIn page, and the development was a typical one where they pretended to be a think tank offering to pay for policy papers, then later, after establishing a relationship, offered more money for more sensitive information. In terms of motivation, the Mallory case was the exact opposite of the Squillacote case. Mallory was not motivated by ideology. He was motivated purely by money.

During this time frame, I was advising on several Chinese espionage investigations that were maturing into prosecutions, but the Mallory case was the low-hanging fruit of the bunch, thanks mostly to Mallory himself. For Mallory was, frankly, an inept spy.

In an inartful attempt to obtain current classified information he could sell to the Chinese, Mallory started asking old colleagues who were still working at the CIA about current intelligence matters. This was an obvious red flag, and his colleagues reported him. The reports started a counterespionage investigation by my old friends in CEG, who were as paranoid as ever, and, in this case, appropriately so. Sometime later, when Mallory was traveling overseas to meet his Chinese handler, he got caught bringing into the United States almost $20,000 in cash without claiming it on his customs form. Mallory was also carrying a new phone (still in a box) that he told customs was a gift for his wife. The phone was actually given to Mallory by his Chinese handlers and had been loaded with special software to permit covert communications between Mallory and Chinese intelligence.

Mallory was spooked by the incident with U.S. customs, and he assumed he was under some type of investigation, so he devised a plan to cover his tracks that might have even worked had he been a little more technically savvy. Mallory reported to the CIA that he had been approached by Chinese intelligence, to include that the Chinese had provided him with the phone. Mallory even permitted the U.S. government to inspect the phone, after he had permanently deleted some very incriminating text messages he had already sent to his Chinese handlers. Or so he thought. As hard as this is to believe, Mallory had mistakenly not deleted the messages, and he handed the federal government the nails to his own coffin. He was arrested shortly after and charged under Section 794 of the espionage statutes. Classic espionage. Espionage heavy. Up to life in prison or the death penalty.

Spies are trained to evade detection, and, among other things, they may have multiple identities and travel documents. As a result, when a spy is being prosecuted, they represent, in legal terms, a "flight risk." Facing decades in jail for committing espionage could be a powerful motivator to flee the country, and given the training and skills that spies possess, DOJ will normally seek court permission for a current or former spy to be held in custody pending trial.

Presiding over the Mallory case was Judge Ellis of the EDVA. Judge Ellis had presided over other espionage prosecutions and had strong opinions on the Espionage Act and how related proceedings should be handled. I always enjoyed watching him on the bench. Ellis was incredibly sharp, witty, and possessed a booming command voice. He also had a quick temper that would explode out of him if he thought an attorney appearing before him was giving him the runaround. Regardless of the temperature of the proceedings, there was never a dull moment in Judge Ellis's courtroom. And it was, most definitely, His Courtroom.

Judge Ellis was unwilling to keep Mallory in custody pending trial unless DOJ made a sufficient preliminary showing that Mallory had been passing NDI to Chinese intelligence. He expressed serious reservations over whether the government had, in charging Mallory, made a sufficient showing that NDI was at issue in the case. No one had expected Judge Ellis to push the government so hard so early in the case. At the early stages of an espionage prosecution, the government will usually just charge that NDI was being gathered or transmitted and then, much later, nearer to trial (if there even is one) decide specifically what NDI it will rely on to prove this critical element of the crime. This requires a great deal of collaboration with the agencies and departments whose NDI is at risk of public disclosure (the equity owners) so there is good reason for putting these difficult trial issues off for as long as possible. But as Judge Ellis wanted a preliminary showing, and the NDI at issue was classified CIA information, the task fell to a CIA original classifier to provide a sworn declaration (at least this time, given the early stage of the prosecution, we did not need a live witness) to sufficiently show that Mallory had been passing NDI to Chinese intelligence.

By this time, I had risen to chief of the Litigation Division, so I was primarily responsible for the drafting of the affidavit but not doing the actual work. There was an excellent line attorney and deputy doing all the heavy lifting, and they kept me updated and sought guidance when appropriate. We had, as I recall, a very short time, maybe even just one day, to get a signed declaration to the EDVA, and the deputy was working late to fine-tune the draft affidavit so it could be signed and filed the next morning. The timing was so tight we did not have an opportunity to share a draft with the EDVA before the declaration was signed, as we would in the normal course of business, and I knew the prosecutors would be nervous about whether we were going to provide enough information to satisfy Judge Ellis that the case involved NDI.

The CIA General Counsel's office had a long-term relationship with the U.S. Attorney's Office for the EDVA. I always considered the agency fortunate to be within the jurisdiction of a U.S. Attorney's Office of such a high caliber. Due to the nature of the CIA's work, almost all of which is classified, the CIA complicates just about every case in which it is involved. Even what would normally be relatively minor ministerial actions in a litigation can, when a clandestine intelligence service is involved, become quite complicated and involve a spectrum of unique legal issues and challenges. And this is not just on the criminal side. Civil cases (yes, the CIA can be sued in civil cases just like any federal agency) can be even more complicated than the criminal cases. The attorneys in the EDVA know the agency better than any U.S. Attorney's Office, and with all they have done for the agency over the years in both the civil and criminal arenas, I did not want to let them down.

Late that night, I checked in on my deputy—politely, as she did not take kindly to being micromanaged (that is as graciously as I can put it, Smythe)—and the declaration was coming nicely, except for the most important part: describing the NDI. My deputy was a gifted writer and an excellent litigation attorney, but she had no experience with the operational components of the CIA (where I had spent half my career), and she did not have the background to understand what was staring her in the face. When she showed me copies of what Mallory was caught passing to Chinese intelligence, I immediately recognized the code words and related information, as I had served as a legal advisor to the operational component whose classified information Mallory was passing. This is a good example of how important experience is in government, and especially in the intelligence business, where information, and hence knowledge and experience, is tightly compartmented.

Having recognized the equities, the delicate part was describing the sensitive information in sufficient detail for DOJ to meet the evidentiary burden and to do it at an unclassified level so the evidence could be placed on the public record. Luckily, I had decades of experience doing exactly that. For me, it was as natural as breathing.

The next morning, my not-to-be-micromanaged deputy and I drove the declaration over to the EDVA U.S. Attorney's Office. The atmosphere was tense. These were seasoned prosecutors—some of the best in the country—and they comfortably carried enormous amounts of stress. But they were also accustomed to having more than just a few moments to read a critical piece of evidence about to be filed and argued over in open court minutes later. The prosecutors were speed-reading the declaration, nervously flipping pages, until they hit the sweet spot where the original classifier described (generally, but sufficiently) the classified information at issue and explained why it was NDI. Their reading slowed, their demeanor eased, and I could feel the tension dissipate. They knew they had enough to carry their burden to keep Mallory behind bars. And they filed the declaration immediately.

Judge Ellis came to the bench a little late for the morning hearing, and it was obvious he had been reading the declaration. His sharp command voice sternly repeated his serious concern over whether there was NDI at issue in the case. He then stated that after reading the recently filed CIA declaration from "Officer Shiner" (the CIA original classifier), he was now more than satisfied that the case involved NDI. The chief of the EDVA National Security Section, a wonderful man whom I had known for over two decades, looked over at me and gave me a thumbs up. Looking back on my career, it is those moments that I cherish the most.

From your first year as a plebe at West Point, you are taught to memorize and internalize the Principles of War: Mass, Offensive, Objective, Security, Economy of Force, Maneuver, Unity of Command, Simplicity, and Surprise. These principles served me well throughout many long campaigns waging bureaucracy. Given I had risen to division chief level by the time Mallory was being prosecuted, I was akin to a commanding general deploying forces, and I fully embodied Economy of Force (although my deputies might disagree), which boils down to not committing too many resources or too much energy to a particular area so you can conserve them to use elsewhere.

This is a long way of saying I was not involved in the details of the actual Mallory trial, as I had top attorneys working on the case, and I wanted to give them the freedom my managers had given me in the Squillacote case and many others. I was always available when they needed guidance, which they would seek from time to time, and I would require frequent updates. But I have no firsthand account of the trial.

Mallory was found guilty and sentenced to twenty years in prison. *60 Minutes* subsequently did a segment on the Mallory case. They told the true story. For once. During the *60 Minutes* segment, they showed a video of Mallory being interviewed at CIA headquarters when he was pretending that he had not yet been recruited as a Chinese spy. I recognized the room as one of the CEG interview rooms. The video does not show the face of the CEG officer interviewing Mallory, but it shows the back of his head, which I recognized as belonging to a CEG investigator I had enjoyed working with for many years. Not long after the episode aired, I saw him in the hallway at CIA headquarters. I came up from behind him and said, "Hey, I have seen that bald spot before. Were you on *60 Minutes*?" We both had a good long laugh, and I congratulated him on his success in the case, which was well deserved. Then I told him to stop reading my emails and following me. He laughed. But it was a nervous laugh.

Espionage prosecutions often do not go to trial. There tends to be a mountain of evidence against the defendants, which, combined with the potential for lengthy prison sentences and maybe the death penalty, mitigates toward plea agreements. For example, the other two Chinese spy cases I had been consulting on both resulted in plea agreements (Jerry Lee, a former CIA officer, received nineteen years, and Ron Hansen, a former Defense Intelligence Agency employee, received fifteen years). By chance, my lengthy career in the CIA Litigation Division was bookended by espionage trials and assisting DOJ prosecutors to establish the national defense relatedness of classified information that was central to the prosecutions.

CHAPTER 4

Major Mishandling—Precedents, but Not Presidents

Having reviewed the laws pertaining to classified information and provided some real-life experiences with their application, let us now examine the precedents where senior executive branch officials were caught mishandling classified information. Although none of these cases involved a current or former president, they are the closest precedents we have, thus they merit review. Each story is fascinating from the human-interest perspective and instructive in that they provide a benchmark for federal law enforcement conduct in handling cases where senior executive branch officers mishandled classified information.

Director of Central Intelligence John Deutch

John Deutch, President Bill Clinton's director of central intelligence (DCI), was the first high-ranking official investigated and prosecuted for mishandling classified information.[4]

Deutch served as DCI under President Clinton from May 1995 to December 1996. He had also served as deputy secretary of defense and undersecretary of defense for acquisitions and technology in the mid 1990s, and he was known throughout Washington as being an arrogant and abrasive man. Soon after Deutch's appointment as DCI, CIA officers learned that the reputation was well earned. Intelligence officers tend to have irreverent senses of humor and, in that vein, quickly nicknamed their new DCI "Deutchbag."

Shortly after Deutch's appointment as director, he fired two well-respected senior Directorate for Operations (DO) officers. The two officers had been involved in the case of a CIA asset who they kept on the CIA payroll even after receiving reports that the asset had been involved in the murder of a U.S. citizen. In addition to firing the DO officers, Deutch also ordered a file review of all CIA human assets so that those with unsavory backgrounds could be removed from the CIA payroll. This exercise became known as "the dirty asset scrub" and was regarded as one of the stupidest endeavors in the history of the intelligence business. If you want intelligence on what a terrorist cell is planning, you recruit one of the cell members to be an asset, and you pay him well so he tells you what is going on inside the cell. You don't fire the asset you recruited because he is . . . part of a terrorist cell. But that is what Deutch directed, and it turned an already unlikable man into a thoroughly disliked man.

Deutch also took the unusual step of bringing his own team with him to the CIA, to include a close friend from his previous work at the Pentagon, Nora Slatkin. Deutch made Slatkin his second-in-command and gave her authority over operational matters, even though Slatkin had no experience in the day-to-day spy business. Slatkin had all the charm and warmth of Deutch, coupled with an explosive temper, which soon earned her the nickname "Tora Tora Nora." Slatkin was even more disliked than Deutch himself. And that was a high bar.

After his brief tenure as DCI, Deutch maintained possession of unclassified government computers that had been loaned to him for unclassified work at his private residences. Before returning the government computers, Deutch deleted a high volume of classified documents he had unlawfully been keeping on the computers. For one computer, Deutch deleted so many classified documents that he crashed the hard drive and had to call CIA technical support to get the computer running again. When the computers were eventually returned to the CIA, a security review discovered a large volume of classified documents—up to TOP SECRET SCI—on the unclassified computers. I don't recall the exact number, but press reports described the volume as hundreds of classified documents and about 17,000 pages.

In addition to the high volume of classified documents, the CIA security review also discovered that Deutch was keeping a detailed diary on the unclassified computers. Many of the diary entries also contained classified information. I am one of the handful of individuals to have read the Deutch diary, as I was shepherding the classification review. While I am not at liberty to discuss specifics, it was reported at the time, and well known amongst senior CIA officials (as acknowledged in a subsequent public CIA Inspector General [IG] report) that Deutch's diaries were filled with unflattering opinions of other U.S. officials and foreign counterparts Deutch was meeting with across the globe. This added an additional sensitivity to the documents, separate from the typical national security harms at issue in these types of cases.

Slatkin put herself in charge of the internal investigation, and, along with other senior CIA officers, covered up Deutch's crimes. They destroyed evidence, delayed decisions, and failed to notify DOJ of the incident as was required by law. Pursuant to a presidential executive order and federal statute, members of the intelligence community have crimes reporting responsibilities. There is a 1995 Memorandum of Understanding (MOU) between the intelligence community and DOJ (publicly released and available online) that outlines the types of potential crimes that intelligence community officers are required to report to DOJ if they learn of the conduct as part of their official duties. This responsibility is well known within the CIA Office of General Counsel and is part of the culture of the CIA. Under the applicable laws and the MOU, Deutch's conduct should clearly have been reported to DOJ, but it was not.

Eventually the CIA IG—which is an independent office within the CIA—learned of the incident and reported it to DOJ. Attorney General (AG) Janet Reno declined to prosecute the case without even requesting a preliminary investigation. The CIA also neglected to conduct, as they normally would in a situation like this, an assessment of the likelihood of compromise and potential damage. Meanwhile, a new CIA IG, apparently based on a whistleblower complaint, investigated Deutch's conduct and the cover-up by senior CIA officers. The IG issued a classified report in July 1999, and, at the request of the Senate Intelligence Oversight Committee, a sanitized unclassified version (over eighty pages) was publicly released in February 2000. It contained many damaging conclusions:

- Throughout his tenure as DCI, Deutch intentionally processed on unclassified computers "large volumes of highly classified information to include TOP SECRET Codeword material."
- All classified information on those computers was at risk of compromise.
- Even after Deutch was made aware that computers with internet connectivity were vulnerable to being hacked, he continued his practice of processing highly classified material on unclassified computers.
- Deutch took no steps to restrict unauthorized persons from using the government computers at his residence.
- The CIA Office of General Counsel violated a presidential executive order and federal law by not reporting Deutch's conduct to DOJ.

Shortly after Congress released the unclassified report, and after significant public backlash, AG Reno reversed herself and appointed a retired senior prosecutor to conduct a criminal investigation of Deutch. As too much time had passed to appoint what at the time would have been an "independent counsel," the appointee was given the title "special assistant to the assistant attorney general for the Criminal Division."

I was the CIA attorney assigned to support the DOJ investigation and eventual prosecution. The special assistant investigating Deutch was very professional and a man of few words. He was stoic and all business, and I never blamed him, given that he knew my agency—and specifically my office—at the most senior levels, had covered up Deutch's unlawful conduct. I did my best to honor his requests in a timely and professional manner. And I gave him a wide berth.

Deutch ended up signing a plea agreement for a single misdemeanor for "unauthorized removal and retention" of one document. One single document. Classified SECRET.

You may recall that "unauthorized removal and retention" was the misdemeanor charge that I characterized as the go-to charge when DOJ only wanted to give the proverbial slap on the wrist to a high-level official. The Deutch case paved the way for this tactic. Deutch was not charged with obstruction of justice, even though he had gone to great efforts to destroy the evidence of his crime. Deutch's inner circle was never investigated or charged with any crimes, despite also destroying evidence, never filing a crimes report, and taking other active measures to cover up Deutch's illicit activities. Under the terms of Deutch's plea agreement, he would serve no jail time and would pay a $5,000 fine.

Deutch never even had to uphold the terms of this incredibly lenient deal. Right after he signed the plea—the very next morning—President Clinton pardoned Deutch as one of his last official acts in office. It was fascinating to see the politics playing out. It was no coincidence that Deutch did not sign his plea agreement until the evening before Clinton's last day in office: Deutch had obviously been hoping to receive a pardon.

It appears nearly certain that President Clinton did not inform Deutch that the pardon was going to issue, as had Deutch known a pardon was coming, he would not have signed a plea agreement admitting to a misdemeanor the night before. Given Deutch's acknowledgment of mishandling of classified information, his successor as DCI, George Tenet, revoked Deutch's security clearance. In 2007, CIA Director Michael Hayden restored Deutch's clearance.

And that is the sordid tale of the first cabinet-level official to be prosecuted for mishandling classified information. But I also have an interesting epilogue.

Due to my work on the case, I was nearly certain I had figured out the identity, or rather identities, of the CIA whistleblowers (I deduced that there were two) who had gone to either the CIA IG or Congress to blow the whistle on Deutch's conduct and the cover-up. I took no umbrage with their actions. They followed the correct procedures; they were right to report what they reported; and they used the appropriate channels to file their reports. Too often, people who leak classified information to the press are referred to as "whistleblowers." That is a misnomer. They are leakers. They usually have a personal or professional vendetta or are trying to achieve a political goal, and if they are leaking classified information, they are also criminals. Whistleblowers follow established procedures, and in the intelligence community that means reporting something you think is wrong to an IG office or a Congressional Oversight Committee, or both.

All I am willing to say is that I deduced that one of the whistleblowers was a senior CIA attorney in my office. After the entire affair was over, I took two copies of the plea agreement, framed them, and brought them to this senior attorney's office and handed them to him. He asked me what they were. I told him they were copies of the Deutch plea agreement, and I thought he might like them. He gave me a nervous smirk, and said nothing, at first. He was literally speechless. And nervous. The exchange confirmed my suspicions. He looked down at the two frames, holding one in each hand with his eyes going from one to the other, laughed as his face turned red, and said, "Why two?" And I said, "The other is for ______." (The name of the other whistleblower, who was also very senior, and a friend of his.) Then I turned and left. I could still hear him laughing as I walked out.

National Security Advisor Samuel "Sandy" Berger

Samuel "Sandy" Berger was President Clinton's national security advisor (technically "assistant to the president for national security affairs") from March 1997 to January 2001. In 2003, Berger was at the National Archives and Records Administration (NARA), reviewing classified presidential records from the Clinton administration to prepare for his testimony before the National Commission on Terrorist Attacks upon the United States (the 9/11 Commission) and to assist former President Clinton to decide whether Clinton would claim executive privilege over any of the documents requested by the 9/11 Commission.

During his review, Berger stole at least five highly classified documents by stuffing them in his socks and down his pants and then hiding them under a trailer at a nearby construction site. When questioned about the missing documents, Berger lied, blamed NARA, changed his story multiple times, and then eventually admitted to the theft and to destroying three of the TOP SECRET presidential records.

Berger claimed that going to NARA to review the documents was inconvenient and stealing them made it easier for him to prepare his testimony. This made no sense, as even if it was true, he would not have needed to steal every copy he found of the same document. The full extent of Berger's thievery was never ascertained, as before the archivist became suspicious and started tracking documents, Berger had enjoyed unsupervised access to uncategorized original presidential records.

As far as we know, the documents Berger stole were all related to a terrorism after-action report that was critical of the Clinton administration.

While I did not work on Berger's case, I do recall a rumor going around Washington that the documents showed that the Clinton administration had a chance to kill Osama bin Laden well before 9/11 but decided not to take the action. This may have been just a rumor, but the documents were apparently embarrassing enough to him and the Clinton administration that a man of his stature would risk jail time to erase them from history.

Like Deutch, Berger's plea agreement was for a single misdemeanor for "unlawful removal and retention of classified information." The Bill of Information accompanying the plea was two short paragraphs and did not list the specific documents, did not describe their classification levels, and omitted that they were presidential records. The one count simply described them as "certain materials which contained classified information belonging to the United States." DOJ's Sentencing Memorandum briefly described one of the documents as having been sent to NARA from the Clinton Library in Arkansas. A later House of Representatives report revealed that the document was highly classified and that the Clinton Library was not authorized to store classified information. The public record does not reflect whether there was any investigation of the Clinton Library or any attempt to assess whether the library contained any additional unauthorized documents.

DOJ never sought any warrants. Berger's home was never raided or even consensually searched. Per his plea agreement, Berger received probation and one hundred hours of community service. No jail time. DOJ only sought a $10,000 fine, but the presiding judge increased it to $50,000. Berger also agreed to not seek a security clearance for three years, but the plea agreement allowed for the government to grant Berger a clearance during those years.

CIA Director David Petraeus

David Petraeus was a four-star general who served as President Obama's CIA director from September 2011 to November 2012, during which time a truly bizarre series of events uncovered Petraeus's mishandling of classified information. Petraeus was having an affair with his biographer, Paula Broadwell, who was jealous of a third woman who Broadwell apparently felt was too close to Petraeus. Broadwell sent anonymous threatening emails to the third woman, who then reported the threats to the FBI. The FBI investigation led to a raid of Broadwell's home, wherein the FBI discovered TOP SECRET SCI information Petraeus had unlawfully provided to Broadwell. Petraeus was questioned by the FBI and lied about providing Broadwell with the classified information. A subsequent FBI raid of Petraeus's home discovered eight notebooks containing what DOJ described as "classified information regarding the identities of covert officers, war strategy, intelligence capabilities and mechanisms, diplomatic discussions, quotes and deliberative discussions from high-level National Security Council meetings, and . . . discussions with the President of the United States of America."

Petraeus was, like John Deutch, arrogant and abrasive. Intelligence officers are good at keeping secrets, but they also love to gossip, and stories quickly spread through the CIA of Petraeus's massive ego, demeaning behavior toward subordinates, and sense of entitlement. One popular story involved Petraeus losing his temper over a briefing he received. Part of CIA culture is to have experts, regardless of rank, personally brief issues within their expertise rather than following a more hierarchical structure where managers would do the briefing even though a manager would not have as much granular detail on the topic. This culture went all the way up to briefings for the director. After Petraeus was briefed by one expert, he enquired as to the rank of the individual, and when he was informed that the expert was of a comparatively low rank, he became furious and shouted, "So, I was just briefed by a private!"

Petraeus was incredibly fit for his age, and his CIA security detail had trouble keeping up with him on his daily runs. A trustworthy source confided to me that while Petraeus was difficult to keep up with on a running track, the real reason no one wanted to be on his workout detail was because Petraeus treated them like serfs. Members of the security detail were not allowed to run within his shadow (as that could interfere with his running stride). As he entered his cool-down phase and transitioned to a brisk walk, he would drop his hands to his sides. That was the signal for one serf to place a fresh towel in one of his hands and another serf to remove the cap from a fresh water bottle before placing the bottle into Petraeus's other hand.

These were just rumors and may or may not have been true, but I was privy to similar conduct. When I was serving as the legal advisor to the CIA's Computer Operations Group (COG),[5] Petraeus visited COG for briefings. Because of the nature of COG's work, which occurred within different vaults with different types of highly specialized equipment, Petraeus had to move around for the briefings. We were required to have Petraeus's favorite type of chair in each separate space where he was to be briefed, even if the briefing was only for a short period. There were many such stories going around CIA headquarters, and the result was that Petraeus was considered to be the biggest Deutchbag since Deutch himself. No one at the agency shed a tear at Petraeus's departure or steep fall from grace.

By the time Petraeus was prosecuted, I was toward the end of my CIA litigation career, serving as chief of the Litigation Division. The twilight of my CIA Litigation Division career had come full circle to near where it started: prosecution of a CIA director for mishandling classified information. The Petraeus case dragged on for a while, but it was resolved in 2015 without much fanfare through a plea agreement, as is customary.

DOJ charged Petraeus with—you guessed it—one single misdemeanor for unauthorized removal and retention of "documents and material containing classified information." This was particularly lenient, as Petraeus had also provided the classified information to his biographer and mistress, who lacked the requisite clearances, and because Petraeus had obstructed justice by lying to the FBI. Like Berger, Petraeus received probation and no jail time. DOJ sought a fine of $40,000, but the presiding judge increased it to $100,000.

There is no public information to indicate whether Petraeus maintained his security clearance, but well after his plea it was reported that Petraeus was still informally advising President Obama on foreign policy and military matters, which would presumably entail needing a security clearance.

Secretary of State Hillary Clinton

The fourth precedent is the most infamous. In 2016, while she was running for president, classified information was discovered on home email servers Hillary Clinton had established during her tenure as President Obama's secretary of state.

While I did not work directly on the FBI investigation, I was doing related work in the context of civil litigation. Private entities were seeking copies of Clinton's emails through the Freedom of Information Act (FOIA), and as I was serving as chief of the CIA's Litigation Division, I was responsible for the review of Clinton's emails referred to the CIA by the State Department as part of the litigation. While I cannot discuss the specific content of the emails, I can say that I am one of the few people to have read the most sensitive of the fabled Clinton emails. And for the record, I want to state—unequivocally—that I am not suicidal. I love myself. Probably too much.

Clinton initially refused to give the federal government access to her servers, and DOJ accommodated Clinton's desire to have her own private attorneys review the contents of the private servers Clinton had established for her official emails (about 60,000 emails). After Clinton's private attorneys reviewed the emails, approximately 30,000 were deemed federal records and returned to the government. Out of those 30,000, a government-wide classification review determined that more than a hundred—at least—contained classified information when they were sent, and about a dozen of those were classified TOP SECRET.

By reviewing tidbits in the slack space of some of Clinton's servers (later provided to the government, after Clinton's attorneys wiped the servers with a software called "BleachBit") and looking at email accounts of other government officials, the FBI determined that there were thousands of other federal records that Clinton's lawyers had deleted—some of which were classified.

Clinton's private lawyers, it turned out, had searched Clinton's emails by running search terms and reading subject lines (in other words, they destroyed federal records, classified documents, and evidence in a criminal case without attempting to read the content). Clinton publicly claimed that none of the emails on her server were marked as classified, that none of the sensitive information was classified at the time it was sent, and that her use of a private server had been authorized. None of those statements were true.

According to the testimony of FBI Director Comey, some of Clinton's emails were marked as classified when they were sent, and over one hundred contained classified information when they were sent. Additionally, the State Department IG Steve Linick (an Obama appointee) conducted a review and published a report that found there was "no evidence" that Clinton sought or received any approval for storing her official email correspondence on a private server in her home. The IG report also concluded that if Clinton had sought such approval, it would have been denied.

Clinton and seven of her aides refused to cooperate with the State Department IG review, so they were never interviewed. Even after the IG report was published, Clinton continued to publicly claim that her use of a private server "was allowed."

Working with the State Department on the classification review of Clinton's emails was, in a word, *tense*. Normally, the people you need to watch out for as a government lawyer are the political appointees. They were nominated to those positions because of party loyalty and will protect their party and its officials at all costs—including leaning on career government lawyers to cross ethical lines. I have many such war stories that would truly shock you, but they will have to wait for another day.

In the Clinton email classification review, however, I was surprised to find the exact opposite: the political appointee I met with—an undersecretary at the State Department—was professional, polite, and never attempted to unduly influence the outcome of the classification review process in any way. However, a career senior State Department officer who was working on the classification review repeatedly tried to influence classification decisions to benefit Clinton. Maybe the State Department was just trying to avoid embarrassment, but it appeared to me that the goal was to protect Clinton. Either way, I witnessed the department purposefully skewing its review. It is a near certainty that many more of Clinton's emails were classified when they were sent, and the claim that only slightly over one hundred classified emails were found on her private servers is not accurate.

It never got much publicity, but toward the end of the Clinton email scandal, FBI Director Comey publicly stated that around 2,000 of Clinton's emails were determined to be presently classified, even though they were not classified when they were sent. Comey described these emails as having been "up-classified." That is not a thing. I spent twenty-five years steeped in the world of classification, and I had never heard the term "up-classified" before Comey uttered it, and I've never heard it after.

Having seen firsthand how the State Department was handling the classification review, I would wager that most, if not all, of those 2,000 emails were classified when sent, but Clinton and her aides had just not properly marked the classified communications. Failure to properly mark classified documents does not excuse the negligence. It makes it worse.

This would, of course, not be a revelation to anyone who has worked extensively with classified information. One of the primary categories for classified information is the "foreign relations or foreign activities of the

United States." Clinton was secretary of state. What percentage of over 30,000 official government emails to and from the secretary of state would you think discussed "the foreign relations of the United States"? According to the State Department and the FBI, the rough estimate is about 100 out of over 30,000. That would be less than .33 percent. That is what we were to believe: that only one-third of 1 percent of the secretary of state's official emails discussed sensitive matters pertaining to the foreign relations of the United States.

Not every email of the secretary of state discussing U.S. foreign relations would carry a sufficient likelihood of harm from unauthorized disclosure to merit classification. But the actual percentage would with near certainty be a good deal more than one-third of 1 percent. While I don't need to rely on the data alone, having read many of the emails and seen firsthand how the classification review was being handled, any unbiased individual experienced with classified information and the higher levels of government would see that the results of the State Department classification review did not comport with reality.

After the FBI investigation concluded, Comey held a press conference and publicly declared that Clinton and her aides had been "extremely careless" in handling classified information but lacked "criminal intent" and that "no reasonable prosecutor" could pursue criminal charges against Clinton. DOJ never filed any charges against Clinton or any of her aides, all of whom apparently kept their security clearances. One of Clinton's senior aides, who was on some of the more classified emails, was Jake Sullivan, who became President Biden's national security advisor. In testifying before Congress, Comey summarized his views as follows:

> I see evidence of great carelessness, but I do not see evidence that is sufficient to establish that Secretary Clinton, or those with whom she was corresponding, both talked about classified information on email and knew when they did it they were doing something that was against the law.

Secretary Clinton was an original classifier. She was required under Executive Order 13526 to have yearly training that "must include instruction on the proper safeguarding of classified information and on the sanctions . . . that may be brought against an individual who fails to classify information properly or protect classified information from unauthorized disclosure." It bears repeating that failure to properly mark classified information is not an excuse for negligent handling: it makes it worse. Especially for someone who is an original classifier and should absolutely know better.

You will recall that one of the executive order requirements to be granted a security clearance is signing a nondisclosure agreement, and that this requirement applies even to cabinet-level officials. The State Department uses a standard government form, the SF 312. Secretary Clinton's signed SF 312, which is publicly available, clearly states the following:

> I have been advised that the unauthorized disclosure, unauthorized retention, *or negligent handling of classified information by me* could cause damage or irreparable injury to the United States or could be used to advantage of a foreign nation. [emphasis added]

The textbook definition of gross negligence is "conscious and voluntary disregard of the need to use reasonable care." You be the judge as to whether Clinton's conduct met that standard.

Similarities & Anomalies

While none of these historical cases involved a current or former vice president or president—an important fact considering the uniqueness of those elected positions—they are the closest precedents and merit deeper scrutiny. Analyzing these cases reveals a few commonalities and a couple of notable anomalies.

As for the commonalities, all the cases involved very senior executive branch officials with high-level clearances who were presumably well versed in the spectrum of rules concerning creation, marking, access, transportation, and storage of classified information. All of these high-ranking officials engaged in egregious mishandling of highly classified information, and despite that conduct, all were treated with incredible leniency and deference.

In Deutch's case, AG Reno initially declined to even have a preliminary investigation of his blatantly unlawful conduct. Only after a public backlash did Reno reverse herself and order an investigation. And even then, DOJ permitted Deutch to plead to a single misdemeanor for mishandling a single SECRET document, despite Deutch having stored hundreds of classified documents, classified up to TOP SECRET SCI, on unsecured computers with internet access. Deutch's home was never raided, despite the obvious potential for Deutch to have printed some of the hundreds of highly classified documents he unlawfully retained; Deutch was not charged with obstruction of justice even though he attempted to destroy evidence; and no one in Deutch's inner circle was investigated for obstruction of justice despite destroying evidence, and engaging in other unlawful conduct to protect Deutch.

The Deutch pardon received very little publicity because the other pardon President Clinton issued the morning of his last day in office was to Mark Rich, a fugitive financier who had fled the country after he was indicted in the Southern District of New York for tax evasion, wire fraud, racketeering, and trading with the Iranians during the Iranian Hostage Crisis. The Rich pardon got all the publicity because Rich had been on the FBI's Top Ten Most Wanted List and because Rich's wife had coincidentally donated over $1,000,000 to the Democratic party, $450,000 to President Clinton's library, and $100,000 to Hillary Clinton's Senate campaign. Unbelievably—or perhaps not—the Rich pardon was never even reviewed by the DOJ Pardon Office. Instead of following the normal process, the pardon was reviewed and approved by a little-known deputy AG. His name was Eric Holder. But I digress.

As for Sandy Berger, his home was also never raided, even though Berger stole TOP SECRET documents from our National Archives, lied to investigators, admitted to destroying documents, and the full scope of his thievery was never ascertained. Berger was only charged with a single misdemeanor for mishandling classified information and was never charged for false official statements or destruction of evidence. Berger received no jail time and DOJ's requested fine was so lenient that the presiding judge increased it five-fold. Perhaps most incredibly, Berger's plea permitted Berger to seek a new security clearance in just three years.

Petraeus was allowed to plea to a single misdemeanor for unauthorized removal and retention of classified information despite unlawfully retaining, in his home, for years, eight notebooks containing TOP SECRET SCI information. Petraeus was also not charged for providing highly classified information to his mistress or for making false statements or obstructing justice for lying to the FBI about providing her with TOP SECRET information.

The Petraeus case does, however, present two interesting anomalies. The first is that the FBI raided Petraeus's home. While this would be expected in a typical criminal investigation, it is abnormal compared to how similarly situated high-ranking executive branch officials were treated by law enforcement. The second anomaly is that the Petraeus plea contained an unusually detailed statement of facts wherein Petraeus acknowledged deliberately and intentionally lying to FBI agents. This was quite odd. DOJ did not charge Petraeus with false official statements or communicating or transmitting national defense information (NDI) to someone not entitled to receive it, even though the facts that clearly supported such charges were included in the plea. The atypical treatment of Petraeus can with some confidence be attributed to one person: Sean Joyce. Sean Joyce was the deputy director of the FBI at the time, and he oversaw the Petraeus investigation. Joyce was an experienced agent who rose up through the ranks and was aggressive, highly ethical, and known for refusing to let politics impact a criminal case. We cannot know for sure, but it is highly likely that Joyce's leadership accounts for the anomalies in the handling of the Petraeus investigation, and if true, a very good example of how one person with a strong moral compass can ethically lead a large bureaucracy and set an example for government officials to venerate and emulate.

While the FBI, likely due to Joyce's leadership, handled the Petraeus investigation "by the book," DOJ has unfettered discretion over charging decisions, and DOJ was incredibly lenient. Petraeus was charged with only one misdemeanor when other crimes were not only obvious, but acknowledged by Petraeus in the very plea agreement he signed.

As for Hillary Clinton, you would be hard pressed to find any individual in U.S. history treated so leniently by the FBI and DOJ. Clinton purposefully established unsecured private email servers in her home to store sensitive government communications. Any reasonable government official would know that classified information would be captured in the work emails of such a high-ranking official. This is a basic fact that has been glossed over, but any competent official at her level of government would know that her emails would routinely contain classified information. Much of it might only be CONFIDENTIAL, and in my experience, prosecutors won't charge individuals for the lower spectrum of classification, but the fact remains that given her position and her official duties, even the most dim-witted government official would have known that Clinton's emails would frequently contain classified information.

Clinton was given such a wide berth by federal law enforcement that the FBI even permitted Clinton's lawyers, who did not have security clearances, to search a massive tranche of documents that absolutely would contain classified information. Clinton and her inner circle destroyed their personal communications devices, and Clinton's lawyers even wiped their own hard drives after completing the email review "in a such a way as to preclude complete forensic recovery." Clinton was never charged with any crimes, and the investigation did not resemble a typical criminal investigation. No FBI raid. No subpoenas. No effort to compel any testimony. No obstruction charges. No targeting of her closest aides who were obviously complicit.

Given my decades of experience in working on these types of cases, I can state unequivocally that any rank-and-file officer in the executive branch engaging in the same conduct as John Deutch, Sandy Berger, David Petraeus, or Hillary Clinton would absolutely have been prosecuted, would almost certainly have received jail time, and would without doubt have been barred from ever holding a security clearance again. So yes, these high-ranking executive branch officials—all of whom belonged to the Democratic party—were all treated by federal law enforcement with a degree of leniency and deference few ever see.

To get a sense of what would happen to a lower-level government employee for unauthorized removal and retention of classified information, consider the case of Kenneth Ford. Ford was an employee at the National Security Agency (NSA), and when he left service, he took two boxes of TOP SECRET documents with him, allegedly because he thought the information in those documents could help him obtain future employment. Ford kept one box in his kitchen and another in a bedroom closet, and apparently, he only showed them to his girlfriend, who, after they broke up, made an anonymous tip to the Feds that Ford was headed to the airport to sell classified documents to a foreign country. The latter claim was false (hell hath no fury), but it was enough for a warrant and the FBI found the classified documents in a quickly organized raid of Ford's home. Ford was found guilty of violating the Espionage Act (a 793 charge for unlawfully possessing NDI) and of making a false statement, and he was sentenced to six years in a federal penitentiary. *Six years*. That is how normal people are treated.

The final commonality between the precedential cases is that they all involved some degree of politics. Some more blatantly than others. This is not surprising, given all the officials were well-known, high-ranking political figures.

DCI John Deutch was a Democrat, appointed by a Democrat, President Clinton. The Democratic party was in power when Deutch was prosecuted, and it was a very reluctant and gentle prosecution. AG Reno declined to even have the FBI conduct a preliminary investigation until she was shamed into reversing herself by a public backlash. Despite having purposefully kept a high volume (hundreds) of classified documents on his home computers connected to the internet, Deutch was permitted to plead to a single misdemeanor for one single SECRET document, then pardoned by the same Democratic president who had appointed him as DCI.

The Sandy Berger prosecution, viewed through the lens of politics, was an anomaly. Berger, a Democrat, was treated with great leniency by a Republican administration. All the other precedents involved Democratic appointees being treated leniently by Democratic administrations, but Berger was prosecuted under the reign of George W. Bush. The Bush administration was not generally known for a laid-back approach to protecting national security, yet it was incredibly deferential to Sandy Berger, and we can only speculate as to why. Maybe Bush did not like the optics of using the criminal justice system to go after a high-ranking figure from a rival political party. Maybe he was concerned about inviting a quid pro quo. Maybe he just had bigger fish to drown.

While the Berger prosecution appears to have lacked political bias, there was a strong political undercurrent. Both the factual basis for the plea agreement and the DOJ Sentencing Memorandum for Berger's prosecution contained an odd statement: "The 9/11 Commission received copies of each of the documents the defendant removed in the normal course of the production of documents." The DOJ Sentencing Memorandum added, "There is also no evidence that any unique document was destroyed or lost." Both of those statements are at a minimum misleading and may also be false. DOJ never told anyone that Berger had access to uncategorized original presidential records before the NARA staff suspected Berger of theft and started marking documents. Only when Congress subsequently conducted its own inquiry did these additional facts come to light, and Congress also discovered that there had been heated debate between the NARA IG and DOJ over whether Congress should be informed about Berger's unsupervised access to other original documents that had been requested by the 9/11 Commission and which Berger could have easily stolen. DOJ prevailed, Congress was not notified, and the House of Representatives issued a formal report accusing DOJ officials of making misleading statements to hide that the full extent of Berger's theft was unknown and that Berger may have destroyed other documents sought by the 9/11 Commission.

CIA Director David Petraeus was appointed by a Democrat, President Obama. The Obama administration permitted Petraeus to plea to a single misdemeanor despite Petraeus keeping eight notebooks containing highly classified information in his home and giving unlawful access to his mistress and biographer. There were noteworthy apolitical actions taken in the Petraeus investigation, likely attributable to the FBI deputy director, but DOJ has unfettered discretion on charging decisions and Obama's DOJ was incredibly lenient and deferential to Petraeus, a Democratic appointee.

There were no anomalies in the Clinton case. Clinton was the Democratic nominee for president, being investigated by a Democratic administration, that of President Obama. The DOJ IG reviewed the FBI investigation of Clinton and published a report ("A Review of Various Actions by the Federal Bureau of Investigation and Department of Justice in Advance of the 2016 Election") thoroughly detailing the deference and political bias that permeated the Obama administration's Clinton investigation. Among other things, the DOJ IG noted the following:

- The FBI decided not to obtain or even seek specific evidence, such as the personal devices used by Clinton and her senior aides, because the FBI was anxious to complete the investigation, believed the evidence would be of limited value, and because of "limitations [the FBI] . . . imposed on the investigation's scope."

- The FBI used voluntary witness interviews instead of grand jury testimony, claiming it was concerned about exposing grand jurors to classified information.
- The FBI used "consent agreements" to obtain the laptops of Clinton's private attorneys instead of subpoenas, and then they never even searched the laptops.
- The FBI permitted fact witnesses (and potential co-conspirators) in the criminal case to be present for the sole interview the FBI conducted with Clinton. (The DOJ IG's idea of a strong rebuke was to describe this unbelievably biased event as "inconsistent with typical investigative strategy.")
- The FBI decided not to seek permission from DOJ to review highly classified materials that may have included information that was relevant to the investigation.
- During the criminal investigation, AG Loretta Lynch—our nation's top law enforcement officer—directed the FBI to publicly refer to the criminal investigation of Clinton as a mere "matter."
- While he was in a supervisory role in the criminal investigation, a DOJ assistant AG tried to get his son a job with the Clinton campaign.
- The FBI ignored obviously relevant evidence that was found on the laptop of a Clinton aide's husband and hid the evidence from DOJ prosecutors.

The last finding involved particularly egregious conduct, because the FBI did more than just ignore relevant evidence: it purposefully buried it. DOJ only found out about the buried evidence because a DOJ prosecutor in New York (working on a related case) made an inquiry to Deputy Assistant AG George Toscas in Washington. Toscas was the most senior career DOJ official with supervisory responsibilities for the Clinton investigation. Toscas, like Sean Joyce, was an experienced career official who rose up through the ranks and was aggressive, highly ethical, and known for refusing to let politics impact his work. Here, again, is an example of the impact one person with a sound moral compass can have on a large bureaucracy. Once Toscas learned about the buried evidence, he started asking questions, which forced the FBI to concoct a proverbial laundry list of excuses as to why they had been hiding the evidence against Clinton. For a month. After examining the dog-ate-my-homework FBI excuses, the DOJ IG wryly concluded, "We found these explanations to be unpersuasive."

Let me elaborate on two of the FBI excuses for not doing their jobs, as they could appear reasonable to the average person, are national-security based, and run counter to my extensive experience in this arena.

In all my experience working on hundreds of high-profile criminal cases involving classified information, I never had a case where the FBI or DOJ was "concerned" about exposing grand jurors to classified information. Section 9-90 of the U.S. Attorneys' Manual outlines a process for providing classified information to grand jurors, and I have never known any law enforcement officer to be shy about pursuing those procedures. Yet the FBI used that as an excuse to not pursue leads in the Clinton case. The FBI also claimed that it did not review relevant information because it was highly classified. My extensive experience with FBI agents was just the opposite: the more sensitive the information, the more the FBI agents pushed to see it. These examples may seem small, but they show that the FBI agents handling the Clinton investigation acted contrary to typical law enforcement practices and used "national security" as an excuse to avoid taking logical and routine investigative actions.

The DOJ IG review of the FBI Clinton investigation also discovered that five FBI officers working on the case—*five*—had sent messages on

FBI systems that "reflected political opinions in support of former Secretary Clinton and against her then political opponent, Donald Trump" and that some of the messages "raised concerns that political bias may have impacted investigative decisions." The DOJ IG was most concerned with a specific text message between the FBI deputy assistant director and the FBI special counsel to the deputy director:

FBI special counsel to the deputy director:

> **"[Trump's] not ever going to become president, right? Right?!"**

FBI deputy assistant director:

> **"No. No he's not. We'll stop it."**

The DOJ IG, ever cautious in its use of the English language, described these texts as being "indicative of a biased state of mind" that "implies a willingness to take official action to impact the presidential candidate's electoral prospects." There are many more such texts, such as this:

FBI deputy assistant director:

> **"Also CNN poll. Has me stressed out."**
>
> **"Poll Finds Emails Weighing on Hillary Clinton, Now Tied With Donald Trump."**

This text shows the FBI deputy assistant director working on the Clinton investigation was "stressed out" that the investigation he is working on is hurting Clinton's candidacy. Again, there are many more such texts, but you get the picture.

While it may be a truism that a few rotten apples can spoil the whole barrel—particularly when they are the biggest apples in the barrel—we should be mindful that there are, throughout federal law enforcement, many very good people working hard every day to make sound ethical decisions in the performance of their duties, regardless of their personal political opinions or preferences. Throughout my twenty-five-year career as a government attorney specializing in federal prosecutions involving classified information, I was privileged to work with many top-notch FBI agents and DOJ prosecutors. One commonality amongst all the top-tier prosecutors was their highly ethical adherence to their legal responsibility to provide specific categories of information to criminal defendants. They wanted successful prosecutions, no doubt, but they insisted on a fair fight. If I suggested a creative way around implicating classified information in criminal discovery that these prosecutors considered too close to the line, they would remind me, politely, that it was their law license, and their soul, that was on the line, not mine. And they were right. One senior DOJ prosecutor I worked with many years ago had a Shakespeare quote on his computer screensaver I have never forgotten: "He Who the Sword of Heaven Will Bear Should Be As Holy As Severe."[6] He obviously wanted a constant reminder of his dual roles as a prosecutor.

Throughout my career, I have, unfortunately, also worked with some in law enforcement who, let's just say, could have benefited from having the same screensaver. Those were the types working on the Clinton investigation. And those same officers were simultaneously investigating the Trump campaign in 2016.

As a practical matter, the Clinton investigation was a sham from the start, as even the DOJ IG acknowledged that the FBI, right from the beginning, focused on "whether Clinton intended to transmit classified information on unclassified systems." If you have worked on these types of cases, you really don't need to know anything else to see the inherent bias, because one of the relevant criminal laws *does not require intent.* As discussed earlier, "gross negligence" is sufficient to violate one of the relevant criminal laws, and negligence does not require intent. Yet, the FBI focused on intent from the start, and lack of criminal intent was former FBI Director Comey's excuse for stating that "no reasonable prosecutor" could charge Clinton.

A basic fact that merits emphasizing: the FBI director is not the AG. Director Comey's job (at which he clearly failed) was to oversee an unbiased and thorough criminal investigation, not to make charging decisions. Charging decisions are DOJ's prerogative. Comey's actions in unilaterally proclaiming that "no reasonable prosecutor" could charge Clinton usurped DOJ's authority and were subsequently, and correctly, described by the DOJ IG as "extraordinary and insubordinate." We all do things from time to time that are spontaneous and ill conceived, but Comey had begun drafting his statement clearing Clinton *two months* before the investigation had concluded and before Clinton and key witnesses had even been interviewed. When subsequently called to testify before Congress, Comey contumaciously defended his indefensible conduct. Comey's congressional testimony merits a thorough analysis, because it centered on a relevant aspect of the Espionage Act: the 793 language that criminalized gross negligence in the handling of NDI.

James Comey v. The Espionage Act

Gross negligence in the handling of NDI is expressly criminalized by the Espionage Act, so Comey could not claim otherwise when he testified under oath before Congress. Comey also could not dispute that former Secretary Clinton had TOP SECRET SCI emails on a private server she had purposefully set up in her home (along with at least a hundred other classified emails), as he had already publicly acknowledged this fact. And given Comey had publicly described Clinton's conduct as "extremely careless," he would have looked ridiculous if he tried to claim that Clinton was not "grossly negligent," as "gross negligence" is so closely synonymous with "extremely careless." So, Comey did the only thing he could do: he attacked the law itself.

Comey testified that when Congress was debating criminalizing gross negligence in handling NDI, "there was a lot of concern in the House and the Senate about whether that was going to violate the American tradition of requiring that before you're going to lock somebody up, you prove they knew they were doing something wrong." First, there is no "American tradition" of not prosecuting someone unless they knew they were violating a law. There are many examples of criminal laws where lack of knowledge or negligence will still get you prosecuted. Statutory rape. Negligent homicide. Involuntary manslaughter. Negligent endangerment of a child. There are probably others, but these all came immediately to mind, and they expose the fallacy of Comey's "American tradition." Second, in Clinton's case, her signed SF 312 specifically warned against negligence in the handling of classified information, and Clinton was one of the few original classifiers in the executive branch. Those facts alone show that Clinton should have known that she was "doing something wrong."

According to Comey's logic, if members of Congress expressed concern about a proposed law during debates, even if the proposed law is enacted, it should not be enforced. This is, of course, absurd and would undermine our legal system. Comey claimed that comments during the congressional debates were the reason DOJ did not want to enforce the law concerning gross negligence and the reason DOJ had only invoked the law once: "as best as I can tell, the Department of Justice has used it once in the ninety-nine years since [it passed], reflecting the same concern." Notice the qualifier: "as best as I can tell." That is legal terminology for "I am not sure if this is true." So, Comey's own words show that he did not know why DOJ had rarely charged gross negligence in the handling of NDI. Contrary to Comey's assertions, the public record indicates that the law criminalizing gross negligence in handling NDI has rarely been used because DOJ was either being lenient and only charging misdemeanors (such as with high-ranking officials), or because DOJ was charging more heavily (such as with classic espionage that carries the death penalty) and not interested in more lenient charges.

Comey also made the dubious claim that if a criminal law is rarely charged, then that rarity supports the law not being enforced: "no reasonable prosecutor would bring the second case in one hundred years." But there is no correlation between the frequency in which a criminal law is invoked and that law's constitutionality or usefulness. A good example from the national security arena is the nuclear option for disloyalty: treason. Treason is the only crime expressly defined in the U.S. Constitution.[7] And "as best I can tell," only one person has been charged with treason in over seventy years. Under Comey's logic "no reasonable prosecutor" would charge treason given that the law has not been used in decades *even though the crime is embedded in the Constitution.* There are probably more criminal laws that are rarely charged but perfectly acceptable, but this example sufficiently exposes the fallacy of Comey's logic.

Apparently, no one thought it suspicious that Comey did not mention the name of the one case in the last hundred years where gross negligence in handling NDI had been charged. But it stuck out to me. Right away. Why would he not even mention the name of this one case and at least give a summary? It was not difficult to find the case, which I knew well but had admittedly forgotten. And having refreshed my recollection, it was not difficult to see why Comey had conveniently neglected to identify the case in his testimony.

FBI Counterintelligence Officer James J. Smith was prosecuted in 2003 for gross negligence in handling NDI. That was the case Comey slyly avoided identifying by name. Smith's friends and associates called him "J.J." Although I never worked with J.J. Smith, I did work closely with FBI agents who knew him quite well, and from what they told me, Smith was a wonderful man whom everyone in the FBI respected and liked. Unbeknownst to his colleagues, however, Smith was involved in a twenty-year intimate relationship with Katrina Leung, one of the top FBI China sources. Leung was also a Chinese double agent, reporting everything she was learning from the FBI to Chinese intelligence.

According to Leung's statements to the FBI (after her arrest), Smith would let her review and take notes of classified documents he would bring to her home. She would also surreptitiously remove the documents from Smith's briefcase (conveniently left open) and copy them. One particularly sensitive document Leung copied and then passed to Chinese intelligence was a TOP SECRET document Smith had "checked out" overnight from the FBI and unlawfully brought to Leung's house. Another document the FBI seized from Leung around the time of her arrest was a TOP SECRET transcript from an electronic surveillance wherein Leung was caught talking to a Chinese intelligence officer. After his arrest, Smith admitted that he continued to provide Leung with classified information *even after he discovered she was a Chinese spy.* Smith even allowed Leung to attend and videotape his retirement party, which included CIA officers who were almost certainly undercover operations officers whose affiliation to the CIA was classified. When questioned by his fellow agents, Smith initially denied having a sexual relationship with Leung, and repeatedly lied about trips he had taken with her, to include two weeklong trips to Hong Kong. Smith showed the FBI agents several journals containing extensive notes from his debriefings with Leung over a twenty-two-year period, along with videotapes and other miscellaneous documents he had kept. Before Smith was arrested, he removed twenty-five of these notebooks from his home and tried to hide them in his lawyer's office. The FBI was surveilling Smith and seized the documents.

Smith was indicted for gross negligence in handling NDI and making false official statements to the FBI about his affair with Leung. Smith's conduct could have easily justified a 794 charge under the Espionage Act, but DOJ chose to charge Smith with the more lenient 793 charge involving gross negligence. Leung was indicted for unauthorized copying of NDI with intent to injure the United States or to benefit a foreign nation. That, you may recognize, is also a 793 charge. For inexplicable reasons, Leung was not charged under 794, even though she was obviously stealing classified information to provide it to a foreign adversary (classic espionage).

The lenient charging of Smith and Leung was minor compared to the leniency shown in their prosecutions. Smith was permitted to sign a plea for making false official statements. All other charges were dropped. All of them. His punishment under the plea was three months of home confinement, three years of probation, one hundred hours of community service, and a $5,000 fine. Smith was also permitted to keep his FBI pension. Astonishingly lenient given Smith's conduct looked more like a 794 violation, and even under the 793 charge originally filed, which was mysteriously dropped, Smith could have received ten years in prison. Leung's case was dismissed in 2005 due to prosecutorial misconduct based on DOJ forbidding Smith, as part of his plea, from speaking with Leung or her defense counsel. DOJ appealed the dismissal and in the interim Leung signed a plea admitting to one count of lying to the FBI and one count of tax fraud. As part of her plea, Leung received no jail time, three years of probation, and a $10,000 fine. This, mind you, was a known Chinese spy who almost single-handedly crippled the FBI's China Counterintelligence Program and who engaged in classic espionage for over twenty years. During her time as a double agent for China, the FBI paid Leung around $1.7 million. She was not required to return any of the money.

DOJ's IG's office did a thorough review of the case. The DOJ IG reviewed more than 300,000 documents and conducted over 100 interviews. The final report, over 200 pages long, was classified, but a short unclassified summary is publicly available. According to the public summary, because of the DOJ IG investigation, the FBI updated its procedures for handling human assets and substantially revamped its China Counterintelligence Program.

This was the one case in history where someone was charged with gross negligence in handling NDI. Ironically, given that Smith purposefully brought classified documents to Leung's house in an unlocked briefcase, for decades, the gross negligence charge against Smith fit perfectly for much of his conduct (that is, if you believe Leung, who was a Chinese spy, and Smith, who lied repeatedly to the FBI for over twenty years). Also ironically, the gross negligence charge appears to have been used as a matter of leniency to avoid more serious charges against a beloved career FBI agent whose conduct was grossly negligent but also could have supported a much harsher 794 charge. No wonder Comey did not mention the name of the case.

PART II

The Biden Cover-up

CHAPTER 5

The Presidential Records Act

In the President's Hands

Before we can analyze the cases of President Biden and former President Trump, we first need an understanding of one additional federal law: the Presidential Records Act (PRA). This will likely come as a surprise to many, but the PRA is not a criminal law. You could have easily believed otherwise, given how this law has been publicly portrayed, but the PRA is a purely civil law with no criminal provisions. Additionally, courts have ruled that the PRA provides no enforcement mechanism, civil or criminal, against a president or vice president, current or former. Let's briefly examine the law's history and practical application.

The PRA governs the preservation and disclosure of presidential and vice-presidential records. Up until President Richard Nixon's administration, records from a presidential administration were considered private papers of the president. Congress passed the PRA in 1978 to address lingering issues from the Nixon era concerning preservation of historical records, and with the passage of the PRA, "presidential records" were deemed public property. But critically, to avoid potential separation-of-powers issues inherent in Congress telling the executive how to keep his own records, under the PRA, only a president or vice president decides what is a "personal" and what is a "presidential" record. So, to a president or vice president, the law is practically toothless. Yes, the law does specifically define what types of documents should be presidential or vice-presidential records, but it leaves the critical decisions on categorizing records completely up to the president and vice president. The practical result is that the PRA is a mere guide for a president or vice president, and nothing more.

In federal court cases involving the PRA, the courts have ruled that courts lack the authority to even review a president's decision as to whether a document is a personal or presidential record. In a case called *Armstrong v. Bush*, a private group sued President Bush seeking a declaration from the court that the records they wanted were presidential records.[8] The D.C. Circuit Court ruled that the PRA precluded judicial review of the "president's recordkeeping practices and decisions," given that such review "would upset the intricate statutory scheme Congress carefully drafted to keep in equipoise important competing political and constitutional concerns." While acknowledging that the statute contained requirements for the president's disposition of records, the D.C. Circuit clearly ruled that the statute "leave[s] the implementation of such a requirement in the president's hands."

A few years after the *Armstrong* decision, the D.C. Circuit pulled back a bit of the sweeping language in a follow-on case, but only to permit judicial review of *guidelines* for determining when a federal agency record was a presidential record.[9] And the clear reason for re-engaging on the topic was that the court was concerned that *agencies would designate too many records as presidential records* and circumvent the Freedom of Information Act (FOIA) (under the PRA, presidential records are generally not subject to FOIA for many years).

Closest to current events is the case *Judicial Watch v. NARA* (National Archives and Records Administration).[10] In this case, a private group brought a lawsuit against the National Archives to try to force the archivist to designate material from the Clinton administration as presidential records instead of personal records. Clinton had, while president, met with an author in the Oval Office, and the author taped the conversations. After leaving office, Clinton kept the tapes (in a sock drawer in his bedroom), which allegedly included things like phone conversations between Clinton and foreign heads of state (which would be presumptively classified). The lawsuit alleged that the tapes should have been designated as presidential records and transferred to the archivist after Clinton's presidency. The court ruled that (1) Clinton's decision to keep the tapes as "personal records" was solely the president's decision; (2) that the National Archivist had no authority to reverse that decision; and (3) that no court could even review the decision. In making its ruling, the court highlighted that "under the statutory scheme established by the PRA, the decision to segregate personal materials from presidential records is made by the president, during the president's term and in his sole discretion." Emphasizing that "NARA does not have the tapes in question" and that "NARA lacks any right, duty, or means to seize control of them," the court clearly ruled that "the PRA does not confer any mandatory or even discretionary authority on the archivist to classify records. Under the statute, this responsibility is left solely to the president."

Generally, under the PRA, presidential records are unavailable to the public for five years, but the PRA also permits a president or vice president to further restrict access to records containing information such as classified information, confidential communications amongst senior advisors, and personnel and medical files. Those restrictions can last over a decade and are themselves subject to exceptions, some of which we will examine later. Nowhere in the PRA does it state that classified documents must be considered presidential or vice-presidential records, which makes sense given that the statute leaves those decisions up to a president and vice president. Legal scholars can debate the meaning of congressional silence, but as written, there is an argument that a president or vice president could decide that classified documents are personal records. I do not like that—and I am uncomfortable with that being the law—but I must concede that it is at least a viable argument given the way the law was written.

To summarize, the PRA is a purely civil statute with no criminal provisions, it has no enforcement mechanisms to force the compliance of a president or vice president (current or former), and it gives the president and vice president unfettered discretion to decide which of their records are presidential or vice-presidential records and which are personal records. Despite the existence of the PRA, presidents and vice presidents maintain significant control over public access to their records, regardless of content. In the closest legal precedent, the court ruled—in the context of audiotapes (some likely classified) that President Clinton kept after his presidency—that a president has the sole, unfettered, unreviewable discretion to decide what is and is not a presidential record, and NARA's only job is to accept what a president provides. Keep all this in mind as we delve into the cases concerning our current and former presidents.

CHAPTER 6

From Locked Closet to the Adjacent Room

On November 2, 2022, President Biden's private lawyers reportedly found about ten classified documents in a locked closet in Biden's office in the Penn Biden Center for Diplomacy and Global Engagement (a non-governmental entity affiliated with the University of Pennsylvania). Some documents were marked TOP SECRET SCI. After the discovery, Biden's private lawyers contacted the White House; the White House contacted the National Archives and Records Administration (NARA); and NARA contacted the private lawyers to take custody of the documents. None of these entities contacted the FBI or DOJ. The next day, NARA informed the NARA inspector general (IG), a statutorily independent office, and the day after that, the NARA IG contacted DOJ.

When NARA contacted Biden's private lawyers, it learned that the lawyers had already taken nine boxes of documents from the Penn Biden Center and shipped them to a law office in Boston. NARA General Counsel Gary Stern emailed Biden's private lawyers asking them to "please ensure that the boxes in your office in Boston remain secure in a locked space and are not accessed by anyone." Stern's request for additional security and sequestering indicates that the boxes were known or thought to contain classified documents. There would be no other reason for Stern to request that the documents be locked up to restrict access.

Having overseen the review and inventory of large tranches of documents throughout my career, I know that lawyers do not just throw documents into boxes: they review them first and create an inventory. So, Biden's private lawyers must have known what was in the nine boxes, as they almost certainly would have created an inventory before packing them. Emails between NARA senior officers and Biden's private lawyers indicate that the lawyers informed NARA, verbally, via phone conversations, that there was something particularly sensitive about the boxes' contents. For just over an hour after NARA's initial request to have the boxes secured and sequestered, NARA's Chief Operating Officer William Bosanko sent an urgent email to Biden's private lawyers. "Based on some discussions this evening, we need to change our approach. I believe that tomorrow we will need to take temporary physical custody of all of the textual (or other) record material." This email shows NARA's increased concern as it learned more information, and it shows that NARA senior officials were having detailed phone conversations about the boxes *while purposefully avoiding putting any details in their emails*. That is very suspicious behavior. Especially for senior officers at the National Archives. Normally archivists are in the business of documenting and preserving government conduct, not hiding it.

For decades, I worked with senior government officers, especially lawyers, who would purposefully avoid emails or any written record memorializing their thoughts, opinions, or directions. Sometimes I would send an email to a client, colleague, or boss memorializing exactly what they had suggested or ordered, only to have them send a reply claiming that they had said something quite different or the exact opposite. I learned to be very careful when working with someone who wanted to avoid putting something in writing. So, I, of course, noticed that the senior NARA officials were purposefully avoiding putting any substantive details about the nine boxes in their email exchanges with Biden's private attorneys.

On the evening of November 8, Bosanko sent a cryptic email to another NARA official informing the official that the next day Bosanko would be asking him "to send two staff to retrieve and then secure some materials from a law firm" and that this task would need "to be done with the utmost professionalism and discretion." The email was titled "URGENT." Like other NARA emails concerning Biden's documents, the communication purposefully avoided substantive details. Again, archivists are normally focused on documenting the internal work of government, not hiding it. This may just be a coincidence, but typically transporting TOP SECRET documents requires two people, and Bosanko specifically requested "two staff." Lastly, while a request for "professionalism" is understandable, a request for the "utmost discretion" implies that NARA was conspiring to keep the recovery of Biden's vice-presidential records, and likely classified documents, hidden from the public.

On November 9, NARA took control of the nine boxes but did not—according to NARA—inventory or examine the contents. Given the urgency NARA expressed in gaining possession of the boxes, NARA's lackadaisical approach to reviewing the contents defies logic.

Within a week, the attorney general (AG) assigned U.S. Attorney John Lausch to conduct a preliminary investigation of Biden's possession of classified documents at the Penn Biden Center. In mid-November, the FBI searched Biden's Penn Biden Center office. No information pertaining to any of these events was made public. Everything was handled secretly.

Over a month later, on December 20, Biden's private lawyer informed DOJ that more classified documents (described only as a "small number") were found in Biden's Wilmington, Delaware, garage. We do not know when the lawyer discovered the classified documents, only that he reported the discovery to DOJ five days before Christmas. When the FBI gathered the documents, it did not fully search the garage or any part of the home, despite there being an open investigation and this being the second discovery of classified documents in Biden's possession.

A few weeks later, on January 5, 2023, U.S. Attorney Lausch advised AG Garland that a special counsel should be appointed to investigate the mishandling of classified documents found in Biden's D.C. office (about ten) and Wilmington garage (a "small number"). Up to this point—over two months after the initial discovery in Biden's D.C. office and almost three weeks after the discovery of additional classified in Biden's garage—the Biden administration handled the entire matter in secret. No press releases. No leaks. No photos. No NARA statements about recovering vice-presidential records. No public knowledge of what was transpiring. You can maintain secrecy like this when you control the entire executive branch.

On January 9, 2023, CBS News broke the story of classified documents being discovered in a locked closet in Biden's D.C. office. Having worked on a broad range of investigations and prosecutions involving the mishandling of classified information—and more high-profile government scandals and crises du jour then I care to recount—I viewed the breaking news story with an admittedly critical eye, and I will share my reactions in no particular order.

First, it struck me that the context of the discovery was odd and highly suspicious. Why would President Biden's private lawyers travel all the way from Boston to clean out Biden's personal office in D.C.? Those are high-priced lawyers who presumably bill by the hour, and the administrative task of packing boxes does not need to be done by lawyers. That Biden's private lawyers traveled from another city to remove documents from Biden's D.C. office (which had been vacant for some time) indicated to me that Biden or someone close to him knew that there was something that merited sensitive handling. And again, lawyers don't just throw documents into boxes: they inventory them first (unless they are trying to hide what they are taking). So, where was the inventory? Also, why weren't the documents being sent to Biden's home, or, if they were vice-presidential records (which they were) to the National Archives?

Second—and what struck me the most—was that the detail about the "locked closet." The Biden administration emphasized this detail, probably to imply that the TOP SECRET SCI documents were stored safely. But storing them in a more secure manner than other documents indicated to me that someone knew they merited additional safeguarding. That is admittedly speculation, but reasonable, and to me, the "locked closet" seemed more damaging than favorable for Biden. Also, the Penn Biden Center was still being built when Biden left the White House (the center did not open until over a year later). This means the classified documents were not always in a locked closet, unless that closet was originally in another place and then somehow magically transported into the Penn Biden Center.

Third, I focused specifically on who did what. The mantra from the Biden administration was that Biden did the right thing and reported the infraction to DOJ immediately. But none of the entities involved in the initial discovery attempted to contact law enforcement. Not Biden's private attorneys. Not the White House. Not even NARA. It was the NARA IG—an independent office within NARA—who contacted DOJ. Biden's private attorney obliquely addressed this inconvenient fact by stating in a press release that "the President's personal attorneys were in regular contact with NARA and anticipated that NARA would notify the Department of Justice."

Lastly, we soon learned that the breaking news neglected to mention the second set of classified documents already found (three weeks prior) in Biden's Wilmington garage. The disclosure of only selective, dated facts, just days after the AG was advised to appoint a special counsel, indicated with near certainty that the breaking news was leaked from the Biden administration, likely part of a media strategy to start addressing a growing scandal that would soon be public, given the recommendation to appoint a special counsel. Within hours of the story breaking, the

White House Counsel's Office issued a statement from a relatively new hire, the "Special Counsel to the President" Richard Sauber. Do you recognize the name? Coincidences are sometimes just coincidences, and this may be one of those times, but the special counsel to the president handling issues related to Biden's mishandling of classified documents was the same Richard Sauber who defended Kurt Stand (Theresa Squillacote's husband) in the first espionage case I worked on in the late 1990s.

Sauber was hired by the White House Counsel's Office in May 2022. At the time, the White House announced that Sauber was hired to handle potential congressional investigations, and maybe that is true, as that was about five months before Biden's private attorneys reported they had discovered the first set of classified documents found in Biden's possession. Sauber is a top-tier criminal defense attorney and a Democrat, and maybe that alone is why he was hired by the White House. But it is nonetheless a fact that five months before President Biden's personal attorneys reported discovering classified documents in Biden's personal office, the White House just happened to hire one of the few criminal defense attorneys in the world who has defended Espionage Act charges. Maybe just a coincidence. But maybe not, and I found myself wondering if maybe the classified documents had been discovered sooner than we had been led to believe (more on that later).

Putting aside the background of the newly hired special counsel to the president, there were several substantive issues I noticed with Sauber's statement. First, Sauber described the discovery as involving what "appear to be Obama–Biden Administration records." The language is a clever way of avoiding the more accurate term "vice-presidential records," given the more accurate term would directly implicate Biden's six-year violation of the Presidential Records Act (PRA). Sauber also very cleverly side-stepped providing information on the volume of vice-presidential records: after admitting that "Obama–Biden" records had been discovered, he quickly narrowed the focus, adding that a "small number" bore classification markings, without ever providing any information as to the overall volume of

"Obama–Biden" records. To this day, we have no idea how many vice-presidential records Biden had at the Penn Biden Center.

Having spent a career helping the executive branch hide uncomfortable facts, deceptive wordplay tactics are familiar to me, and I spot them instinctively. And so, I also noticed that Sauber avoided providing the number, or classification levels, of the classified documents Biden had retained, describing them only as a "small number." Those are tactics I would have used, and I appreciated the tradecraft. I also noticed (a few days later) that Sauber's statement, like the breaking news story, completely omitted any information about the classified documents discovered in Biden's garage three weeks before. As the garage discovery was not yet publicly known, the White House was hiding it from the public for as long as possible. You can keep secrets like this when you control the entire executive branch, and you have made sure that the other two branches are kept in the dark. Lastly, Sauber stated that Biden's private lawyers were cooperating with the Archives and DOJ in "a process" without providing any details about what the "process" entailed. Almost every subsequent statement from Biden's private attorneys, the White House Counsel's Office, spokespersons for the president, and President Biden himself, referenced cooperation in "the process" *while omitting any details about the process.*

One day after CBS broke the initial story, President Biden briefly spoke to reporters, downplaying the growing scandal. Biden began by stating, "Well, let me get rid of the easy one first. People know I take classified documents, classified information seriously." Biden then emphasized that his lawyers "did what they should have done: they immediately called the Archives—immediately called the Archives . . ." In fact, from what we know, Biden's lawyers did not call the Archives at all, let alone "immediately." President Biden also—just like the breaking news story and Sauber's statement—conveniently neglected to mention the second set of classified documents already discovered in his Wilmington garage three weeks prior.

Once the story broke, it became obvious that NARA had never made any press release or congressional notification back in November 2022 when it recovered (six years late) a large volume of Biden's vice-presidential records. NARA was criticized for helping cover up Biden's PRA violations and retention of classified documents. Debra Steidel Wall, the acting archivist, responded to the criticism in a letter to the chairman of the House Committee on Oversight and Accountability, insisting that NARA had conducted itself "without any political bias." Steidel Wall claimed that NARA did not publish a press release in November 2022 because NARA's policy was not to divulge confidential communications with current or former presidents or vice presidents unless and until those matters are reported in the press.

There are two fatal flaws with the acting archivist's excuses for NARA having hidden that it had recovered, six years late, a large volume of Biden's vice-presidential records. The first flaw is that NARA did not need to divulge any confidential communications at all, as NARA could have just released a statement that it had recovered Biden vice-presidential records and informed the public of the approximate volume and when those documents would be available for public access through the Freedom of Information Act (FOIA). Instead, NARA kept its collective mouth shut. The second flaw is that despite the purported NARA policy to not divulge communications unless and until the matters are reported in the press, NARA still failed to make a press release *after the story broke*.

When examining government actions, the closest you will get to the truth is usually gleaned from contemporaneous records, such as emails and instant messages. Even when officials are being cautious in what they memorialize—and trust me, officials are very aware that their writings are being captured for posterity—the best chance you have of ascertaining truth is from records drafted at a time when they were under pressure to get things done. If there are no contemporaneous records, the lack of documentation is itself telling, and in those circumstances, the best option for finding truth is to put the relevant officials under oath for testimony. NARA's decision not to publish a press release, even after the Biden story broke, is a good example, because NARA's internal emails concerning the decision have been released through FOIA, and the NARA general counsel testified to Congress about the decision.

NARA internal emails show that NARA was not relying on any policy when it kept silent even after the story broke. Throughout the day of January 10, NARA's most senior officers were editing draft documents titled "Draft Statement Regarding Biden Records" and "Draft NARA Notice Penn Biden Materials," obviously believing that NARA would be publishing a press release that day or January 11. After editing and fine-tuning the drafts all day, in the evening, NARA's Chief Operating Officer Bosanko abruptly stated in an email "we will not be issuing a statement at this time. Many thanks to all who helped dial in the message we would have issued."

There was no reference to, or reliance upon, any NARA policy. It was just a decision. NARA did publish an internal notice to the NARA workforce the next day, noting the breaking news story concerning Biden's retention of classified documents and informing the workforce that NARA was "unable to comment on the specifics of the matter." Again, the internal NARA notice made no reference to any NARA policy. That same day, the Archives board members received an email from Patrick Madden, the executive director of the National Archives Foundation. "Biden Classified Documents News Story" was the subject of the email, which stated, "The Archives has opted not to release any press statements about this story." Again, there was no mention of any policy dictating that NARA make no comment. Use of the word "opted" implies that NARA could have "opted" to issue a press release concerning the breaking story, or at a minimum, inform the public that NARA had obtained a large volume of Biden's vice-presidential records, *six years late*. NARA chose to make no comment, which you will see in due time, is the exact opposite of what NARA chose to do in Trump's case.

As part of a later congressional interview, the NARA general counsel admitted that someone in the Biden administration—outside of NARA—had directed NARA not to make a press release after Biden's possession of classified documents became public. This direction obviously came on the evening of January 10, when Bosanko sent the email telling NARA senior officials that NARA would not be making any public statement. When asked by Congress who in the Biden administration ordered NARA to not publish the press release, the NARA general counsel refused to answer the question. His refusal to answer was based on "DOJ guidance."

On the same day as NARA's "unable to comment" notice to the NARA workforce, January 11, President Biden's private attorneys—without the FBI being present—began a two-day search of President Biden's Delaware homes (Wilmington and Rehoboth Beach). You don't need to have any experience investigating the mishandling of classified information to see how odd it is that, at this juncture, Biden's residences were being searched by Biden's private attorneys and not by the FBI. A U.S. attorney had been appointed to conduct a preliminary investigation in mid-November; the FBI had searched the Penn Biden Center in mid-November; and yet, almost two months later and weeks after classified documents were also found in Biden's Wilmington garage, President Biden's private attorneys were the ones searching Biden's residences, not the FBI. Biden's private attorneys did not even have security clearances. That means they were not even supposed to have *access* to classified information, which means the FBI arguably facilitated additional crimes. This is the kind of anomaly that the DOJ IG would matter-of-factly describe as "inconsistent with typical investigative strategy."

To me, the most shocking aspect of Biden's private lawyers searching Biden's personal residences for evidence of crime was not just that they did it, with FBI knowledge, but that they kept searching even after they found more evidence. No one seems to have caught this, but after the private lawyers discovered classified material at the Wilmington home, they did not inform DOJ. Only after conducting an additional search of the Rehoboth Beach home, *the next day*, did Biden's private attorneys inform DOJ that they had found evidence the previous day in Wilmington. The only reason for the delay, that I can see, is that Biden's private lawyers wanted to ensure that they searched the Rehoboth Beach home before the FBI, as if they had made a timely report to DOJ of the evidence they had found in Wilmington, DOJ might have asked them to cease work and not search the Rehoboth Beach residence.

On January 12, Sauber released two statements concerning additional classified documents discovered in Biden's Wilmington home. Sauber emphasized that the White House was cooperating with the Archives and DOJ "in a process" to ensure "Obama–Biden Administration records" were "appropriately in possession of the Archives." Sauber acknowledged that Biden's private lawyers had searched Biden's two Delaware homes, and that Biden's private lawyers had discovered a "small number" of classified documents. Sauber's statement is misleading in that it conflates the recent discovery of classified documents in Biden's Wilmington home with the classified documents discovered in the garage almost a month before. One of the classified pages was described as located not in the garage itself but in an "adjacent room." That vague language hit me right away, but I will address that later. While much of Sauber's statement was misleading, one sentence was outright false: "As was done in the case of the Penn Biden Center, the Department of Justice was immediately notified." Reasonable people could debate the scope of "immediately," but in the context Sauber was using the word, it is not synonymous with "two days later."

On the same day as Sauber's public statements, January 12, AG Garland announced the appointment of Robert Hur as special counsel to investigate the discovery of classified documents in the Penn Biden Center and Biden's Wilmington home.

"Special counsel" are sometimes mistakenly referred to as "independent counsel," so let me briefly explain the difference. Independent counsels no longer exist. They were appointed under a law that expired in 1999, and under that law, independent counsels reported to Congress, not DOJ. Both political parties had been so sufficiently spanked by independent counsels over the years, that in 1999 Congress permitted the law to expire. (The law had a built-in shelf life, often referred to as a "sunset provision.") DOJ then promulgated new regulations for appointing "special counsel." Under DOJ regulations, special counsel are appointed by the AG when a criminal investigation "would present a conflict of interest" for DOJ or there are "other extraordinary circumstances," and the appointment is in the public interest. While special counsel have day-to-day independence and the authority of any U.S. attorney, they are bound by DOJ policies and procedures, and the AG maintains the authority to reject any investigative or prosecutorial steps a special counsel wanted to pursue. So, a special counsel has room to run, but the AG, and hence the incumbent administration, *still holds the reigns.*

Decisions of whether to appoint a special counsel, and whom to appoint, are inherently political. Robert Hur was a very smart choice for special counsel to investigate President Biden, as Hur, on the surface, has conservative credentials, but underneath that conservative veneer is a moderate who had participated in Democratic party anti-Trump endeavors. Hur clerked for Chief Justice William Rehnquist, a well-known conservative chief justice of the U.S. Supreme Court, and Hur was nominated to a U.S. attorney position by President Trump. Stellar conservative credentials. In practice, however, Hur also served closely with senior DOJ officials who took notable actions against President Trump. He served as the special assistant and counsel to Christopher Wray, Biden's FBI director, when Wray was the assistant AG in the DOJ Criminal Division. He also served as a senior aide to Deputy AG Rod Rosenstein when Rosenstein appointed Robert Mueller as special counsel to investigate collusion between the Trump campaign and Russia. Hur then served as Rosenstein's top liaison to Special Counsel Mueller's investigation. Hur is known to be an excellent attorney; a kind, decent man; and not a pit-bull prosecutor. Make no doubt about it: the Biden administration put great thought into the selection of Robert Hur as special counsel. And a very smart choice he was.

AG Garland's order appointing Special Counsel Hur only mentions one criminal law: "unauthorized removal and retention of classified documents." Recognize the language? It is verbatim from the law, discussed earlier, that used to be a misdemeanor but was recently upgraded to a felony and which *does not apply to elected officials*. Biden's government service has always been as an elected official. I saw this immediately. It is inconceivable that the multiple DOJ attorneys drafting and reviewing a formal AG order appointing a special counsel to investigate President Biden did not know that the only law cited in the order did not even apply to Biden. Hur was expressly permitted to investigate other related crimes, so he was not limited to the only law cited in the order, but the fact remains that the only law listed in the AG order appointing a special counsel to investigate Biden *did not apply to Biden*.

On the same day Hur was appointed, Biden finally acknowledged the classified documents found in his Wilmington garage about three weeks prior. When asked what he was thinking by keeping classified documents in a garage, next to his Corvette, Biden testily responded, "My Corvette's in a locked garage, okay, *so it's not like they're sitting out in the street*." Biden also emphasized that he was cooperating fully with his DOJ and that "as part of that process" his private lawyers "reviewed other places" where he had stored documents from his vice presidency and that "they discovered a small number of documents with classified markings in storage areas and file cabinets in my home and my personal library." Biden added that "as was done" with the material from his D.C. office, DOJ was "immediately notified."

Almost everything in Biden's statement was false or misleading. DOJ was not "immediately" notified about the initial discovery; classified documents in his home were not secure; and Biden's lawyers did not "review" other places—they *searched*. Biden emphasized "the process" to give the illusion of normalcy, when in reality, *the process* was far from normal.

On January 14, Sauber released another statement concerning a third set of unsecured classified documents discovered in Biden's possession. This third set Sauber described as "six pages" with "classification markings" found in "a room adjacent to the garage." Sauber's description of where the third set of classified documents was found—"a room adjacent to the garage"—had me laughing out loud. Who describes a room in their house as "adjacent to the garage"? Not me. And not you. Maybe an English nobleman. But other than aristocracy, a government attorney trying very hard to hide something. No one seemed to focus on the description, but I spent a career helping the government bury bodies (figuratively speaking . . . mostly), so I can spot government sophistries scattering brush over a freshly dug grave. I knew the "room adjacent to the garage" was either something embarrassing, like a bathroom, or more incriminating, like a personal library. It turned out to be the latter.

It also struck me that while the description of where the most recent classified documents were found was odd and vague, the description of the material itself was very specific: "six pages." I could see how carefully the narrative was being crafted: unfavorable information was being hidden through either omission or clever wording, while anything the Biden administration viewed as favorable was described in detail. You can do these things when you control the entire executive branch. Most people would understandably think six pages was not a big deal, but I viewed this differently. The description "six pages" told me that the discovery was not a single document. Otherwise, it would have been "one six-page document" or just "one document." These were six separate pages in Biden's personal library in his private home. We can only speculate as to how six separate pages of classified information got into Biden's personal library, but the likely scenario is that Biden (or someone in the house) was rummaging through boxes, selecting individual pages to review, and bringing them into the personal library. How else would six separate pages of classified information get into Biden's personal library? This is not a minor issue because the narrative the White House had been fostering was that negligent staffers must have mistakenly put classified information into boxes that were sent to Biden's home. And that narrative could well be true. But six single pages in Biden's personal library does not fit the narrative.

Sauber's statement also provided no information as to the nature of the classification markings on the six pages. *What were the markings*, I wondered? *CONFIDENTIAL? SECRET? TOP SECRET? TOP SECRET SCI?* With near certainty, the classification markings were on the more sensitive end of the spectrum. Because if the documents were only CONFIDENTIAL, the Biden administration would have been eager to provide that detail.

In a sign that the Biden administration knew it needed more damage control, on January 19, President Biden again addressed the issue of his retention of classified documents. By this time, classified documents had been found in the Penn Biden Center, Biden's garage, and his personal library. Biden described the discoveries as just "a handful" of documents that were "filed in the wrong place." He downplayed his potential malfeasance by claiming that the "American people don't quite understand" why reporters were asking questions about the unsecured classified documents found in his possession. "I think you're going to find there's nothing there . . . I have no regrets . . . There is no *there* there."

The next day, January 20, yet another set of unsecured classified documents was discovered in President Biden's possession. This fourth set of classified material was also found in the Wilmington home, pursuant to an actual FBI search (with President Biden's private lawyers and White House lawyers present). The FBI search discovered what Biden's private lawyer described the next day as "six items consisting of documents with classification markings and surrounding materials." The description of "six items" and "surrounding materials" was yet another vague and brilliant description that I noticed instantly. This grave was dug a little deeper than the "room adjacent to the garage," and the scattered brush was thicker, but the odor of cadaver was wafting through the press release.

Previous classified material discovered in Biden's possession was described by the Biden administration or Biden's private lawyers as "documents" or "pages." But this time the classified material was described as six "items." Lawyers are very specific about their wording. Use of the word "item" was not happenstance. And an "item" could be a folder of documents. Or a box of documents. Or a trunk full of documents. It was possible that the "six items" was just six documents, and no one in the Biden administration paid any attention to the difference in language. But my experience told me otherwise. I may have retired a few years ago, but the lingering dirt under my fingernails and my well-worn shovel told me that if it was just six documents, the Biden administration would have been happy to widely disseminate that description. Above ground.

You may think me paranoid, but you should never underestimate the deviousness of government officials and particularly that of government lawyers. I know. I was one of them. While I kept chalk on my cleats throughout my career, I insisted on staying within ethical boundaries. This was not the case with many of the government officials, and especially lawyers, I was exposed to in my career. Bending the law clearly past the breaking point was often excused as providing "what the client wants." And at the political-appointee level, "what the client wants" is often for senior career lawyers to provide cover for the ruling political party to break inconvenient laws to achieve political goals, score political points, protect a party loyalist, or just pander to a party base. I have numerous real-life examples that I witnessed, and I could write an entire book with stories that would shock your conscience. For now, I will just say that I don't blame the Biden administration for doing what any administration would do—mobilizing all the Kingdom's considerable resources to protect the Throne—but I am also not willing to uncritically consume the waxed fruit placed out for the serfs to devour.

Another interesting aspect of the description of the fourth set of classified documents found in Biden's possession was that some of the documents were "from the President's service in the Senate." This added an interesting plot twist, as unlike the previous sets of classified documents discovered in Biden's possession, which were all apparently from his vice presidency, this fourth set included material from Biden's time as a senator. That is not a minor fact. Some would conclude that, given the passage of time since Biden was a senator, any classified information he possessed from that time frame would be dated and likely of lesser sensitivity. That is likely true. But even if true, this classified material presents a very interesting scenario for which a bit of background is required to fully appreciate.

U.S. senators sometimes receive classified information from the executive branch, despite it being under the president's control. This practice extends to members of congressional Intelligence Oversight Committees for oversight purposes. Unlike executive branch employees, senators and federal judges granted access aren't subjected to security clearances, polygraph tests, or pre-publication reviews due to their high-level roles. However, this doesn't extend to congressional staffers or judicial law clerks, who require security clearances for access. For instance, while Senator Biden had access, his staffers might not have had the necessary clearances or need-to-know for lawful access.

Additionally, to gain access to classified information, a senator would need to go to a sensitive compartmented information facility (SCIF). There are SCIFs on Capitol Hill, but classified documents are not supposed to leave the SCIF. So, if classified documents from President Biden's time as a senator are in his personal residence, it is likely—perhaps even a near certainty—that Senator Biden himself unlawfully removed the classified documents from a SCIF and later took them home. There is admittedly some speculation involved in this scenario, but it is nonetheless the likely scenario, and it is not covered by the White House narrative of "staffers must have negligently packed some boxes."

During the Squillacote espionage prosecution, I recall the FBI agents being quite pleased when the forensics came back, and they included one of Kurt Stand's fingerprints on the SECRET CIA finished intelligence product his wife had stolen from the Pentagon. Do you think Special Counsel Hur attempted to lift fingerprints from any of the classified documents discovered in Biden's possession? Fingerprinting would be especially important for documents from Biden's time as a senator, because if the only fingerprints on those documents belong to Joseph Robinette Biden, that is what the law enforcement folks call "strong circumstantial evidence."

After the January 20 search that discovered the "six items" with classification markings in Biden's Wilmington home, Richard Sauber also released a statement that was mostly devoid of detail but described the special counsel's criminal investigation as "a review" and emphasized that President Biden "takes this seriously." The talking point that President Biden "takes this seriously" has been another mantra from the Biden administration and President Biden himself since Biden's unlawful possession of classified documents became public. But compare the mantra with Biden's words.

When Biden finally publicly acknowledged the initial discovery, he started by saying, "Well, let me get rid of the easy one first." So right from the beginning, Biden downplayed a question concerning a potential mishandling of classified documents that could harm national security as "the easy one." When asked about his keeping classified documents in his garage, next to his Corvette, President Biden angrily responded: "My Corvette's in a locked garage, okay, *so it's not like they're sitting out in the street*." And after at least three sets of unsecured classified documents had been found in his possession, Biden claimed they were just "a handful" of documents "filed in the wrong place" and chastised reporters *for even asking* about the mishandling. (The "American people don't quite understand" why reporters are asking such questions, he reprimanded, and then added "I think you're going to find there's nothing there . . .

There is no *there* there.") You decide if those responses from President Biden comport with the mantra that Biden "takes this seriously."

In February 2023, Biden's DOJ obtained a guilty plea from twenty-nine-year Air Force veteran Lieutenant Colonel Robert Birchum, for unlawful removal and retention of classified information. Birchum had retained—in his home, overseas office quarters, and driveway storage pod—about 300 classified documents or files, more than thirty of which were TOP SECRET/SCI. Birchum was sentenced to three years of incarceration in federal prison and a $25,000 fine. Maybe this is what President Biden was referring to when he assured the American public that he takes protecting classified information "seriously."

Also in early February 2023, the FBI searched Biden's Rehoboth Beach home. Biden's private lawyer made a press release stating that the FBI seized "some materials and handwritten notes" relating to Biden's time as vice president. The public was not provided with any information concerning the volume of material that was seized or whether any of that material was classified. President Biden's private lawyer stated that the search was conducted pursuant to "DOJ's standard procedures." DOJ standard procedures do not involve permitting a subject's private lawyers to search the subject's home before the FBI.

Also in early February, the FBI searched the University of Delaware, which houses approximately 2,000 boxes of documents that Biden donated to the university. This massive number of documents is reportedly from Biden's time as a senator and vice president, and the volume is so large that the FBI only searched a sample (about 350 boxes). CNN reported that the FBI seized several documents from the school. No official statements were made about the results of this FBI search. There were also no photographs released, so the public has no visual of the 2,000 boxes piled up somewhere within the University of Delaware.

In early March 2023, four months after NARA received the nine boxes that Biden's private attorneys took to Boston, NARA informed Congress that it had not examined the contents of the nine boxes. Four months. Without so much as opening a box to peep inside. About seven months later, in early October 2023, Special Counsel Hur interviewed Biden in a voluntary interview. Such interviews usually signal an investigation's end, and the interview being voluntary usually indicates that no criminal charges would be filed.

Just as Hur was completing his investigation, the U.S. House of Representatives Committee on Oversight and Accountability revealed it had "obtained information that contradicts important details from the White House's and President Biden's personal attorneys' statements about the discovery of documents at Penn Biden Center." According to the Oversight Committee, since May 2022, senior White House officials were visiting Biden's D.C. office to discretely coordinate the removal of documents. That is *seven months* before Biden's private lawyers allegedly "discovered" classified documents at that location. This was May 2022—the same month the White House Counsel's Office hired Richard Sauber. Maybe not so much of a coincidence after all.

The Oversight Committee reported that in June 2022, Dana Remus (then serving as the White House counsel) and Anthony Bernal (senior advisor to the first lady) went to the Penn Biden Center to take "boxes of documents and materials but could not fit all of the boxes into their vehicle." White House personnel were apparently removing a large volume of Biden's records from the Penn Biden Center. And not just any White House officials: Remus was *the* White House counsel, and Bernal was a long-time confidant and advisor to the Biden family. Basically, they sent the executive branch version of Winston Wolfe. In my extensive government experience, you do not send such high-level officials to run ministerial errands. It appears the document removal was considered a very sensitive mission, although we may never know why. We do know this: Remus and Bernal should have taken two cars. Or an SUV.

CHAPTER 7

The Hur Report

Special Counsel Hur's team devoted considerable resources to their investigation, interviewing 147 witnesses and collecting over seven million documents. Hur's final report, released in February 2024, was almost 400 pages long and concluded that no criminal charges should be filed. Some aspects of the Hur report were good, some were bad, and many were downright ugly. We can start with the good.

The Good

Describing the Extent of Biden's Mishandling

Overall, the Hur report did a good job describing the amount, nature, and location of the classified documents recovered from the Penn Biden Center, Biden's Wilmington home, and two different repositories at the University of Delaware (UD). There were some notable gaps, but the report provided a much more comprehensive accounting than the statements from Biden and his defenders. Biden's mishandling, the report confirms, was extensive and far beyond what the public had been led to believe.

At the Penn Biden Center, ten documents from Biden's vice presidency were recovered, totaling fifty-four pages, classified up to TOP SECRET/SCI. Hur described these as "the most highly classified, sensitive, and compartmented materials recovered during our investigation." Biden's Wilmington home had about one hundred classified documents in the main-floor personal library, basement den, second-floor office, third-level den, and the garage, with dates spanning five decades and classification levels up to TOP SECRET/SCI. From the UD library and the UD Biden Institute, investigators sampled boxes, recovering about twenty classified documents dating from Biden's senate tenure. Two contained formerly restricted data (FRD), which, as noted earlier, sounds ominous but has been downgraded from restricted data (RD). These two documents were only CONFIDENTIAL, but they merit mention, as they show that when serving as a senator, Biden had, with near certainty, removed documents with "nuclear information" from their proper place.

Included in the report was a twenty-two-page appendix of "recovered documents" with about one hundred entries, but the number of entries does not equate to the total number of documents recovered. Some entries cover more than one document, such as an entry for a "stack" of notecards, some of which contained highly classified information. Seventeen highly classified notebooks, all in Biden's handwriting and from his vice presidency, were also not listed. Biden had not properly marked the notebooks, so Hur chose to have sample paragraphs reviewed for classification, listed in a separate appendix. Also, due to the passage of time, some of the classified documents recovered were, upon review, downgraded to unclassified. As a result, the exact number of classified documents Biden possessed is unknown, but it was a large number—around 130 that we know of—dating from the 1970s forward for five decades.

While 130 is a good estimate of the documents we know of, I know from experience that prosecutors generally don't consider CONFIDENTIAL documents in espionage or mishandling prosecutions, and several of the documents Biden possessed were only CONFIDENTIAL. I also know from experience that the documents recovered from the UD library and UD Biden Institute would also probably not be considered, as even though some were still classified, they were decades old and were likely sent to UD because of lapses that would normally be handled as security violations. Also, a few of the documents recovered from Biden's Wilmington home, although still classified, would also probably not be considered because they were dated and to avoid policy issues related to prosecuting Biden for conduct he engaged in while serving as a senator. When you discount all these categories of documents, you end up with roughly thirty-five TOP SECRET and thirty-five SECRET documents from the Penn Biden Center and Biden's Wilmington home. Those are the real numbers. Those are the numbers that count. And that is where a prosecutor would focus.

Out of the seventy more sensitive classified documents, twelve were particularly sensitive. These twelve documents were not just TOP SECRET—they were TOP SECRET SCI, marked with multiple codewords for compartments that remain so sensitive that even the codewords themselves are still classified. Think TOP SECRET with whip cream, sprinkles, bananas, fudge, and a cherry on top. Biden's seventeen notebooks and undisclosed number of notecards also contained particularly sensitive national defense information, including contemporaneous notes Biden took while performing sensitive official duties, such as attending daily intelligence briefings and meetings in the White House Situation Room. These notes included information on U.S. intelligence sources, methods, and capabilities; human intelligence sources; U.S. intelligence activities; activities of foreign intelligence services; U.S. military programs and capabilities; foreign military program and capabilities; and plans and capabilities of foreign terrorist organizations. Some of the most highly classified documents were related to Afghanistan, and the FBI found these documents in files Biden must have personally created, as labels were in his handwriting and contained "memos and intelligence products he removed from the ordinary flow of paper he received as vice president."

Contrasting details in the Hur report to public statements from President Biden and his defenders show clearly that the American public was greatly misled as to where Biden's classified documents were discovered; the total volume; Biden's knowing possession of classified documents; and who reported what and when. As I will later elaborate, Biden even lied about his reputation for handling classified documents, which was not one of him taking his duties "seriously." Even the most basic facts the public was led to believe, such as the Penn Biden Center documents being found in a "locked closet," turned out to be of dubious veracity. When interviewed by the FBI, Biden's private lawyer was suddenly not so sure the closet was locked. His memory was "fuzzy" on that point.

Acknowledging Political Bias

One good aspect of the Hur report was that it recognized that a prosecutor should only seek criminal charges when "the fundamental interests" of our society require that the federal criminal law be applied to the specific circumstances of the case, and that one of the circumstances in the present case was that Biden was "someone for whom many jurors will want to search for reasonable doubt." This, to me, was one of the highlights of the report, as it is the closest Hur comes to acknowledging the inescapable reality saturating the entire case: political bias. For Hur could have also stated that Biden was "someone for whom many jurors will want to *avoid* searching for reasonable doubt." Both are true statements, and both acknowledge that due to political bias, prosecuting a vice president or president should be avoided given that an *unbiased jury is likely unattainable*. That is a raw truth. Hur approaches that truth obliquely, but acknowledges it nonetheless, and it reinforces that our nation's highest elected officials should be judged through political processes: the voting booth, or impeachment in Congress, or both.

The Final Decision

Among the good aspects of the Hur report, the most outstanding, for me, was Hur's decision not to file criminal charges. If a special counsel is going to get anything right, it should be the decision of whether to pursue a criminal prosecution. Reasonable people could disagree, but I think Hur's decision not to indict Biden was as good as it gets.

Hur based his decision, in part, on DOJ's handling of former President Reagan's diaries. Reagan's diaries—written after the Presidential Records Act (PRA) became law—contained classified information, as did Biden's notebooks and notecards. Shortly after Reagan left office, DOJ concluded that it was lawful for Reagan to keep his diaries, because under the PRA, a president had the right to keep his diaries no matter the content. Hur's analogy between Reagan and Biden was a rough one, as Biden's notebooks and notecards were not diaries: they were contemporaneous notes taken while performing sensitive official duties. Nonetheless, Hur concluded that given DOJ's position on Reagan's diaries, "an about-face, without previous public warning that is sharper than the relevant executive order and regulations, would be seen by many to violate basic principles of notice and fairness." Personally, I found the analogy between Reagan and Biden to be weak, but still enough to mitigate against charging Biden.

While a very basic fact, Hur also emphasized the practical reality that "Biden did not move the files himself at the end of the Obama administration." One of Biden's aides, the report related, described the pack out process as "random" and "a challenge," as everything had to be packed in "maybe a couple of days." This excuse, like the Reagan analogy, was more than a bit strained. Biden was not running for re-election. He knew well in advance—four years in advance—exactly when he would be departing the White House.

Not leaving enough time to pack, however, is a common human tendency, and despite the chaos being a self-inflicted wound, it is understandable that that there was a lot to pack in a short time frame, and Biden was not packing the boxes himself. A prosecutor must consider those facts, and it would have been a stretch for Hur to blame Biden for classified documents staffers packed into boxes, even if Biden's poor planning had caused the time crunch. Hur emphasized similar facts in deciding not to recommend charging Biden for the classified documents discovered at the University of Delaware, pointing out that Biden "depended on staffers" for maintaining files and to "pack them, transport them . . . and review them" and that there was no evidence suggesting that Biden knew classified documents were being donated to UD. These were all valid points.

Longstanding DOJ policy is that a sitting president cannot be prosecuted. Hur expressly stated that this policy did not impact his decision not to charge Biden, but even if Hur had decided to indict Biden, no prosecution could occur until Biden left office. No Democratic administration would support a prosecution of Joe Biden (and the attorney general [AG] can prevent a special counsel from filing an indictment), so Biden would only be prosecuted under a Republican administration. If a Republican administration prosecuted Biden, the entire Democratic party and over 90 percent of the mainstream media would be manning barricades à la *Les Misérables*, screaming of political persecution and demagoguery.

Putting aside the manifest hypocrisy, they would, in a sense, be right: because no Republican administration would prosecute a former Republican president in similar circumstances. That is why a prosecution of a former president in such circumstances will always be tainted by political bias, and that is another reason Hur was correct to decline pursuing what could only be a politically charged prosecution of the highest magnitude. It is true that Biden was not a president during the relevant time frames, but he would be a former president when prosecuted, and that matters, along with his record of service to the country, which is considerable. Love him or hate him, the man was a senator, vice president, and president, and that all carries weight.

Right about now, many people would be thinking, *But this is America, and no one is above the law!* Whenever I hear this platitude, I sigh. Almost always, it is pundits and politicians using the phrase as a cudgel to bludgeon members of the opposing political party, while ignoring similar conduct within their own. The hypocrisy gnaws at me. Even when the speaker lacks the pious pretensions (which is rarely), the naivety is alarming, as the statement is provably false. Throughout American history, there have always been—and will always be—those who are very much above the law. Examples are plentiful. Just look at the cases of John Deutch, Sandy Berger, David Petraeus, Hillary Clinton, and Joe Biden, and compare them to Kenneth Ford, Robert Birchum, and—as we will in due time—former President Trump.

Perfect equity in any justice system is, with certainty, unattainable. Justice systems are created and implemented by humans, and so will always be, to varying degrees, flawed and biased. And powerful and wealthy people have the most resources to take advantage of those inescapable flaws and biases. So, whenever anyone utters the "no one in America is above the law" platitude, I know with near certainty they are about to advocate for some hypocrisy, some harsh action that they would not extend to members of their own political party. One can aspire to make the platitude a reality (I do) but should not confuse aspiration with actuality, or confuse a utopian fantasy with historical reality. The next time you hear this platitude—it won't be long—take a moment to analyze the speaker's motive. Especially if it is you.

The Simply Bad

Although declining to file charges was, I believe, the correct decision, Hur took many wrong turns along the way. Important laws were misinterpreted, relevant facts were omitted, and politically charged commentary was gratuitously included. Admittedly, the charging decision was most important, and Hur deserves credit for getting that right. But the logic behind the decision is also important, as it sets precedent, and much of Hur's logic was deeply flawed. I will address the simply bad, before moving to the more grievous ugly.

Misinterpreting Executive Order 13526

One of the biggest mistakes in the report—though not entirely Hur's fault—was assuming that Executive Order 13526 applies to a former vice president retaining classified information from his time in office. The order doesn't actually say this. This mistake is important, because it resulted in Hur wrongly labeling Biden's retention as "unauthorized," which is how Hur wrongly concluded that the section of the Espionage Act criminalizing unauthorized retention was the best fit for analyzing Biden's conduct. Even though Hur ultimately decided not to charge Biden for unauthorized retention, this mistake led Hur to focus on the wrong part of the Espionage Act. For if there was no unauthorized retention—and there simply was not—this part of the Espionage Act did not apply to Biden's conduct. Let me explain.

Hur cited three authorities to support the mistaken assumption that the executive order required a former vice president retaining classified information from his vice presidency to seek and receive permission for access from a subsequent administration. Those three authorities were section 4.1 of the executive order, section 4.4 of the executive order, and the DOJ indictment of former President Trump for alleged mishandling of national defense information (NDI).

Section 4.1 of the executive order is titled "General Restrictions on Access." Access requirements established by section 4.1 (security clearance; nondisclosure agreement; need-to-know) do not even apply to a vice president, so Hur should not have been relying on section 4.1 to justify any limitations on Biden's retention of classified information. Interestingly, section 4.1 does expressly state that an "official or employee leaving agency service may not remove classified information from the agency's control." The words "official or employee" do not include a vice president, and if the intention was to place such a restriction on a departing vice president, this would have been the place to do it. Yet no such restriction was included here or anywhere else in the order.

Similarly, section 4.4 of the order also has no relevance to a vice president's retention of classified information from his time in service.

Rather, section 4.4 establishes a process for specific individuals to obtain formal waivers to the need-to-know requirement for *access* to classified information. Historical researchers, former senior policymakers, and *former* presidents and vice presidents can request these waivers. On its face, the waiver process only applies to individuals seeking access to classified information. It does not take a law degree to see that you don't need to seek access to something you already possess. Yet the report ignores this fact and conflates a vice president's *retention* of classified information from his tenure with *seeking access* to classified information *after having left office*.

No matter how much we want them to, laws rarely cover all eventualities. They have gaps. Filling those gaps is a job that often falls on the federal judiciary and one for which judges are better suited. When prosecutors fill gaps in the law, there is a high risk, given human nature, that the results will tend to advance a prosecution. Manifest injustice can result, given there could be no notice to impacted individuals that their conduct was unlawful. Hur acknowledged this policy concern when concluding that Biden's classified notebooks could be excused because DOJ had accepted Reagan's classified diaries as authorized. Analogizing Biden's situation to Reagan's was a stretch, but still enough to support Hur's conclusion that charging Biden, given the Reagan precedent, could be viewed as violating "basic principles of notice and fairness." Hur got that right. But when examining whether the executive order covers a former vice president's retention of classified information from his service, Hur abandoned his fidelity to notice and fairness.

Filling in the gap in a way that departed severely from the plain text of the order, Hur's interpretation gave no meaningful notice to the man being held to the newly forged standard. That was wrong and unfair. But not completely unprecedented. Which is why it was not all Hur's fault. For there was one case in history—recent history—for which DOJ had already condoned this novel expansion of the order's reach: Special Counsel Smith's indictment of Donald Trump for mishandling classified information. That indictment, which we will analyze later, merely cited to the same sections of the executive order (4.1 and 4.4) to expand the order to cover a former president's retention of classified information from his presidency. An unprecedented interpretation that just coincidentally supported charging former President Trump. Surprise, surprise.

As DOJ approved this novel and expansive theory to support indicting Trump, and given the theory applies equally to a former vice president, Hur was stuck with it. Unlike Smith, who only needed to state the theory, Hur had to justify it in his report. Tip-toeing around the obvious—that the executive order sections he was citing did not support the novel expansion of the order—Hur referenced section 4.4, then deduced "by implication" that "the restrictions on access to classified information in the order appear to govern a former vice president." There is no "appearance" that this section applies to a former vice president: it *expressly* applies. Hur uses words like "appear" and "implication" because when he uses the word "access," he is not talking about access at all: he is talking about storage and handling—and not just storage and handling, but storage and handling of retained documents from a vice president's tenure. This is a federal prosecutor, mind you, interpreting a law weakly and speculatively, potentially imprisoning someone based on implications. It's a clear example of overreaching beyond the law's intended scope.

To be clear, I am not saying that all provisions of the executive order did not apply to Vice President Biden. Most did. But not the access provisions Hur cited. What this all means is that Biden did not violate any rules controlling access to classified information, because *there were no rules* limiting Biden's access to classified information. Biden did—undoubtedly, routinely, and flagrantly—violate the rules for handling and storage. But whether Biden also violated criminal law is a separate analysis, which we will get to in due time.

Initially, I considered labeling Hur's expansion of the order as "ugly," but I reconsidered. As a special counsel, Hur was bound by DOJ positions and Biden's DOJ had already endorsed Smith's broad interpretation to indict Trump. While Hur could have stated that the theory was a DOJ theory that he was following, he instead adopted the flawed interpretation as his own, making him a good soldier but still incorrect.

Ignoring Critical Aspects of the Presidential Records Act

Another bad aspect of the Hur report is how it treated the Presidential Records Act (PRA). While the report has very little discussion of the PRA, what little there is neglects important aspects of the law. You will recall that the PRA is a purely civil statute, with no criminal provisions, no enforcement mechanism against a vice president, current or former, and under which designations of vice-presidential records are completely up to a vice president. These are all critical aspects of the law, and yet Hur does not mention any of them. Hur's omissions perpetuate the myth that this federal law somehow legally binds a president or vice president. It does not. If it did, it would likely be found unconstitutional for violating separation of powers, given that Congress cannot dictate to the executive how the executive must maintain executive records.

Interestingly, the report discloses that Biden's personal lawyers and the White House counsel claimed that Biden's highly classified notebooks and notecards were "personal records" under the PRA. This was a good argument—a winning argument, I believe—not because Biden's notebooks were diaries (they were not), but for the simple fact that Biden decided they were personal records, and that decision is non-reviewable. Hur rejected that argument by first reiterating the erroneous expansion of the executive order to cover a former vice president's retention of classified information, then compounded the error by mistakenly claiming that "courts and the Department have determined whether possession of national defense information is authorized principally based on the terms of the executive order." This claim is provably false, by Hur's own report, in which Hur acknowledges that DOJ "repeatedly asserted" that Reagan's diaries "were Mr. Reagan's personal property," even though DOJ knew the diaries contained classified information. As Reagan's diaries were written after passage of the PRA, DOJ must have considered the PRA to authorize Reagan to keep, in his home, NDI.

In rejecting the argument that the PRA gave Biden a viable defense, Hur claimed that, "The approach that the Department and courts have taken in Espionage Act cases after passage of the Presidential Records Act cuts against this view." This was quite misleading. First, contrary to Hur's assertion, courts have not considered this issue. Maybe Hur was referring to the preliminary ruling over Trump's attempt to dismiss his indictment under the Espionage Act, but that ruling only stated that Trump's motion to dismiss was insufficient to dismiss the indictment "pre-trial." Hardly an established history where "courts" have established and reinforced some established precedent. Second, there was only one Espionage Act case where DOJ's approach went against the idea of using the PRA as a defense, and that was the same case: the recent indictment of former President Trump under the Espionage Act. Hur misleadingly describes the history as involving espionage "cases." Plural. But there was only one: Trump's.

Notable & Suspicious Omissions

While not as bad, the report also has inexplicable omissions that are bad enough to merit mention. Most glaring is the report's failure to address the contents of the nine boxes Biden's private lawyers took from the Penn Biden Center just before informing the White House they had found classified documents in the maybe-locked closet. Emails between the National Archives and Records Administration (NARA) and Biden's private lawyers indicated the nine boxes contained classified documents. And when Congress asked NARA about the boxes—four months after NARA took possession—NARA incredulously claimed that it had not yet examined them. The contents of these boxes could significantly increase the total number of classified documents Biden had retained.

This is highly suspicious behavior, and at a minimum, Hur should have stated that his team reviewed the boxes and related the findings. Details about other Biden documents that the White House may have removed from the Penn Biden Center have also been omitted from the report. Since May 2022, White House Counsel Dana Remus and other Biden aides were removing documents from Biden's Penn Biden Center office. Hur's team interviewed Remus, who stated she was "gathering materials to prepare for potential congressional inquiries about the Biden family's activities" and that she "decided to ship material that could be relevant to future congressional inquiries to Patrick Moore, one of Mr. Biden's personal counsel in Boston." Whatever Remus removed—we have no idea what—appears to be in addition to the nine boxes that were shipped to Boston, and again, whatever was removed could increase the total count of the classified documents Biden had retained.

A few other omissions struck me as suspicious enough to briefly mention. Many would consider these small oversights, and maybe I am overreacting. You be the judge.

First, the report does not mention the search of Biden's Rehoboth Beach home. Biden's private lawyer acknowledged that the FBI searched that home, and seized "some materials and handwritten notes that appear to relate to his time as vice president," but Hur never mentions the search or the results. This, to me, was a material omission. If this were a Hardy Boys book, it would be titled *The Mystery of the Disappearing Beach House.*

Second, the report's appendices list a computer hard drive labeled "VP Records" seized from the Penn Biden Center, yet there is no discussion of the hard drive. Odd, at least to me. *The Vanishing VP Hard Drive.*

Before leaving the topic of omissions, there is one for which I will just, for now, lay down a marker: nowhere in the report will you find the words "damage assessment." Keep that in mind. Later, I will explain in detail what damage assessments are; when they are done; when they are not done; and why this is not a minor issue.

Using Politically Charged Language

The last bad aspect of the Hur report is the inclusion of politically charged language. Specifically, Hur referred to Biden as a "sympathetic, well-meaning, elderly man with a poor memory"; and in describing how Biden sounded on tape recordings made from as far back as 2017, stated that Biden's memory "appeared to have significant limitations," as evidenced by Biden being "often painfully slow" and "struggling to remember events and straining at times to read and relay his own notebook entries." These descriptions received the most publicity and the most criticism from Biden's defenders. In my opinion, bluntly describing Biden's diminished mental acuity was unduly direct, but in Hur's defense, the context—which critics ignored—necessitated a description along these lines. Let me explain.

During their investigation, Hur's team discovered tape recordings of highly incriminating conversations between Biden and a ghostwriter writing a book for Biden. Apparently with Biden's consent, the recordings were made by the ghostwriter to assist in writing the book.

One of the recordings (dated from 2017) captured Biden proclaiming that he had "just found all the classified stuff downstairs." This is about the best evidence any prosecutor could hope for in such a case, as it evidences that Biden knew he possessed classified documents, and that Biden made no effort to return the classified documents after he found them.

Other incriminating recordings captured Biden reading "his notes from classified meetings" to the ghostwriter "nearly word-for-word." On one occasion, when Biden was showing a passage in one of his classified notebooks to the ghostwriter, Biden warned the ghostwriter that "some of this may be classified, so be careful."

Despite all this highly incriminating evidence, Hur still concluded that the evidence was "insufficient to meet the government's burden in a criminal prosecution." But there was a price to be paid.

Hur avoided filing charges, despite Biden's taped admissions, by claiming that Biden's memory was so poor that a jury could find that Biden had forgotten that he had "just found all the classified stuff downstairs." This was in 2017, mind you, *years before Biden even ran for president*. Hur must have recognized that his decision not to charge Biden was exceptionally weak, given that he had caught Biden elbow deep in the cookie jar with a fistful of oatmeal raisin. As Hur put great weight on Biden's poor memory as an excuse to not charge Biden, he likely felt the need to use forceful language to describe Biden's cognitive decline.

In his congressional testimony, Hur defended his blunt descriptions on the grounds that his report was confidential (not in the classified sense) and a candid assessment to the attorney general (AG), not for the public. I found those statements to be not credible. Yes, the report was for the AG, but it was also clearly written for a public audience, and there was near certainty the report would be publicly released. Hur must have known this, and could have, and should have, been more sensitive in describing Biden's age and cognitive decline. Especially in an election year, when Biden's age and mental state are primary issues.

However, there is a huge irony here: Hur's frank assessment of Biden's mental decline was, if anything, understated. Throughout his presidency, Biden's inner circle has done its best to hide Biden's cognitive impairment. Public appearances are few and tightly controlled; interviews are only granted to friendly personalities; and even Biden admits that aides identify the friendly reporters he is permitted to call on for obviously pre-screened questions.

One particularly bizarre example of shielding Biden from reporters occurred at the 2022 White House Easter Egg Roll, where a costumed Easter Bunny, later identified as a White House press official, jumped between Biden and a reporter when the reporter asked Biden a question and Biden tried to answer. Waiving furry paws frantically in Biden's face, the Bunny not only interrupted the president, but it did not stop gesticulating until Biden was directed away from the reporter. Pretty extreme. Many excuses have been proffered by Biden's defenders, but any unbiased person can see that Biden is wandering around the presidency like Mr. Magoo.

Hur's interview of Biden is probably the only time in Biden's presidency that someone not in the business of protecting Biden was granted meaningful access to the throne. And sure enough, Biden's cognitive decay was laid bare: he could not even recall which year his son died or which years he was vice president. Seeing Biden as he truly was, Hur's reaction reminded me of Hans Christian Andersen's fable, *The Emperor's New Clothes*, in which one person not infected by delusion comes close enough to the emperor to observe and speak an obvious truth. Brainwashed supporters of the emperor, previously unwilling to acknowledge what was plainly before their eyes, have a mass epiphany and finally see the truth.

Unlike the fable, however, in Hur's case, the Democratic party—mental decline denialists—rejected the truth and attacked the messenger. Meanwhile, despite the interview transcripts having already been released, AG Garland has adamantly refused to release the interview recordings, as they likely reveal the mutterings of a tired and confused elderly man. Biden has even claimed executive privilege to prevent the interview recordings from being made public. After the presidential debate in June 2024, no one was criticizing Special Counsel Hur anymore. While the mental decline denialists will never admit to their gullibility—or complicity—and will never apologize to Hur for vilifying him as a Republican party stooge, after the debate, Hur's maybe too-frank-at-the-time assessment appears restrained and gracious.

Lost on commentators was the far worse derogatory comments Hur made about Trump. After acknowledging that it was not his "role to assess the criminal charges against Mr. Trump," Hur proceeded to do exactly that, stating that the allegations, if proven, "would clearly establish not only Mr. Trump's willfulness, but also serious aggravating facts." Hur also attempted to distinguish Biden's case from Trump's by highlighting allegations that Trump failed to return classified documents; enlisted others to help cover up his crime; and failed to cooperate. Odd categories to claim as distinctions, given Hur's own report showed Biden doing all these things that Trump is merely alleged to have done, including Biden knowingly possessing classified information and not returning it; Biden's underlings secretly removing documents from the Penn Biden Center and misleading the public to cover up Biden's malfeasance; and Biden's "cooperation" with an abnormal process that was created by his own administration.

Whereas there was significant outcry over the unfortunate yet painfully true statement that Biden was "an elderly man with a poor memory," I saw no such outcry concerning the unjustified and inappropriate speculations about Trump's case, which might have even violated DOJ policy concerning publicly commenting on an ongoing prosecution. It is a sign of our times that the worse language about Trump was ignored, while the at least arguably defensible language about Biden's age and mental decline was railed against.

Weighing the good and bad in the Hur report, I believe the good far outweighs the bad. But when you place the report's uglier aspects on an unbiased, properly calibrated scale, the weight shifts. Perhaps not dispositively, but definitely dramatically.

And the Ugly

For those who know little to nothing about classified information or Espionage Act prosecutions, the Hur report likely appears to be a thoughtful, principled assessment of President Biden's criminal liability for unauthorized retention of classified information. From an experienced insider's view, however, the report contains deeply flawed, disingenuous, and convoluted analysis. These are the ugly aspects of the Hur report. And they are many.

Disregarding Gross Negligence

Right from the beginning of his legal analysis, Hur disingenuously directed the focus away from where Biden was most vulnerable (which I will get to), to an area of law that was more conducive to clearing Biden. "The criminal statutory provision that best fits the facts of our investigation" Hur claimed, was the "section of the Espionage Act that proscribes unauthorized retention and disclosure of national defense information." Under this section of the Espionage Act, a person must have had (1) unauthorized possession of NDI; and (2) the violation must have been willful. As discussed in the previous chapter, Hur was bound by Special Counsel Smith's expansive interpretation of the executive order, and therefore concluded that Biden's possession of classified documents post–vice presidency was "unauthorized." National defense relatedness was unquestionable, so that requirement was easily met. That left the intent element: willfulness.

Like James Comey in the Clinton "matter," Hur used the intent element of the crime to excuse Biden's conduct. Throughout his analysis of the most incriminating evidence (classified documents pertaining to Afghanistan and Biden's notes), Hur conceded that there was evidence of willfulness, but claimed it was not enough to meet the government's burden. Despite having more evidence of willfulness than any mishandling case I have ever seen—including that of Deutch, Petraeus, and Clinton—Hur claimed that the evidence was "short of proof beyond a reasonable doubt." This is what DOJ does when it does not want to prosecute someone—it focuses on the intent element of the crime and claims that it would be too difficult to prove criminal intent beyond a reasonable doubt.

Contrary to Hur's assertion that the "best fit" under the Espionage Act was willfulness, it was actually *gross negligence*, a concept familiar to Jim Comey. Hur did eventually analyze gross negligence, but in a stunningly disingenuous manner. As a reminder, gross negligence involves conscious and extreme carelessness. Here is the pertinent language from this section of the Espionage Act:

> Whoever, being entrusted with or having lawful possession or control of . . . [national defense information] . . . through gross negligence permits the same to be removed from its proper place of custody or delivered to anyone in violation of his trust, or to be lost, stolen, abstracted, or destroyed.

Hur dismissed gross negligence by focusing solely on the language requiring removal "from its proper place of custody." It would be difficult to apply the law to Biden, Hur claimed, because it was "at least arguable that as vice president, Mr. Biden could not have removed national defense information 'from its proper place of custody'" given that "presidents and vice presidents are generally permitted to retain classified information in their residences while in office." While it is true that presidents and vice presidents are authorized to retain classified information in their homes, Hur's statement is, nonetheless, very misleading for two reasons.

First, when it comes to abiding by handling and storage requirements for classified information, presidents and vice presidents are not the same. One is the commander in chief. The other is not. Yet, Hur erroneously equates the two positions, cloaking Vice President Biden with the full vestiges of presidential power. For instance, Hur stated that DOJ's "prior treatment of former presidents and vice presidents who kept national security materials . . . counsels against prosecution of Mr. Biden." One would assume, given that assertion, that the report included relevant examples of presidents *and* vice presidents. Not so.

The only example provided was Reagan, and Reagan was, obviously, a president. Along the same lines, Hur misleadingly implied that a president and vice president have the same duties under the Constitution: "presidents and vice presidents are constitutional officers whose handling of classified information supports their Article II functions of conducting foreign affairs and providing for the national defense." Conducting foreign affairs and providing for the national defense are powers expressly granted to the president, not the vice president. Hur clerked for a Supreme Court justice. The man can read the Constitution. Blurring the authorities, and conflating the roles, was not an oversight.

Vice president is a unique position, I would concede. Below the president, vice president is the only elected position in the executive branch. Everyone else is an employee or appointee. Also, in the event of "the Removal of the President from Office, or of his Death, Resignation, or Inability to discharge the Powers and Duties of the said Office," the vice president assumes presidential duties.[11] But being next in line to the throne does not make one King.

Second, it is true that some senior members of the executive branch (such as a CIA director) are permitted to retain classified information in their homes, but that does not excuse them from handling and storage requirements. And the executive branch dedicates significant resources to ensure that any senior official with authority to bring classified documents home also has the resources for proper storage and safe handling. Inappropriately conflating these two separate issues—(1) authorization for home retention; and (2) security requirements for handling and storage—permitted Hur to excuse Biden's flagrant violations of the latter just because he had the former. That is not how it works, and it is difficult to understand how Hur could have missed this distinction. His own report quoted President Biden acknowledging that there is a difference between the two:

> **Reporter:** Mr. President, in simple terms, is it ever appropriate for a president to take home with them classified and TOP SECRET documents?
>
> **Biden:** Depending on the circumstances. For example, I have in my home, a cabined-off space that is completely secure. I'm taking home with me today's PDB [president's daily brief]. It's locked. I have a person with me—military with me. I read it, I lock it back up, and give it to the military.
>
> **Reporter:** Without a specialized area in which you can declassify documents, is it ever appropriate for a president to bring classified and TOP SECRET documents home with them?
>
> **Biden:** It depends on the document, and it depends on how secure the room is.

For me, the most fascinating part of this exchange is that Biden was president when he made these remarks. And he was describing his alleged practices as president to follow his own rules, which, as president, he was not bound to follow, but as vice president he *was bound to follow*, and yet knowingly and routinely disregarded.

To reiterate, even for senior officials who are approved to possess classified documents in their homes, up to and including a vice president, the authority to retain does not equate to authority to violate the rules pertaining to handling and storage. Those rules become *even more important* in those circumstances, not less important. Conflating these two separate issues was either an error or a clever way to avoid the obvious conclusion, as you will see presently, that Biden was, throughout his vice presidency and after, grossly negligent in the handling of NDI. Again, I will highlight that Biden being grossly negligent as a factual matter does not mean that he is criminally liable for the gross negligence. That is a separate issue.

Executive Order 13526 does exempt vice presidents from typical access requirements. Specifically, the executive order exempts a vice president from the rigid and extensive pre-requisites for *access* to classified information that apply to every other executive branch officer under the president. This shows, however, that when the executive order treats a vice president differently, it does so explicitly. One need not speculate or guess which requirements a vice president is excused from, because they are expressly stated, and excusal from handling and storage requirements *is not among them*. There is no doubt Biden violated these rules—routinely—but as stated here, that does not mean he also committed a crime.

Perhaps the greatest deception Hur employed to hide the issue of gross negligence was to completely ignore the concept of gross negligence. This part of the report is so disingenuous that when dismissing the law against gross negligence Hur never even informs the reader that he is talking about gross negligence. Instead, Hur describes the subsection by numerical designation and briefly summarizes it as a section of the law requiring "removal of national defense information from 'its proper place of custody'" by a person who has lawful possession. Compare Hur's summary to the actual language of the law:

> Whoever, being entrusted with or having lawful possession or control of . . . [national defense information] . . . (1) *through gross negligence* permits the same to be removed from its proper place of custody. [emphasis added]

Hur's analysis of the law omitted the term "gross negligence." This took effort. Hur had to literally jump over the express legal standard, "gross negligence," by craftily summarizing this section of the Espionage Act in a way that no one would even know the actual crime being analyzed. This may be hard to believe, but the term "gross negligence" is nowhere in the report. That is not an oversight. Hur artfully hid the 800-pound gorilla in the room.

Although the Hur report cleverly avoided analyzing whether Biden was grossly negligent, it did relate the following facts concerning Biden's conduct as vice president:

- "In 2010, the Executive Secretary team raised concerns about the number of classified briefing books that Mr. Biden had not returned" and "even when they were returned, some of the content was missing."
- "Nearly thirty of the classified briefing books [given to Biden] from the first six months of 2010 were outstanding."
- Biden failed to return TOP SECRET/SCI contents of a classified briefing book provided to him while he was vacationing in the Hamptons.
- After Biden's TOP SECRET/SCI briefing book contents went missing, Biden's counsel prepared a memo for Biden stating that "our procedures for handling your classified briefing material . . . must be maintained at all times."
- Biden's counsel also met with Biden to discuss proper procedures for handling classified information and told Biden "that any classified material taken from the White House

must be transported by military aides in locked bags and that military aides must retrieve the classified material when Mr. Biden was done with it.

- Biden "continued frequently to leave classified documents unattended, outside of safes, at the Naval Observatory and his Delaware home."
- Biden wanted to take copies of his notecards home, to avoid visiting NARA when writing his book. So, his staff made notecard binders for Biden to take home, even though the notecards were highly classified. Two aides raised issues about this, and one felt strongly enough to memorialize in a memo that the aide had "requested to not participant [sic] in any project or meetings that involve these records."

Biden had been in government for decades and enjoyed access to classified information since he was a senator. It is inconceivable that he did not know the rules. Given all Hur's report uncovered, the available facts are enough for any reasonable, unbiased person to see that Biden was grossly negligent in the handling of classified documents. For years, and probably decades. But again, just because Biden was grossly negligent does not mean he violated criminal law. That is a separate question, and the answer is straightforward.

Hur concluded that no matter how strong the evidence against Biden, a former vice president could not be prosecuted for violating the law against gross negligence (without, of course, Hur ever using that term) because it would raise "significant separation of powers concerns." For support, Hur cited to purely presidential authorities under the Constitution and Supreme Court cases holding, generally, that criminal laws do not apply to a president unless expressly stated. As he needed to extend those Supreme Court opinions to cover Biden, Hur further relied on DOJ opinions extending the same policy concerns to a vice president. A correct statement of the law, in my opinion, but predictably, I saw no commentators clutching pearls over Hur's near blanket immunity to Biden.

Crafting Get-Out-of-Jail-Free Cards

Aside from Hur avoiding gross negligence, the other stunning aspect of the report was the stream of *get-out-of-jail-free cards* that Hur created, many so outlandish that Hur pointedly avoided claiming that he himself found them persuasive. Instead, Hur projected the reality-bending excuses onto a patsy: the gullible juror, hidden under a cloak of reasonableness. Having created this patsy, Hur then sat him front and center, and dealt him every *get-out-of-jail-free card* hidden up Hur's sleeves. And the amount was, to borrow a phrase, "not small."

We have already covered the boldest card: the *he-could-have-just-forgotten card*. This was Hur's primary means to dismiss Biden's admission that he had "just found all the classified stuff downstairs." Closely related to the *he-could-have-just-forgotten card* was the *loose-talk card*. "Given Mr. Biden's tendency towards loose talk" with his ghostwriter, "reasonable jurors may hesitate to place too much evidentiary weight on a single eight-word utterance." Have you ever heard of a federal prosecutor who, despite having a recording of someone admitting to a crime, decided not to press charges because they thought a juror might not take the admission seriously enough? Worse yet, Hur dismissed this confession, which was essentially caught on tape, partly because it was *too brief* (an "eight-word utterance"). "I killed him" is just three words. Can you imagine a federal prosecutor dismissing such an admission, captured on tape, because a juror might find the murder confession *too succinct*?

In addition to the *he-could-have-just-forgotten card*, the *loose-talk card*, and the *too-succinct card*, Hur added the *too-casual-for-crime card*. This was based on Hur's view that in the taped admission, Biden's "tone was remarkably casual," and if Biden knew he was breaking the law, he would not have been so casual about it.

After pulling all those *get-out-of-jail free cards* from his sleeve, Hur kept dealing, adding the *lousy-criminal card*. You see, if Biden knew he was breaking the law, he would not have had classified documents strewn all over the house, and in the garage for God's sake. A reasonable juror might find that only a lousy criminal would do such a thing, and since Biden is so wise, if he knew he was breaking the law, he would have been better at hiding his loot: "A reasonable juror could conclude that this is not where a person intentionally stores what he supposedly considers to be important classified documents."

Any DOJ attorney who prosecuted a mishandling case must have audibly gasped when they read Hur justifying not charging this crime because the stolen loot was not better protected. Kenneth Ford had a box of classified documents in his kitchen and another in a bedroom closet (maybe locked—my memory is fuzzy on that point). Robert Birchum had classified documents in his home, office quarters, and driveway storage pod. Many other mishandling cases prosecuted over the years had this one commonality: the defendants kept classified information in places that were, most definitely, "not where a person intentionally stores what he supposedly considers to be important classified documents." Yet all were charged and successfully prosecuted. Quite successfully.

Probably the weakest card Hur dealt was the *only-briefly-broke-the-law card*. Under this theory, although Biden illegally possessed, in his home, classified documents, it was not worth pursuing because Biden only broke the law briefly: "It may be difficult to convince a jury they should care about Mr. Biden's brief illicit possession . . . particularly since he was allowed to possess the same documents both before 2017 (as vice president) and after (as president)." Notice how cleverly this is written. "Before 2017" refers to Biden's vice presidency, which ended at the beginning of 2017, and the "after" was the beginning of 2021, when Biden became a president. The intervening period was four years. *Four years.* Hur describes a four-year violation as "brief."

Perpetuating "Full Cooperation"

Amongst all the bad aspects of the Hur report, particularly disappointing to me was the report's perpetuating the myth of Biden's "full cooperation." From the moment the news first broke about the Penn Biden Center documents, Biden's private lawyers, White House counsel, friendly news outlets, and President Biden himself, all repeatedly emphasized that Biden had "fully cooperated with the process." This mantra effectively deflected attention from whether a crime had occurred in the first place, and purported to distinguish Biden's case from that of his political rival. Fact-checking the myth, however, shows that it does not comport with reality.

One component of the myth of cooperation was that Biden "immediately" reported the discovery of classified documents to the proper authorities. A "pro-active self-disclosure," in the words of the Hur report. This is provably false. No reasonable person could claim Biden did not know, given the 2017 taped admission, that he possessed classified documents. Yet, Biden made no effort to report that discovery, which is itself a crime under the Espionage Act. *Fact check #1.*

Five years later, when classified documents were discovered in Biden's office at the Penn Biden Center, neither Biden nor his private lawyers reported the discovery to law enforcement, as we have covered. *Fact check #2.*

When the FBI first discovered a highly classified notebook at Biden's Wilmington home, Biden's private lawyer told the FBI that Biden had *not consented* to the FBI taking the evidence. This is clearly stated in the report. White House Counsel Richard Sauber came to the house, handled the evidence, and apparently prevented the FBI from physically seizing the document. Two days later, the White House agreed to provide the evidence to the FBI. Refusing to permit the FBI to seize relevant evidence—even for just two days—is inconsistent with "full cooperation." So is a White House lawyer inserting himself into the chain-of-custody. *Fact check #3.*

During his voluntary interviews with the special counsel, Biden refused to answer many relevant questions. This is all documented in the Hur report:

> He [Biden] declined to answer several questions about whether he believed his notes contained classified information; whether he believed he was authorized to possess classified information after his vice presidency; and whether he took steps to avoid writing classified information in his notebooks.

The refusal to answer relevant questions is also incompatible with "full cooperation." *Fact check #4.*

Even when Biden did answer questions from the special counsel, he lied. When confronted with the 2017 tape recording admitting he had "just found all the classified stuff downstairs," Biden claimed that when he said "classified" he didn't mean that they were actually "classified.'" Hur concluded that Biden's explanation was "not credible." Lying about a central piece of evidence in a criminal investigation is not cooperating. *Fact check #5.*

Of all the lies concealed under the veil of "cooperation," the biggest was the implicit one: that Biden was cooperating with a fair, normal process. The reality is that the process was not normal and very deferential to Biden. The list of process fouls is extensive, including:

- Biden's private attorneys conducting searches in lieu of the FBI (while there was an open investigation)
- A White House attorney inserting himself into the chain of custody
- No grand jury
- No search warrants
- No subpoenas
- Voluntary interviews
- Interviewees permitted to refuse to answer questions
- No documents fingerprinted
- DOJ making no attempt to coerce anyone to testify against Biden

The last point may sound far-fetched, but it is not: Hur's team caught Biden's ghostwriter destroying evidence. According to the report, the ghostwriter produced transcripts and audio recordings to the FBI, and upon reviewing them, the FBI noticed some of the transcripts had no corresponding audio. When the FBI enquired as to the missing audiotapes, the ghostwriter responded—through his lawyer— that he had in fact destroyed some of the audiotapes *after learning that Biden was being investigated*.

Now, in any normal case, DOJ would have indicted the ghostwriter for obstruction of justice, threatened the ghostwriter with a lengthy jail sentence, and then offered the ghostwriter a lenient plea deal that required the ghostwriter to testify against Biden. In a normal case. Or, as you will soon see, an abnormal case, where the Biden administration is prosecuting Biden's greatest political rival.

Another noteworthy part of "the process" was the lack of media leaks. Although never proper, leaks and "leak strategies" are routine when DOJ and the FBI are motivated to put you in jail. Biden's investigation, however, was kept from the public for months until the Biden administration could no longer contain the growing scandal, and even after the case was public, there were no leaks. All these deviations from normal processes further expose the false foundation upon which the myth of cooperation was built. *Fact check #6.*

Within the normal-process fallacy is a more subtle but pervasive falsehood: the pretense of an apolitical process. I will cover this in greater detail later, but I will highlight for now that nothing in Biden's case was apolitical. Biden was "cooperating" with a process established by his own administration. A Democratic president being investigated by his own Democratic administration. Would Biden "fully cooperate" if he was being investigated by a Trump administration? With a process that his major political rival controlled and directed against him? Of course not. And no reasonable person would expect him to, because of the political context. This last aspect of the myth of cooperation—that it was apolitical—from my perspective, is the most subtle, and the most egregious. *Fact check # 7.*

Mishandling of Precedents

Another particularly bad aspect of the Hur report is how it dealt with the precedents. Admittedly, none of the precedents involved a vice president, but they should have all been analyzed. Deutch and Clinton were never mentioned, and the Petraeus case is only cited in a footnote. To me, it appeared Hur did not want to remind people of the political bias and leniency shown to similarly situated, high-ranking Democrats.

Petraeus was prosecuted for possessing, in his home, eight notebooks of highly classified information. Sound familiar? Petraeus provided classified information to his biographer. Ring a bell? And Petraeus lied to the FBI. Remind you of anyone? Despite the many similarities, Hur relegates the Petraeus case to a footnote, in which he acknowledges that the cases have "significant similarities," but also incredulously claims that "the differences are more significant." Let's look at what Hur deemed "more significant" differences.

Hur highlighted that Petraeus's retention "violated numerous nondisclosure agreements" Petraeus had signed, whereas Biden had never signed any such agreements. Factually, that is true. Like everyone else in the executive branch (excepting the president and vice president), Petraeus had to sign nondisclosure agreements for access to classified information. But cases involving the mishandling of classified information do not hinge on nondisclosure agreements. Just ask Donald Trump. He never signed a nondisclosure agreement: he is facing thirty-two felonies for unlawful retention of classified information. So why is it only an excuse for Biden?

Petraeus's case was also distinguished on the grounds that Petraeus lied to the FBI about sharing classified information with his biographer. Perhaps Hur was having his own senior moment, as this was an obvious *similarity*, not a difference. Hur's own report concluded that Biden lied to DOJ about discovering classified documents in his home in 2017. The lies were slightly different, but both lies were false statements to obstruct justice.

While Hur's attempts to distinguish Petraeus's case are meritless, the cases are truly distinguishable. Just not for the reasons Hur cites. Executive branch rules for handling and storage of classified information applied to both Petraeus and Biden. But the criminal laws did not apply to both men. Only to Petraeus. Because Petraeus was not a vice president.

That is the hard reality. That is the distinction.

Unsettling Future Deterrence

In justifying his decision to not charge Biden with any crimes, Hur examined the issue of future deterrence, which DOJ policy requires a prosecutor to consider. To my knowledge no one spotted this, which is surprising, as it is a jaw-dropping irony: Hur stated that one of the reasons Biden need not be prosecuted was that Biden's prosecution of Trump (for less egregious, lawful conduct) was sufficient deterrence. Lest you think I am exaggerating, here is the language in the report:

> As for general deterrence, future presidents and vice presidents are already likely to be deterred by the multiple recent criminal investigations, and one prosecution, of current and former presidents and vice presidents for mishandling classified documents.

Distilling this logic, it was basically, "I can give Biden a pass, because Biden is already sticking it to Trump." Practically, I suppose the logic is sound, but I personally found it unsettling.

In a perfect world, Hur could have published the facts from his investigation; found that executive branch handling and storage rules applied to a vice president; determined that Biden broke those rules; but then concluded that the criminal laws simply did not apply to a vice president. That would have been an honest analysis, and in a perfect world, accepted.

But Hur was not in a perfect world. Hur found himself in a situation where he was limited by recent DOJ interpretations of laws aimed at prosecuting Trump, as well as by a culture that insists on the belief that laws should be applied equally to everyone in America.

Given the obstacles blocking the honest, direct route, Hur was left looking like a drunken driver erratically swerving about the roadway, plowing over a few garbage cans but making it home safely. And make it home safely he did, the importance of which can be appreciated even more after delving into a much more controversial, and much more political case: DOJ's indictment of former President Trump for retaining classified documents from his presidency. By the time we are done analyzing that case, you will view the Hur report, despite its many flaws, as the work of angels.

PART III

Trumping Up Espionage Charges

CHAPTER 8

The Turbulent Threat to Democracy

About two weeks before President Trump left the White House, aides began packing documents and personal items and sending them to Trump's home. As a general matter, there is nothing nefarious about a president taking a large volume of material from his presidency. You might not know this, given the press reporting and DOJ's portrayal of Trump's departure, but president's keep a lot of stuff from their presidencies, including documents they deem personal records and even gifts, so long as they were personal and under a certain value.

For instance, in addition to President Clinton keeping Oval Office recordings (including likely classified conversations with foreign leaders) as "personal records," Clinton also kept over 14,000 gifts, including around $140,000 worth of government property (furniture, artwork, etc.) and items over the ethics threshold ($260) for keeping without paying for them. Only after a public backlash did Clinton return the government property and pay to keep higher-value gifts, as required by law.

A subsequent congressional investigation found that Clinton was taking government property from the White House a year before he left; that Mrs. Clinton had unlawfully solicited gifts totaling close to $40,000 (china and silverware); and that Clinton had installed a political person from his inner circle, Lori Krause, as head of the White House Gift Unit. Krause was appointed on "special hiring authority," despite having no experience in gift valuation, and she subsequently undervalued an astonishing number of gifts.

About 98 percent of the over 14,000 gifts Clinton retained were either not valued at all, or they were coincidentally valued just below the $260 threshold. One example was a framed and signed John Quincy Adams land grant that Krause valued at $240. But again, I digress. The takeaway here is that presidents are permitted to keep a lot of stuff from their presidencies, and even when some went a little overboard, no one made a federal case out of it.

About four months after Trump left office, in early May 2021, the National Archives and Records Administration (NARA) General Counsel Gary Stern asked Trump's lawyers to ensure that NARA received all of Trump's presidential records. Stern specifically requested the original correspondence between Trump and the leader of North Korea, stating that it was "essential that these original records be transferred to NARA as soon as possible."

Reading the email from Stern—the top lawyer for NARA—I was stunned at how aggressive NARA was in dictating to former President Trump that specific records from his presidency were presidential records. Recall that in the litigation over Clinton's Oval Office tapes, NARA and DOJ took the position that Clinton's tapes were presumptively personal records, even though the tapes captured Clinton's discussions with heads of state (which would likely make them classified). And in that case the court ruled that NARA's only role was to accept what a president decided to give NARA. With Trump, NARA took a completely opposite approach. With Trump, NARA unilaterally decided that specific Trump documents were presidential records. Worse yet, NARA was unlawfully forcing its decision on former President Trump, threatening legal action if he did not comply with NARA's demands.

To be clear, it is indisputable that any reasonable person reading the detailed definition of "presidential records" in the Presidential Records Act (PRA) would conclude, as the NARA general counsel did, that communications between a president and a foreign leader are indeed presidential records. Any reasonable person would also conclude that at least some of President Clinton's Oval Office tapes were presidential records. However, what a reasonable person concludes is irrelevant. What you or I conclude is irrelevant. And what NARA concludes is irrelevant. Under the PRA—and according to the federal courts—the only thing that matters is what a president decides, and that decision—as *unreasonable* as it may be in any given situation—is unfettered and unreviewable.

Laws are not perfect. And given the political and constitutional implications inherent in Congress telling a president how to keep his own records, the PRA was purposefully made toothless against a president. That is why, in practical terms, the PRA serves as nothing more than a guide for a president or vice president. Presidents are politicians and their decisions in designating records will include political calculations that do not follow obvious logic or the guidance in the PRA. For better or for worse, that is the law, and that is how the law must be. The most NARA could state to a president about a record is: "We think such-and-such is a presidential record, and while this is your decision alone, we hope you will agree." And even that statement runs counter to the judicial ruling in the most relevant court case, the Clinton Oval Office tapes litigation, which was that NARA's *only role* was to accept what a president provides.

In his early May 2021 email to Trump's lawyers, the NARA general counsel acknowledged that the gathering of presidential records is often particularly confusing and chaotic for a one-term president: "We know things were very chaotic, as they always are in the course of a one-term transition." This statement, from NARA's general counsel, shows that the challenges the Trump team was encountering were not unique. A later email from William Bosanko, NARA's chief operating officer (responding to a reporter's query) expressed a similar sentiment: "We frequently encounter situations where records are found (classified and not) in places they should not be," and that NARA is often notified "long after the fact."

Sometime in December 2021, President Biden reportedly proclaimed to members of his inner circle that Trump was a "threat to democracy," and expressed frustration that the attorney general (AG) was acting like "a ponderous judge" and not being more aggressive in criminally prosecuting Biden's greatest political rival.

Biden's frustration over his subordinate's lack of zeal against a political rival is reminiscent of the legendary struggle between the Archbishop of Canterbury Thomas Becket and King Henry II. The rift between them stemmed from Becket's transformation from a loyal chancellor to a staunch defender of the church's independence from state, which clashed with the king's efforts to exert royal control over the clergy. This conflict escalated when Becket excommunicated bishops supportive of the king. By 1170, King Henry had grown so frustrated with Becket that he angrily proclaimed his annoyance to his inner circle.

Historical accounts differ as to King Henry's exact words, but the most popular version is: "Will no one rid me of this turbulent priest?" What we do know is that four of King Henry's knights proceeded to Canterbury Cathedral and brutally murdered Becket. Today, the words attributed to King Henry II are often used to describe situations where a cowardly leader directs something illegal or politically unsavory in a manner that is ambiguous enough to avoid responsibility for the outcome. The phrase aptly characterizes Biden's declaring to his inner circle that he was fearful of Trump, and frustrated with AG Garland for not pursuing Trump more aggressively. "Will no one rid me of this turbulent threat to democracy?"

In mid-January 2022, Trump's representatives provided NARA with fifteen boxes of Trump's presidential records. Within a few weeks, NARA issued a press statement claiming that Trump's records "included paper records that had been torn up by former President Trump." NARA's press statement was shocking, as NARA was publicly criticizing a former president for the physical condition of presidential records when NARA apparently had no evidence of who had torn up any particular document. To make up for the lack of evidence, NARA cited press reports, which are not only unreliable, but they also did not establish any linkage between Trump and any specific torn document. NARA's conduct in going out of its way to quickly and publicly criticize a former president reeked of political bias.

Soon thereafter, in early February 2022, NARA released another statement with even more antagonistic language toward former President Trump. In a chastising tone, NARA related that Trump's records "should have been transferred to NARA from the White House at the end of the Trump administration" and that Trump's team was searching for more "Presidential records that belong to the National Archives." NARA's statement stressed the "mandates" of the PRA; NARA's pursuit of errant records that have been "improperly removed" or not "appropriately transferred"; and finally, the importance of "timely transfer" because "records matter." You will find no such condescending and chastising language in any press release concerning Vice President Biden's exceptionally late transfer of vice-presidential records (about six years late) to NARA. You will find no such language in a NARA press release about Biden's records, because in Biden's case, as noted earlier, NARA made no press release.

With Biden, NARA felt no need to publicly scold about the "importance of timely transfer" of vice-presidential records and no need to patronizingly proclaim that "records matter." To the contrary, when NARA recovered nine boxes (and likely much more) of Biden's vice-presidential records in November 2022, NARA never told anyone. NARA never told the public and NARA never notified Congress. Internal NARA emails show that when Biden was caught violating the PRA, and likely possessing classified documents, NARA considered the situation to be something that needed to be kept quiet and handled "with the utmost professionalism and discretion." Compare this dichotomy to Acting Archivist Debra Steidel Wall's August 24, 2022, statement, to all NARA employees, that NARA was "uniquely and fiercely non-political."

William Shakespeare, in my opinion, is the greatest writer in human history. My memory is not what it used to be, but a Shakespeare quote will still pop into my head now and then, as it did when reading the holier-than-thou assertions of former Acting Archivist Steidel Wall: "The lady doth protest too much, methinks."[12]

According to Trump's attorneys, who later reviewed the fifteen boxes of material Trump gave to NARA, during the chaotic final days of the Trump administration, White House staffers were sweeping documents from the president's desk and other areas into boxes. Those boxes contained all manner of documents, loosely grouped by date, and most of the classified documents sent to Trump's home apparently concerned briefings for phone calls with foreign leaders given that the documents were located next to the schedules for the calls.

This is interesting, as the negligent-staffer excuse is the same excuse President Biden gave for his possession of classified documents. The difference, of course, is that Biden's excuse was accepted by DOJ, whereas Trump's led to a criminal prosecution that could put Trump in jail for the rest of his life. It is also interesting in that President Clinton's Oval Office tapes also involved phone calls with foreign leaders, but in Clinton's case, NARA and DOJ took the position that Clinton's tapes were presumptively "personal records" for the simple reason that Clinton kept them. Lastly, it is interesting that the chaotic pack out described by Trump's attorneys aligns with NARA's experience. ("We know things were very chaotic, as they always are in the course of a one-term transition," and "We frequently encounter situations where records are found [classified and not] in places they should not be.")

After NARA completed a preliminary review of Trump's fifteen boxes and concluded that the boxes contained "highly classified documents intermingled with other records," the NARA inspector general (IG) made a criminal referral to DOJ. The timing of the NARA IG referral, which occurred on February 9, shows that NARA completed the preliminary review of the fifteen boxes within the span of three weeks. Three weeks. To review fifteen boxes. Compare NARA's dedication of resources to the fact that *four months* after receiving nine boxes of Biden's vice-presidential records, NARA had *still not even opened the boxes*. Contrast that processing disparity with NARA's January 17, 2023, letter to the House Committee on Oversight and Accountability, in which NARA insisted that, in handling Biden and Trump matters, it's conduct had been "entirely consistent and without any political bias"

NARA Chief Operating Officer William Bosanko received a text in late February enquiring as to whether Bosanko had made any progress in discussing an issue with the White House. Bosanko replied, "None—the 15 boxes from mar-a-lago have consummed [sic] all of our discussions." This text shows that the White House and NARA were having extensive, substantive dialogue over Trump's records, and that NARA may have even granted the Biden White House unlawful access to Trump's presidential records as early as January or February 2022. As discussed earlier, the PRA generally restricts access to presidential records for five years and permits presidents to restrict access to vast amounts of presidential records for up to twelve years. Trump's presidential records must have been restricted in some fashion, because the public record shows that the FBI could not access these records without NARA granting a formal exception under the PRA. And here the plot thickens.

There are two relevant exceptions in the PRA that permit NARA to grant access to restricted presidential records. Both exceptions are expressly "subject to any rights, defenses, or privileges which the United States or any agency or person may invoke." One of the exceptions is "for the purposes of any civil or criminal investigation or proceeding," but that exception requires a subpoena or other judicial process issued by a court of competent jurisdiction. Even though the FBI had an open criminal investigation of Trump, the Biden administration chose not to pursue that exception. Instead, the Biden administration chose to pursue a different exception, whereby President Biden himself made the access request to NARA, which is permitted but only under specific circumstances. NARA can only grant an access exception to an incumbent president "if such records contain information that is needed for the conduct of current business of the incumbent president's office" and the records are "not otherwise available." Pursuant to that PRA exception, on April 11, 2022, President Biden formally requested that NARA grant FBI access to the fifteen boxes of Trump's presidential records.

Generally, I don't like assessing issues or events without examining the primary source documents. Unfortunately, not all the relevant source documents, such as President Biden's April 11, 2022, request to NARA, are available. Although Biden's request has not been made public, a DOJ letter to Trump's representatives described Biden's request as claiming that it was "necessary" for an "ongoing criminal investigation" and that there was "urgency" because "the Executive Branch must also conduct an assessment of the potential damage resulting from the apparent manner in which these materials were stored and transported."

So, President Biden's access request had two bases: (1) to assist with a criminal investigation; and (2) an urgent need to facilitate a damage assessment concerning storage and transportation of classified information. There are fatal deficiencies in both justifications. Some are obvious. Some are not. I will explain both.

Playground Bullies

As discussed, under the PRA, access to restricted presidential records for a criminal investigation requires a "subpoena or other judicial process issued by a court of competent jurisdiction." Instead of seeking judicial process, which would have involved another branch of government, the Biden administration chose to keep the matter entirely within the executive branch. Biden's request to NARA, however, was a clearly improper method to obtain presidential records for a criminal investigation. This basis for Biden's request was blatantly inappropriate, and should have been rejected by NARA. It was not.

President Biden's other basis for seeking access to Trump's presidential records was the timely need to conduct a damage assessment. Recall that in Biden's case, no damage assessment was done, even though Biden possessed a large volume of classified documents, in multiple unsecured locations, some for decades, while claiming he had no idea how any of it came to be in his possession. Contrast that with Trump's case, where Trump also had a large volume, but they were all in one place, that was much more secure, for a significantly shorter time frame, and there was no doubt as to how the documents came to be in Trump's possession. And yet for Trump, the Biden administration claimed an urgent need to conduct a timely damage assessment. To appreciate the fully fallacious nature of the damage assessment justification, we must endeavor another road trip through the federal bureaucracy. So hit the restroom, grab some snacks, and buckle up.

The "Damage Assessment": Learning Lessons & Taking Accountability

As previously noted, NARA can grant access to restricted presidential records when an incumbent president needs access "for the conduct of current business" and the records are "not otherwise available."

In Trump's case, the records were not "otherwise available," so that requirement was met. Also, conducting a damage assessment—when one needs to be done—would be "current business" of the incumbent president's office. *When one needs to be done.*

As a general matter, I try not to speak in absolutes, as there are, it seems, always exceptions to every rule or unqualified statement, and so absolutes are often easily impugned. But given my substantial experience in this arena, I can say with as close to an absolute assertion as I can that no damage assessment in Trump's case needed to be done. And even if a damage assessment was going to be done, it would absolutely not be a priority and would normally be delayed until after the criminal case was over. We have to pass a few mile markers before the falsity of the justification can be seen clearly, so be patient. You can use the restroom when we stop for gas.

Major intelligence failures or instances of mishandling classified information often require formal damage assessments so the intelligence community can assess the likely impact of the events on its mission and intelligence sources. There are also likely important lessons to be learned from such episodes so mistakes will not be repeated. Sometimes, depending upon the nature of the event, the damage is obvious, and the internal assessments are more "after-action reports," as the focus is on lessons learned.

For twenty-five years, I participated in many forms of such autopsies, supporting reviews of some of the biggest intelligence flaps in CIA history. Some are well known and officially acknowledged; some are well known but not officially acknowledged; and some are completely unknown. Such internal reviews are necessarily detailed and candid and are often controversial, as they assign blame and identify individuals. Due to their candor and thorough analysis of intelligence matters, they are among the most tightly controlled documents in the spy business.

After being assigned as the legal advisor to the CIA Counterintelligence Center (CIC), I asked my departing colleague for the combination to the large safe in my new office. He replied that he had no idea, as he had never even tried to open the safe. When I finally got the safe opened with the help of a security officer, there was only one document inside: the Aldrich Ames after-action report. Ames was the worst known traitor in CIA history, and his treacherous conduct, working for Russian intelligence as a double agent, cost many intelligence assets their lives.

I read the whole report, which took a few days. It was so thick that Sandy Berger would have had to stuff it down his pants one chapter at a time. The report was thorough and candid. Brutally candid. Dusty and aged, the copy in my safe was numbered, and listed the total number of copies made, which was small. I could not help but think that the few remaining copies had probably met similar fates, gathering dust, in safes, with long-forgotten combinations.

This is not to say that the lessons learned were lost. Many reforms were put in place because of the Ames report, so it had a meaningful impact. But the specific mistakes and failures that led to the updated practices were almost certainly forgotten, even to the select few who had been given access to the Ames after-action report, many years before.

When I was chief of the Litigation Division in the CIA General Counsel's Office, I started an informal program where officers from the CIC would come to the division and give a briefing every couple of months. Based on damage assessments and after-action reports from some of the major events in CIA history, the briefings were informative and fascinating because they were from real life. I started the practice because I was amazed how little of the important history of the intelligence business was known to the junior officers. The program was a big hit with the division, and it was always good to see some of my old colleagues from the counterintelligence world, who were as psychotically paranoid as ever and always up for an opportunity to preach the gospel of counterintelligence. This is but one example of how the lessons learned from damage assessments and after-action reports can be lasting, even when the reports themselves are decaying, under dust, in solitary confinement.

Lessons learned are only one aspect of these postmortems. Another is accountability. Even when I did not participate in the investigation or drafting of such reports, I was at times asked to read drafts before they were finalized to assess potential civil liabilities, given my unique expertise in national security–related civil litigations. For one matter I was deeply involved in—and I am not at liberty to relate any facts—the conduct of certain CIA officers was so egregious that they were fired, demoted, or reprimanded. In addition to participating in the investigation, I personally handled settlement negotiations with private parties to mitigate some of the damage. Very direct orders were given to me by the CIA director himself on how to handle settlement negotiations: "Be generous and get this done: I want it in my rear-view mirror." After reading the final after-action report, the CIA director held a mandatory briefing in the CIA auditorium for all CIA senior intelligence officers. This was unprecedented. Because the details were sensitive, the director never mentioned what had actually happened. You may find that hard to believe, but it is true. The director lectured on accountability, professionalism, and candor, and if you did not know why, before entering the auditorium, you would have been none the wiser upon leaving. But you would have gotten his points.

Around the time of the CIA director's lecture to the senior officers, I was sent to the West Wing with my boss, the legendary John Rizzo, to brief the president's lawyer, the White House counsel. I had fifteen minutes on his schedule. When I entered the White House Counsel's Office, there were about a dozen senior White House lawyers around the table, which I had not expected. It sounds intimidating, but it was not. By this time in my career, I was quite senior myself, had briefed other White House counsel, and was never nervous to brief any person on a topic that I knew more about than anyone. The White House lawyers were mesmerized by the story, which was like the script of a Hollywood spy movie that I would tell my friends not to watch because something like that could never happen in real life. Forty-five minutes later, I was still talking, answering questions from around the table. By this time the White House counsel had his elbows on the table and his head in his hands, looking down at the table in disbelief. Occasionally, he would glance sideways at me with a look on his reddened face that said, *Are you kidding me, son? How could you people have let this happen?*

Learning lessons and assigning accountability are important aspects of a damage assessment or after-action report, but when there has been a potential disclosure of classified information, the most important aspect of the assessment is just that: assessing potential damage from possible disclosure. Given my unique experience with intelligence community postmortems and prosecutions involving the mishandling of classified information, I have perhaps more experience than any government lawyer in history with the complex interplay between potential-disclosure damage assessments and DOJ criminal prosecutions, and that interplay may be quite different than what you would expect.

One of the learning lessons for DOJ from the Aldrich Ames prosecution was to be wary of the intelligence community forging ahead on a damage assessment while a DOJ prosecution was ongoing. That concern was well founded. Prosecutors have obligations to provide certain categories of information to a criminal defendant in what is called "criminal discovery," and, while I don't need to get into all the details of a prosecutor's discovery obligations, I can tell you that it is a nightmare for a prosecutor if the intelligence community is conducting a parallel investigation that DOJ is not in charge of, has little to no insight into, and yet could have significant impact on a prosecutor's discovery obligations.

To properly conduct a damage assessment or after-action report, witnesses need to be interviewed; information needs to be gathered; documents need to be collected; emails need to be sent; memos need to be written; thoughts need to be memorialized; and analytical assessments need to be made—among many other things. Any one of these areas could greatly complicate a DOJ prosecutor's discovery obligations. That happened in the Ames case, and after the Ames case, DOJ learned to ask the intelligence community to hold off on any type of internal postmortem until after the prosecution was complete. The intelligence community, I can tell you, often did not take kindly to this request, which was basically: "Don't do your job until we do ours." But I understood the dynamics and was completely on DOJ's side, as the honest answer was that the damage assessment could wait. DOJ prosecutors have one of the most difficult jobs in all of government, and they don't need the intelligence community complicating it by conducting a concurrent investigation.

Of course, all that only matters when a damage assessment is necessary. And of all the cases I have seen, the one case that stands out as *not* needing a damage assessment is Trump's case. There was no mystery as to when the documents were taken or how they were transported; they were in hard copy and not on unsecured computers with internet capability; and the time frame they were in Trump's possession was relatively short. Given these facts, devoting resources to a damage assessment—at any time—would be a waste for the intelligence community. Even if a damage assessment was to be done for some reason, it would wait until the prosecution was over. Biden's case needed a damage assessment much more than Trump's. Have you heard anyone even mention a Biden case damage assessment?

And that is why Biden's justification to review Trump's presidential records was fallacious: a national security pretext to justify rummaging through the papers of a turbulent political rival, all to support a political prosecution. I will unpack the car. You can stretch your legs.

Selective Justice: Precedents & Political Bias

Let us digress for a moment to compare Trump's case to the relevant precedents and Biden's case. Director of Central Intelligence (DCI) John Deutch had hundreds of highly classified documents (probably more than Trump) on unsecured home computers with internet capability. No damage assessment was conducted. Secretary of State Hillary Clinton had over a hundred classified documents (and likely thousands more) on her unsecured home servers with internet capability. I have no recollection of a Clinton damage assessment being conducted, and none was reported. President Obama publicly proclaimed, *while the Clinton investigation was still ongoing*, in a *60 Minutes* interview: "I can tell you that this is not a situation in which America's national security was endangered." President Obama even went so far as to describe the national security concerns over Clinton maintaining classified information on her unsecured home servers as being "ginned up" because of "politics." So, according to President Obama, no damage assessment was necessary in the Clinton "matter."

Between his office at the Penn Biden Center and his Wilmington home, Biden had at least over 130 classified documents (and likely much more), with dates spanning five decades. Despite Biden claiming he had no idea how he came to possess any of these documents, and some of the material being unsecured for decades, *no one in the Biden administration has mentioned a "necessity" for a Biden case damage assessment.*

So, why a damage assessment for Trump's case?

And what was the rush causing the Biden administration to deviate from historical practices and conduct a damage assessment *during the criminal prosecution?* This is not one of those 3-D posters you need to stare at forever before the true picture reveals itself. It's all there. In plain sight.

Despite the serious deficiencies in both of President Biden's proffered justifications for needing to review Trump's presidential records, NARA readily accepted Biden's request and granted the FBI full access to all fifteen boxes of Trump's restricted presidential records. NARA's approval came so quickly—within hours of NARA receiving the request—that it broke the bureaucratic sound barrier. Trump's team was not even given an opportunity to be heard before NARA notified them it was granting Biden's request.

Trump's lawyers immediately requested FBI access be delayed until a privilege review could be completed to ascertain whether Trump would claim privilege over any material. Such requests are normal and expressly permitted under the PRA. For instance, this was the type of review Sandy Berger was conducting when he stole and destroyed original uncategorized Clinton presidential records. Those Clinton records were requested by the 9/11 Commission, and Berger was reviewing them to see if Clinton wanted to claim privilege over any presidential material to prevent it from being seen by the 9/11 Commission. NARA's response to the delay request from Trump's lawyer was telling. NARA granted a brief delay, and, NARA admitted, only after "the White House Counsel's Office acquiesced in an extension of the production date."

Instead of acting in an independent decision-making role, as NARA should, the evidence shows that NARA was taking directions from the Biden White House. And the brief delay only gave Trump's team about two weeks to review the material (exact dates are not available, but it had to be less than seventeen days). Less time than the three weeks NARA took to review the same boxes, and NARA's review displayed an administrative alacrity akin to the mating ritual of the Patagonian hooded grebe: a spectacle rarely seen.

Given that NARA (after White House approval) only granted a short delay, Trump's lawyer sought additional time from NARA to review Trump's records and to consult with Trump as to whether any privilege claim would be asserted. As a safeguard, in the event NARA denied the request for adequate review time, Trump's lawyer claimed a "protective assertion of executive privilege" over all the material pending his review and consultation with Trump.

On May 10, the Acting Archivist Debra Steidel Wall informed Trump's lawyer that she "decided not to honor the former President's 'protective' claim of privilege," adding that the decision was "not a close one." Steidel Wall admitted that her rejection of Trump's privilege request was based on guidance from Biden's DOJ, and that the guidance hinged on there being no precedent for a former president to prevent an incumbent's access to records "needed" by the incumbent. Factually, DOJ guidance was historically accurate: there is no such precedent. And there never should be. Because when a sitting president truly "needs" to see the records of a former president to carry out duties of the office, the access should always be granted. That is not controversial. The problem—which completely undercuts DOJ guidance and Steidel Wall's rejection of former President Trump's privilege claim—is that a presidential request is not the proper mechanism to obtain a former president's records for a criminal investigation; a damage assessment did not "need" to be done; and if a damage assessment was to be done, it would not need to begin until the criminal case was over.

Steidel Wall's denial of Trump's protective claim of privilege was also much more sinister than it appears on the surface. For in rejecting the protective claim of privilege, the acting archivist also rejected the former president's request to even *review* his own presidential documents for potential privilege assertions. This is not a minor distinction. Under the PRA, a former president has a right to assert any "rights, defenses, or privileges" to prevent disclosure of the records at issue. Inherent in that right must be the ability to review the records to see what information they contain to determine whether any privilege will be invoked. Steidel Wall justified denying Trump's right to a privilege review based on her conclusion that there was "no realistic basis" that the right to review "would result in a viable assertion of executive privilege against the incumbent President."

Think about this: Even with the historic importance of the 9/11 Commission, President Clinton was still given the opportunity for a privilege review of his presidential records that were requested by the Commission. Even with the importance of the 9/11 Commission, this statutory right was afforded to Clinton, as it should have been. But not for former President Trump, under circumstances that I don't think any reasonable person could claim were as important as the work of the 9/11 Commission.

On top of the substantive deficiencies with the acting archivist's decision, the whole affair had an air of comical performative theater. Basically, Biden's DOJ asked the Biden White House to seek access to records held by the Biden-controlled NARA. The Biden-controlled NARA immediately approved the Biden White House request for quick access, and then denied Trump's request to even review his own presidential documents based on guidance from . . . Biden's DOJ, which had originated the request in the first place. You can get away with these things when you control the entire executive branch. You just need a veneer of "process."

All the available evidence shows, to any reasonable person, that NARA, DOJ, and the White House colluded to give Biden's DOJ quick, unlawful access to Trump's records. NARA, DOJ, and the White House acted like a bunch of playground bullies, ganging up on the unpopular kid at school to steal his lunch money. As abusive as this was, it was just a prelude to what was coming. For the bureaucratic bullying quickly escalated. To medieval warfare.

CHAPTER 9

The Siege

Immediately after the acting archivist rejected Trump's privilege review request, Trump received a grand jury subpoena seeking all documents with classification markings. An important milestone, the subpoena was the first instance of legal compulsion in Trump's case—the first flaming boulder catapulted into Trump castle.

Here, again, it is instructive to compare the precedents to DOJ's handling of Trump's case. Director of Central Intelligence (DCI) John Deutch was not a president and was required to abide by all the rules for handling classified information that every other member of the executive branch (except the president himself) was required to follow. Deutch knowingly had hundreds of highly classified documents on unsecured computers in his home, might also have had paper copies, and had attempted to destroy evidence of his unlawful conduct. Yet, DOJ did not pursue any legal compulsion of any kind in Deutch's criminal investigation. Deutch's home was never raided; no search warrants were sought; no grand jury was empaneled; no subpoenas were issued.

Sandy Berger was also not a president. He stole original uncategorized TOP SECRET presidential records from the National Archives; hid them at a downtown D.C. construction site; later took them to his home; and claimed, after he was caught, to have destroyed the records he had stolen. Despite destroying evidence, making repeated false statements to the FBI, and the extent of his thievery being unknown, DOJ did not invoke any legal compulsion of any kind in Berger's criminal investigation. Berger's home was never raided; no search warrants were sought; no grand jury was empaneled; no subpoenas were issued.

Hillary Clinton was also not a president (although she still claims the 2016 presidential election was stolen from her). Clinton knowingly established a home server to store her official government emails, and that server contained at least over a hundred (and likely thousands) of emails with classified information in them when they were sent. DOJ's preference in the Clinton investigation was to seek voluntary cooperation. Clinton's home was never raided; no search warrants were sought; interviews were consensual; and Clinton's lawyers were not forced to disclose discussions they had with their client, *even though they destroyed evidence.*

The comparison to Trump's case is stark. Trump was a former president, which gave him, up until his final moment in office, greater autonomy over classified information than anyone in the world. In Trump's case, the FBI and DOJ moved expeditiously to legal compulsion. A grand jury was empaneled; testimony was compelled; subpoenas were issued; and, as we will soon see, a search warrant was obtained, Trump's home was raided, and 13,000 documents were seized. It was the prosecutorial version of a medieval siege, complete with catapults, flaming arrows, and battering rams.

Now, contrast federal law enforcement's handling of the Trump case to Biden's case. Keep in mind that Biden was not a president during the time frames that he somehow came to possess classified documents, and as such, Biden was required to abide by the rules established by the president for handling classified information. In Biden's case, DOJ never invoked any form of legal compulsion. No warrants; no subpoenas; no raids; voluntary interviews; and the FBI even permitted Biden's private lawyers (who did not have security clearances) to search Biden's house for evidence *after a criminal investigation was opened.* I will cover this disparity in greater detail later, but for now I will just highlight that even though Biden's private lawyers discovered evidence, from multiple searches of Biden's offices and homes, DOJ never compelled them to testify about discussions with their client and never demanded they sign any certifications concerning their searches, as DOJ did in Trump's case.

On the same day Trump's office received the grand jury subpoena, Trump's lawyer received a letter from DOJ Section Chief Jay Bratt asking for a sworn certification that documents produced in response to the subpoena "represent all responsive records" and that if there were "no responsive documents . . . a sworn certification to that effect." This request really knocked me back, and I could not believe what I was reading. Some brief background will help illustrate how nefarious it was for DOJ to request such a certification.

Lawyers, declarants, or affiants should never draft or sign anything stating that the results of a search located "all responsive records" or that "there are no responsive documents." Never. Searches are not perfect. Because people are not perfect. And searches are performed by people. Also, an affiant could never actually know if he or she had located "all responsive records" to a subpoena even if that person had personally executed every aspect of the search. Most importantly, the law recognizes all this, and thus does not require or expect perfect searches: the law only requires *reasonable or diligent* searches. Period.

For over a decade, I was responsible for describing to federal judges the results of CIA searches in support of civil and criminal litigations. The language we used to describe searches would attest to diligent or reasonable searches calculated to locate responsive records. A good example of the fine lines we would draw in describing CIA search results would be what I called the "fraudster cases," where as part of a fraud scheme, a perpetrator had falsely claimed to be a CIA officer. I worked on many such cases over my career. If the miscreant had been a CIA officer, there would be personnel files, security files, polygraph files, etc., which, of course, in these cases, there were not. But to support such fraud cases, the CIA would never submit an affidavit stating that the person was not a CIA officer. We would provide an affidavit stating that we had conducted reasonable searches in all the appropriate places where employee records should exist and found nothing. This may seem overly technical, but it is normal business practice for lawyers who should never—*ever*—draft an affidavit claiming that a search had located "all responsive records" or that "there are no responsive documents." It would be malpractice. DOJ of course knows all this, yet they still requested from Trump's lawyers that very language in a certification. The DOJ section chief was asking Trump's representatives to commit malpractice, and arguably, perjury. Basically, the legal equivalent of an ambush.

Here, again, it is instructive to compare how the FBI and DOJ treated Trump compared to similarly situated senior officials. Clinton's and Biden's lawyers were permitted, by the FBI, to search for evidence of crime in lieu of FBI searches, despite criminal investigations having been opened. Both Clinton's and Biden's lawyers found evidence of crime during the searches that the FBI permitted them to conduct. Yet DOJ never asked Clinton's or Biden's private lawyers to sign any certifications that they had located "all responsive records" or that "there were no responsive documents" or even describing generally the searches they had conducted.

Between May 16 and 18, FBI agents reviewed the fifteen boxes of Trump's presidential records and, according to the FBI's later affidavit, determined that 184 documents bore classification markings (25 TOP SECRET; 92 SECRET; 67 CONFIDENTIAL). Notice the level of detail we have been provided for Trump's case: we even know the number of CONFIDENTIAL documents, which I can tell you a DOJ prosecutor would normally not waste any time on. I would also highlight that this is May 2022. The same month that very senior White House officials, to include Dana Remus, the White House counsel herself, began covertly moving a large volume of Biden's documents out of Biden's personal office in the Penn Biden Center.

In early June 2022, the DOJ Section Chief Jay Bratt and three FBI agents visited Trump's home to collect documents responsive to DOJ's first subpoena. As the subpoena had only issued on May 11, Trump's team only had a few weeks to search what was at least fifty boxes and likely more (remember, National Archives and Records Administration [NARA] previously took three weeks to do a preliminary review of fifteen boxes). Trump's team had asked for more time to conduct a thorough search, but NARA (apparently at White House direction) declined the request. Here, again, is an example of DOJ setting up the Trump team for failure: don't give them enough time to conduct a thorough search, but later criticize, and criminalize, the results of the search. Another ambush.

In addition to providing DOJ with a folder of responsive documents, Trump's lawyers also provided DOJ with a certification that a "diligent search was conducted" of Trump's boxes; that the search "was conducted . . . in order to locate any and all documents that are responsive to the subpoena"; and that "all responsive documents accompany this certification." For the last part of the certification, I personally would have used even more cautious language, something along the lines of "all responsive documents located pursuant to a diligent search accompany this certification," but the language used was sufficient given the certification must be read wholistically, and there were appropriate caveats ("diligent search," "in order to locate" responsive records). The problem with the looser language for the last part of the certification is that it permits someone with nefarious intent to focus solely on that clause, ignore the other caveats, and then misstate that the certification represented that "all responsive documents" to the subpoena were produced. That is exactly what many media outlets did, and even worse, what DOJ shamelessly did in the Trump indictment (which I will cover later).

While at Trump's home, the DOJ attorney and FBI agents were shown a storage room containing about fifty to fifty-five boxes of material from Trump's presidency, and the law enforcement officials requested consent to search the boxes themselves. Trump's lawyers declined the request. That rejection (which was entirely justified and lawful) was likely detailed in the FBI warrant affidavit. I can't say with certainty, because the FBI heavily redacted this portion of the affidavit, but even though the event is not relevant to probable cause, there is a likelihood that the FBI described it to the magistrate anyway, which means that the lawful denial of consent was likely relied upon, in part, by the Biden DOJ to obtain a warrant to raid Trump's home.

Imagine that the FBI shows up at your house and asks for consent to search your home to see if they can find evidence of crime. Your first thought is, *I have nothing to hide*. Then you think of your teenage daughter, and you wonder if she has any marijuana stashed in her bedroom. Then you think about the photos your brother-in-law emailed you of him giving his two-year old a shower after the child slipped in the mud and coated himself. The photos were hilarious. At the time. Now you wonder if they might fit the legal definition of child pornography. And then there are those back tax records you have in the attic. You were a little aggressive on those itemized deductions last year, and DOJ is unlikely to let *your* statute of limitations run. Right next to the tax records is a bunch of old DVDs. You never did pay too much attention to that FBI warning on pirated videos.

After that quick mental inventory, you reply, "No, thanks." The FBI then goes to a federal magistrate seeking a search warrant, and to support the probable cause to believe your home contains evidence of a crime, the FBI tells the magistrate . . . that you refused to let the FBI search your house. Crazy, right? Well, there is a good chance that the Biden administration did that to Trump.

The FBI immediately examined the documents provided by Trump's representatives and ascertained that thirty-eight documents bore classification markings (seventeen TOP SECRET; sixteen SECRET; five CONFIDENTIAL). Again, compare the level of detail provided for Trump's case to the lack of detail provided during Biden's case, where the public was never provided with the number of classified documents found in Biden's possession or the classification levels. In Biden's case, the Biden administration purposefully misled the public about those details. Conversely, in Trump's case, the public was informed of the exact count, classification levels, and even the number of CONFIDENTIAL documents (which normally would not even be considered by DOJ).

On the August 8, 2022, a platoon of FBI agents—unannounced, clad in bulletproof vests, authorized to use deadly force, and armed with pistols and a warrant for forced entry—raided former President Trump's home. Approximately 13,000 documents were seized. Only about 100 contained classification markings.

Crossing the Rubicon

In 49 BC, Julius Caesar was the governor of a Roman province above Rome's northern border, which was marked by the Rubicon River.

Governors commanded their own armies, and through his superior generalship, Caesar had greatly expanded his power and domain. The leadership in Rome came to fear Caesar, and at the end of his governorship Caesar was directed to return to Rome. Roman law did not permit a governor to bring an army into the republic, but Caesar took part of his army and marched south toward Rome, knowing that as soon as he crossed the Rubicon, he would be guilty of insurrection (actual armed insurrection, not a riot, or mostly peaceful protest). The punishment was death, and once Caesar crossed the Rubicon the crime would be complete. There was no going back. That is why, to this day, the phrase "crossing the Rubicon" is used to describe a defining moment from which there is no return.

And so, when the Biden administration forced entry into the home of the former president from a rival political party—a man who was also

Biden's most likely challenger in the upcoming presidential election, and whom Biden had privately impugned as a "threat to democracy"—President Biden crossed the Rubicon. American history was forever changed. Like Caesar, Biden did not cross alone. Unlike Caesar, who only took part of his army, Biden crossed the Rubicon with his entire political party.

From the moment I heard the reports of the Biden administration raiding the home of the former president, I was excited to learn as much as I could about the unprecedented event. As a former student of American history, I was interested to see how my country would react to the seismic event. As a former executive branch lawyer, I was interested to see how the constitutional issues concerning executive power would be treated. And as a former CIA lawyer experienced in investigations and prosecutions involving the mishandling and theft of classified information, I was interested to see how Trump's case would compare to the closest precedents, most of which I had worked on. What surprised me the most was the aggressive campaign to downplay the historic significance of the raid, vilify anyone who criticized the raid, and to deny that a raid had even occurred.

Because of my work as a CIA lawyer, I am sensitive to forms of mass manipulation, or propaganda, and I viewed the raid coverage from that perspective. First, let me provide some background and context, then I will show you what a propaganda cluster bomb looks like when it bursts across the political battlefield of mainstream media.

Back before Al Gore invented the internet and before the existence of television, it was a wise custom to never get into an argument with a man who owned a printing press. Such a man had the means to widely disseminate his side of the story, while ignoring yours, and hence shape public opinion to your detriment. Today, we no longer need to wait for the paper to arrive or for the nightly news to come on, as we carry a constant streaming media feed within arm's reach, all day, every day. It is practically attached to our bodies. For anyone intent on shaping public opinion, the tools of the trade have never been better. As easy as it has become to shape public opinion, when the entity doing the shaping is the U.S. government, it gets a little complicated, so let me provide some background.

The CIA's primary mission is to steal secrets. The agency does much more than that, but that is the primary mission, and many of the other things the agency does is to support the covert CIA officers deployed worldwide to recruit and run agents to steal secrets. Although the specific details as to how the CIA spots, assesses, develops, recruits, and runs agents are classified, the mere fact that this is the primary CIA mission is unclassified. While the CIA's core mission is stealing secrets, the CIA's legal authorities also expressly include another type of mission: conducting presidentially authorized covert action. "Covert action" is defined under U.S. law as an activity or activities of the U.S. government to influence political, economic, or military conditions abroad, where it is intended that the role of the U.S. government will not be apparent or acknowledged publicly. There are some additional complexities, but that definition is sufficient for our purposes. Other large governments engage in the same type of activities. Russian intelligence, for example, engages in similar conduct but they call it "active measures." Regardless of how you label it, covert action includes things like regime change, arms interdiction, and even lethal action or lethal assistance, such as covertly supplying weapons to one side of a conflict.

Covert action can also include more subtle types of activity, such as covert influence, which is when a government attempts to covertly impact public opinion in a foreign country. For example, if a government wanted to covertly achieve a regime change in a specific foreign country, but did not want to use violence, it could try to pollute all that country's media streams with derogatory information about that country's current leadership, thereby persuading the foreign citizens (hopefully) to vote the targeted regime out of office at the next election. That would be covert influence. I want to be clear that I am not saying that the U.S. government does this, it is just a pertinent example because our foreign adversaries target the U.S. population in this manner, and because these tactics are not limited to governments. Political parties do this every day. And you are the target. Every day.

The CIA's legal authority to conduct covert action is expressly granted by federal statute, and because of the aggressive nature of covert action, there are many specific statutory requirements. For instance, under U.S. law, covert action requires a formal presidential finding establishing the need for, and parameters of, a covert action program. There are also reporting obligations to the Congressional Intelligence Oversight Committees.

As a CIA lawyer, I taught classes on covert action to CIA operations officers, and I also learned a great deal about covert action through Freedom of Information Act (FOIA) litigations I handled. FOIA work gave me access to classified details concerning historical CIA covert action programs that had been officially acknowledged and to large extent declassified, because I had to review the information that was still being withheld as well as the information that was being released.

Covert actions have many components and can be implemented in various ways, all of which would broadly be spelled out in the presidential finding authorizing the covert action. Covert influence—commonly referred to as "propaganda"—employs a range of tactics for shaping public opinion, and because of my background, I have an eye for spotting these tactics, and I view media reporting through that lens. It's fun to dissect reporting and other forms of propaganda to try to spot all the tactics—from the subtle to the not-so-subtle—that are employed to shape public opinion. I won't discuss the ones that are not obvious (and there are many), but the obvious and expected tactics include the typical type of spin you would expect from someone like a political pundit: omitting key facts; ignoring counterarguments; shading facts; eliciting emotion to overcome logic or logic to overcome emotion; tone, word choice, inflection; misdirection; driving repetitive themes; etc. Spotting these tactics is instinctive for me, and I see them everywhere. But even I was shocked at the brazenness of the propaganda concerning the unprecedented FBI raid of Trump's home.

In America, when armed police officers show up at your door, *unannounced*, with a search warrant authorizing forced entry into your home, it is commonly (and correctly) referred to as a "raid." *Merriam-Webster's Dictionary* defines a "raid" as "a sudden invasion by officers of the law." *Cambridge Dictionary* defines it as "an occasion when the police enter a place suddenly in order to find someone or something." So, there does not need to be violence for a police raid to be a raid. Even without a battering ram splintering your front door or shaped charges blowing it off the hinges, a raid is still a raid if a warrant authorizes a surprise search of your home without your consent. You may wisely unlock the door, stand aside, and let the police in (whilst still in your jammies), but you have, nonetheless, been raided. The police are coming in, whether or not you put up a fight.

Given all this, it is undeniable that the FBI raid of Trump's home was just that: a raid. This should not be controversial. But despite the raid of Trump's home being, well, obviously, *a raid*, the initial media coverage of the historic event was largely to aggressively deny the incontrovertible fact that the raid was *a raid*; to insist that the FBI and DOJ were non-political law enforcement entities; and to vilify anyone criticizing the motive or means of the raid as *right-wing extremists engaging in dangerous violent rhetoric*. The reporting was like a nationwide Jedi mind trick: this was not a raid, "these aren't the droids you're looking for," and if you dare question this questionable use of unprecedented force, you are a right-wing terrorist.[13] Here is a sample of the post-raid propaganda barrage:

MSNBC Commentator Maya Wiley:

> **"Every person out there attacking this is essentially attacking non-politicized and independent law enforcement."**

CNN Anchor & Senior Political Analyst John Avlon:

> **"This appears to be a non-partisan process."**

NBC Reporter Ryan Reilly:

> **"The FBI is a conservative-leaning law enforcement organization, and we have sort of like lost the thread on that in the last six years."**

MSNBC Legal Analyst and Former Eastern District of Virginia (EDVA) U.S. Attorney Chuck Rosenberg:

> **"It's all legal. It's all lawful. It's not a raid. They are not there improperly or unlawfully."**

> **"This would have been the most fly-specked affidavit for a search warrant in the history of the Department of Justice. It would have been reviewed at the highest levels and multiple times. There are not going to be mistakes in it."**

Member of *New York Times* Editorial Board Mara Gay:

> **"A judge would not have signed off on that if there was not evidence. . . They are basically saying that law enforcement is engaging in some kind of a political attack; well, the fact of the matter is there is no reason to believe that and there is no basis for them to assert that."**

MSNBC Legal Analyst and Former Obama-era Acting Solicitor General Neal Katyal:

> **"The Justice Department is returning to its historical position as a law enforcement agency above politics trying to do the right thing."**

MSNBC Political Analyst and Former Maryland Lieutenant Governor Michael Steele:

> **"Because if anybody on this set had done the same thing, the exact same result would have occurred."**
>
> **"The dangerous rhetoric that is being fomented because of this, because of how Trump talks about a raid on his home—NO MAN—there was no RAID on your home!"**

Political Activist and Co-founder of the anti-Trump Lincoln Project George Conway:

> **"And the fact that a federal judge approved it shows that, hey, they got something there we just don't know what it is."**
>
> **"They are basically saying that law enforcement is engaging in some kind of political attack—well, the fact of the matter is—there is no reason to believe that, and there is no basis for them to assert that."**

NBC White House Correspondent Kristen Welker:

> **"The former president and his allies are escalating their attacks on the FBI claiming without any evidence that the investigation is politically motivated."**

Democratic Representative of California Eric Swalwell:

> **"They are fomenting that violence right now."**

MSNBC Legal Analyst and Former Mueller Investigation Prosecutor Andrew Weissmann:

> **"It's very important to remember this was not a break-in. This was not a raid. This wasn't the attorney general of the United States deciding willy-nilly on his own that he was going to do this search. A court had to approve this search . . ."**

ABC News Senior Political Correspondent Jonathan Karl:

> **"Republican attacks on the Department of Justice and the FBI intensify, prompting fears, the rhetoric, could turn to violence."**

The propaganda was a well-coordinated, relentless, coast-to-coast broadside, and that was just a sampling from a quick internet search. Once the smoke and oakum cleared, you could see the cannister and grape pounded into the cortex of the body politic: the raid was not a raid, it was a peaceful visit; the peaceful visit was not political or partisan; anyone criticizing the peaceful non-political visit is a dangerous and violent right-wing extremist you should vilify and fear.

Aside from my surprise at the level and sophistication of the propaganda downplaying the significance of the raid—and denying that a raid had even occurred—my initial general reaction was, candidly, disbelief. A presidential administration raiding the home of a former president from the opposing political party was so far outside the norms of American culture and history, that, absent some particularly egregious conduct by the former president, it would be a truly shocking abuse of law enforcement power. Given the obvious political overtones, I expected the Biden administration to explain, at least generally, what justified such unprecedented aggression. But that is not what happened. Instead, the Biden administration fought transparency and argued to keep the FBI affidavit supporting the raid off the public record. For me, the lack of transparency fostered the appearance of an unthinkable abuse of law enforcement power to strike a political opponent.

While admittedly stunned by the Biden administration's aggressive action, I wanted to keep an open mind, and I was hoping that as facts surfaced, there would be something of sufficient magnitude to justify the unprecedented raid. Even if I did not agree with it, if there was at least something with merit it would make the action less political and hence less damaging to my country. Unfortunately, I did not find the support I was looking for.

CHAPTER 10

There Are Not Going to Be Mistakes?

As part of the Not-a-Raid! propaganda broadside, the populous was assured that the not-a-raid was non-partisan; that Trump was treated just like anyone else; that there were "really significant" national security concerns (nuclear secrets being sold to God knows who!); and that there were "not going to be any mistakes" in the FBI affidavit supporting the raid. Remember all that while we kick the tires of the FBI affidavit.

Over the objections of the Biden administration, the federal magistrate who granted the warrant ordered DOJ to publicly release a redacted version of the raid affidavit. The released version was heavily redacted, but most redactions related to source protection for law enforcement sources. *Fair enough*, I thought. Thankfully, the section covering the classification system generally, and the specific classified information thought to be at issue in the case, was largely unredacted. I have personally drafted or supervised the drafting of hundreds, maybe thousands, of sworn affidavits describing such matters to federal judges, so for me, examining these types of documents is as effortless as breathing.

What struck me the most was how misleading the FBI affidavit was in describing the origin and applicability of the detailed rules concerning classified information. Ever so briefly, the affidavit stated that information is classified pursuant to executive order, leaving the impression that the act of classifying was just a ministerial matter. Then the affidavit described the strict rules pertaining to classified information *while omitting any reference to the origin and applicability of these rules*. The origin is relevant, and the omission revealing, because all the rules described were created by the president and govern the conduct of subordinates within the executive branch but not the president himself. Reading the affidavit, you would not know that. Along the same lines, the FBI affidavit had no language from, or citation to, section 1.3 of the executive order. Section 1.3, titled "Classification Authority," is a relevant section, as it clearly shows that the legal authority for classified information is presidential power. My overall reaction was that the FBI affidavit was purposefully written in a manner that gives a reader the misimpression that all the rules concerning the handling of classified information are federal law binding on the president. They are not. And DOJ knows they are not.

Even basic concepts pertaining to classified information were materially misrepresented in the FBI affidavit. For instance, the affidavit states categorically that classified information "may be shared only with persons determined by an appropriate United States government official to be eligible for access." That statement is flatly false. DOJ knows that this rule, cited to the court as applying to everyone, does not apply to presidents. Presidents own classified information by virtue of their elected position, and they don't need anyone's permission for access. No one reading the FBI affidavit would know that there is an important legal distinction between a president and every other member of the executive branch.

Another example, which really surprised me, was that the FBI affidavit misstated the standards for classifying information. You would think that the FBI would have at least gotten that right, but it did not, as the FBI affidavit claims that when "unauthorized disclosure could reasonably result in exceptionally grave danger to the national security, the information *may be* classified as 'Top Secret,'" [emphasis added]. Under the executive order, there is no "may" in the classification decision. If the damage standard is met, then the information is classified. Period. I do not see any unfair advantage to the FBI because of this error—it appears to be just sloppy drafting.

As is typical of these types of affidavits, there is an introductory section explaining relevant classification control markings: HCS, SI, FISA, NOFORN, etc. These markings are meaningless to most people, but they are very meaningful to those who spend careers working with classified information. Guess what's missing? The codewords for nuclear secrets. That told me that DOJ did not consider such information to be at risk. The FBI raid affidavit also made no mention of the Atomic Energy Act (AEA), which I would expect to see if "nuclear secrets" were at issue. Yet, at the time of the raid, the Biden administration was, with near certainty, leaking to media outlets that "nuclear secrets" were at risk. For example, after the raid, the *Washington Post* ran an article claiming that "Classified documents relating to nuclear weapons were among the items FBI agents sought in a search of former president Donald Trump's Florida residence . . . according to people familiar with the investigation." A quick internet search would find many other examples of the media hyping risk to "nuclear secrets" in Trump's case. We know the FBI aggressively uses "media leak strategy" as a component of prosecution, and it appears that the nuclear-secrets-at-risk narrative was likely FBI propaganda leaked to give plausible cover for the unprecedented raid of a former president's home.

FBI media leaks are unlawful and yet are part of the culture of the FBI. This is not hyperbole. It is fact. In reviewing the Clinton investigation, the ever-understated DOJ inspector general (IG) had some uncharacteristically harsh words concerning unlawful FBI media leaks:

- "We identified numerous FBI employees, at all levels of the organization and with no official reason to be in contact with the media, who were nevertheless in frequent contact with reporters."

- "We have profound concerns about the volume and extent of unauthorized media contacts by FBI personnel that we have uncovered during our review."
- "In addition, we identified instances where FBI employees improperly received benefits from reporters, including tickets to sporting events, golfing outings, drinks and meals, and admittance to nonpublic social events."

In a typical bureaucratic fashion, the FBI acted—it updated its policy on media contacts. The DOJ IG was not impressed:

> We do not believe the problem is with the FBI's policy, which we found to be clear and unambiguous. Rather, we concluded that these leaks highlight the need to change what appears to be a cultural attitude among many in the organization.

The "cultural attitude" at the FBI could more accurately be described as "unlawful conduct." FBI leaks involve sensitive law enforcement information, along with information protected from disclosure by grand jury secrecy rules, the Privacy Act, court orders, and even presidential executive orders. And when FBI leaks are part of a "media leak strategy," you could perhaps add prosecutorial misconduct to the list of violations, given the possibility (or goal) of widespread tainting of the potential jury pool. Or the voting pool.

From my experience, the apparent FBI media leaks raising the fear of "nuclear secrets" being disclosed had their intended impact. All my neighbors around this time were dutifully echoing their concern over "nuclear secrets" being at risk. One night, I was out to dinner in my neighborhood, and I was chatting with a couple who brought up the raid and shared their concern that Trump had stolen "nuclear secrets" and "could be selling them to anyone!" They were nice people and genuinely afraid. As I find is almost always the case in talking politics with folks in my neighborhood, as soon as I raised alternative views, they withdrew from the topic and said they did not want to talk politics. It always reminds me of the scene at the end of *Invasion of the Body Snatchers* when Donald Sutherland's character screeches and points his finger at the non-converts. I get pointed at a lot. At least in my case, they just retreat instead of screaming, attacking, and turning me into an alien zombie. Anyway, although retreating from the overall topic, this couple did want to know if I thought we were *safe*. The propaganda really worked. At least in my neighborhood, which is admittedly, not a tough sell: I live in the District.

In addition to misleading a reader as to the origin and applicability of the rules concerning classified information, omitting relevant law, and misstating the standards for creation and access to classified information, I also saw problems with the probable cause section. This section of the affidavit was heavily redacted, but it still showed the two primary bases the Biden administration relied on to raid Trump's home: probable cause to believe Trump violated the Presidential Records Act (PRA) and the Espionage Act. There were some lesser offenses piled on, but the thrust of it was PRA and Espionage Act violations. Examining these justifications showed me that they were almost certainly without merit.

The FBI affidavit stated, under oath, that there was probable cause to believe Trump's home contained "Presidential records subject to record retention requirements." There are several basic issues with this sworn statement. First, only a president (not the FBI) decides what is and is not a presidential record. This is not just my opinion; this is what the federal courts have ruled. Second, probable cause for a search warrant should be based on violations of criminal law. Yet, the PRA is a purely civil statute. And not just any civil statute: it is a civil statute that was purposefully designed to have no enforcement mechanism against a president, current or former, and under which only a president can determine his compliance. The PRA should never—*ever*—be used to justify a criminal search warrant against a president who has retained documents from his presidency. But that is what happened.

It took a while for this to come to light, but we can now see the grossly hypocritical conduct that the Biden administration engaged in concerning the PRA. On the one hand, the Biden administration inappropriately used the PRA as a battering ram to force entry into the home of the former president from the rival political party, while on the other hand it was covering up the incumbent president's own PRA violations. Included in the cover-up would be surreptitiously removing what must have been vice-presidential records from the Penn Biden Center starting in May 2022; facilitating Biden's private lawyers moving nine boxes of vice-presidential records to Boston while handling the matter "with the utmost . . . discretion"; hiding the malfeasance from the public for as long as possible; directing NARA to cancel a press release discussing Biden's violation of the PRA; and hiding Biden's retention under the rubric of "Obama–Biden documents." All while denying former President Trump's statutory right to assert any "rights, defenses, or privileges" before the Biden administration was given access to Trump's restricted presidential records.

As for the FBI reliance on the Espionage Act to raid Trump's home, the FBI affidavit specifically listed Section 793(e). This section of the Espionage Act makes it a crime for anyone having "unauthorized possession of, access to, or control over" national defense information (NDI) to willfully retain it and fail to deliver it on demand to an officer or employee of the United States entitled to receive it.

There are many issues in trying to stretch this law to criminalize the conduct of a president, which I will explore in due time. For now, I will give the FBI credit for at least citing to an actual criminal law in trying to justify raiding the home of a former president.

Another major issue with the warrant was the scope: the warrant sought every document dated from Trump's term in office. Every document. "Any government and/or Presidential Records created between January 20, 2017, and January 20, 2021" and "containers/boxes" that were "collectively stored" near boxes that contained classified documents. The breadth of the warrant is stunning, given that a president has the clear legal right to designate records from his presidency as "personal records." As no allowance was made for this obvious fact, the FBI must have seized every document from Trump's presidency, and even boxes (regardless of content) that were stored near a box that contained even one classified document. If the purpose of the raid was to protect national security by seizing classified documents, then the raid warrant would have only sought documents with classification markings, and the government would not have seized *every single document dated within Trump's time in office*. Far beyond the proverbial fishing expedition, the warrant was a deep-sea dredging with sprawled nets and trawler hooks, leaving me with the impression that DOJ's actual goal was to scour up evidence to support the election interference case. This is admittedly speculation, but it would explain why the FBI sought every document dated within Trump's presidency, and why the FBI seized 13,000 documents. Not 130. Not 1,300. The FBI seized *13,000* documents even though only about 100 documents bore classification markings.

To justify keeping the FBI affidavit under seal, the FBI included a claim that disclosing the affidavit could "severely jeopardize its effectiveness by allowing criminal parties an opportunity to flee." Yes, the FBI actually included "fleeing" as a reason to keep the warrant authorizing the raid of the former president's home off the public record. I shrieked with laughter when I read that, imagining comedy skits with Trump pounding vodka with Edward Snowden while hiding in a safehouse in Minsk, playing cards with Julian Assange while holed up in the Ecuadorian embassy, or huddling around a campfire with his gang of former White House aides, pounding whisky while polishing guns, planning their next document heist.

After the raid was over, the Biden administration arranged for the photographs taken during the raid to be placed on the public record. One photo showed dozens of boxes stacked to the ceiling in a bathroom in

Trump's home. Another photo—which appears to have been staged by the FBI—shows the ominous red SECRET and TOP SECRET cover sheets of classified documents all neatly laid out on a table for display. The special counsel later acknowledged that the cover sheets were actually not originally on the seized documents, but were rather attached by the FBI before the photos were taken. A reasonable person could view this conduct as propaganda—the prosecutorial equivalent of a *Victoria's Secret* fashion show—and a reasonable judge could view it as evidence tampering.

The photographed documents are not lengthy, and if they are indicative of the other one hundred or so classified documents seized in the raid, all the classified documents could have fit in one box. So why would DOJ publicly disclose photos of a bathroom full of boxes? Why did it publish any photos at all? Recall that in the Biden "review," the FBI searched a sampling of Biden's boxes at the University of Delaware, which houses approximately 2,000 boxes of Biden's documents. Why have we not seen any photos of Biden's 2,000 boxes?

About a month after the raid, in September 2022, *60 Minutes* aired an interview with President Biden. In the interview Biden was asked about his thoughts on former President Trump retaining classified documents. Although Trump was already under criminal investigation, Biden did not say that he could not comment on an ongoing DOJ investigation. That is the excuse the Biden administration uses routinely to avoid answering questions that could be embarrassing, politically damaging, or incriminating. Yet, when asked about the ongoing criminal investigation of Trump, and specifically what he thought about Trump's retention of classified documents, Biden replied, "How that could possibly happen? How anyone could be that irresponsible?" adding, "And I thought, *What data was in there that may compromise sources and methods?* . . . It's just totally irresponsible." This was September 2022. Biden's White House counsel and other top aides had been covertly moving Biden's documents from the Penn Biden Center for almost six months.

Within six weeks of the *60 Minutes* episode, Biden's private lawyers discovered what as far as we know was the first of many unsecured classified documents found in Biden's possession. That discovery was hidden by the Biden administration until the following year, when the malfeasance widened to a point it could no longer be contained. When Biden finally publicly addressed his own possession of classified documents, in numerous unsecured locations, his curiosity concerning *how anyone could be that irresponsible* had vanished. He was no longer wondering: "*What data was in there that may compromise sources and methods*?" Instead, Biden's concern and curiosity were replaced with dismissiveness and disinterest: "We found a handful of documents were filed in the wrong place." When asked specifically about the classified documents found in his garage, next to his Corvette, Biden testily responded, "My Corvette's in a locked garage, okay, *so it's not like they're sitting out in the street.*"

Biden was not a president during the time frames he came to unlawfully possess classified documents. Which means Biden had significantly less authority over classified information than a president, and he was required to obey the rules, established by the president, for handling classified information. Trump was president. He had complete control over classified information until the moment he left office, and he did not need to follow any of the rules he established for subordinates. Biden faces no criminal penalties for his malfeasance in mishandling classified documents. Trump is facing a lifetime in prison.

Return of the Breathtaking Expansionist

Biden's DOJ kept control over their criminal investigations of Trump for as long as possible, refusing to appoint a special counsel even though Trump was a former president from the opposing political party, Biden's biggest political rival, and the likely Republican nominee in the next presidential election. Finally, in November 2022, a few days after Trump formally announced his 2024 presidential campaign, Attorney General (AG) Garland appointed a former DOJ prosecutor, John L. "Jack" Smith as special counsel to investigate Trump.

Appointing a special counsel would mean losing day-to-day control over its criminal investigations targeting Trump, so the Biden administration was undoubtedly shopping for the right person to appoint. And it found that person in Jack Smith. Smith had proven his bona fides years earlier, when he was still with DOJ, by overzealously prosecuting a high-ranking Republican, Virginia Governor Bob McDonnell. That prosecution was based on Smith's novel interpretation of federal bribery law. Successful in the lower courts, Smith's legal work was rebuked and *unanimously* reversed by the U.S. Supreme Court as being "inconsistent with both text and precedent" and an "expansive interpretation" that raised "significant constitutional concerns."[14] White House counsel from Reagan to Obama went on record in the case criticizing Smith's unprecedented reading of the law as a "breathtaking expansion" that would damage any elected official's ability to perform their duties. That overzealousness in targeting a high-ranking Republican was likely exactly what the Biden administration wanted, and found, in Jack Smith. It probably did not hurt that Smith's wife, a documentary filmmaker, is best known for her work on Michelle Obama's documentary infomercial, *Becoming*.

Most of the order appointing Smith pertained to investigating 2020 election interference. Comparatively little space was devoted to investigating Trump's classified documents, referencing that case only by title, case caption, and docket number. Smith's appointment is also interesting in that it came just a few weeks after the discovery of classified documents in the Penn Biden Center (although the Biden administration would keep that discovery a secret until the following year). Particularly interesting, to me, was that AG Garland's selection of Smith as special counsel likely violated the AG's own regulations. As a career government lawyer, I read the fine print in government regulations, and the published DOJ regulations outlining the requirements for a special counsel state that an "individual named as Special Counsel shall be a lawyer with appropriate experience to ensure . . . prosecutorial decisions will be supported by an informed understanding of the criminal law." Smith was rebuked by a unanimous Supreme Court for having bent criminal law well past the breaking point. A prosecutor who stretched a criminal law in a manner "inconsistent with both text and precedent" and which raised "significant constitutional concerns" is not someone who has an established history making prosecutorial decisions that are "supported by an informed understanding of the criminal law." But that was who AG Garland appointed.

Once appointed, Smith quickly staffed his crusade, and one of the senior prosecutors Smith added to his ranks was Joseph "J. P." Cooney, a veteran of the holy wars against Trump and conservatives generally. Cooney had worked on the overzealous prosecution of Republican Virginia Governor Bob McDonnell and the prosecution of President Trump's personal friend and confidant Roger Stone. Stone was an elderly man with no priors and no history of violence but who had likely lied to Congress and threatened another witness (who himself never took the threat seriously).

Cooney's prosecution team treated Stone's arrest like it was the opening scene of *Saving Private Ryan.* After a platoon of heavily armed federal agents stormed the beach and subdued the lone defender—still in his pajamas— Cooney and his team sought a prison sentence of seven to nine years for Stone. This was a radical departure from the sentences DOJ sought in similar cases, which were more like three years. When his DOJ superiors directed a more appropriate approach to sentencing Stone, Cooney told his team—with no evidence—that the DOJ superiors were meddling in the case because they feared Trump.

All four of the prosecutors working on the case removed themselves in protest and the whole fabricated story was leaked to the media, which hailed the insubordinate prosecutors as heroes. One of the prosecutors even testified before Congress—based on the fabrications that Cooney and another team member had told him—that Trump and DOJ officials who feared Trump had interfered with the prosecution.

During a subsequent DOJ IG investigation—which found no political interference in DOJ's handling of the Stone sentencing—Cooney acknowledged that he had fabricated the political intrigue blaming Trump and senior DOJ officials. This was not a minor event: the entire purpose of the DOJ IG investigation was to determine whether the Trump administration had politically interfered in the Stone sentencing, and the entire allegation turned out to be yet another fabrication, another weapon fashioned by rabidly partisan Democratic party loyalists within DOJ.

Just over six months after Smith's appointment, in June 2023, DOJ filed a thirty-seven-felony-count indictment against Trump based on retention of classified documents. DOJ soon added additional charges in a superseding indictment, bringing the grand total to forty felony counts against Trump. Upon filing the first indictment in U.S. history against a former president, Special Counsel Smith gave a press conference wherein he repeatedly emphasized that America has "one set of laws" that "apply to everyone."

Given my background and the historical nature of the indictment, I was anxious to read the charges, which ended up being unlike any I had ever seen. To illustrate how unconventional and extreme the indictment is, let us compare it to the precedents. Brace yourself. For when you contrast DOJ's treatment of Trump with the senior Democrats in all the precedential cases, including Biden's, the result is jarring. With that disclaimer, let us sharpen Occom's razor and give a close shave to the law, the policy, the precedents, and the politics.

DOJ's indictment of former President Trump is fifty-three pages long, contains forty felony counts, and is based on alleged violations of nine different criminal laws. *Forty felonies.* Attached to the indictment is a "penalty sheet" that lists the maximum sentences for the various charges, and when you add them up, they total 140 years in jail. Keep this in mind.

John Deutch had hundreds of highly classified documents, including TOP SECRET/SCI documents, in his home on unsecured computers with internet capability. Deutch had far more classified than Trump and engaged in the unlawful conduct himself (no negligent staffers packing boxes), and Deutch knew he was violating the law. DOJ permitted Deutch to plead guilty to a one-count misdemeanor for unlawful removal and retention of *one single document.* One document. And the document DOJ chose was only classified SECRET. Deutch had also destroyed evidence, as did members of his inner circle, yet no one in the Deutch case was charged with obstructing justice or related crimes. DOJ summarized Deutch's misdemeanor in just over one page with a two-page statement of facts.

Sandy Berger stole TOP SECRET presidential records from the National Archives, lied to the FBI about it, and destroyed evidence. As with Deutch, Berger knowingly engaged in the unlawful conduct. DOJ permitted Berger to plead guilty to a one-count misdemeanor for unlawful removal and retention of "certain materials which contained classified information." In the documents DOJ filed with Berger's plea agreement, DOJ did not describe the classification levels or the contents of the specific documents Berger had stolen and destroyed. The documents were described simply as "classified documents." Berger was not charged with making false statements, destroying evidence, or obstruction of justice. DOJ summarized Berger's misdemeanor in just over one page with a three-page statement of facts.

David Petraeus knowingly kept eight notebooks of classified information in his home, classified up to TOP SECRET SCI. Petraeus shared the notebooks with his biographer and mistress and lied about it when questioned by the FBI. DOJ permitted Petraeus to plead guilty to a one-count misdemeanor for unauthorized removal and retention of "documents and material containing classified information." DOJ did not pursue obstruction of justice charges, even though Petraeus had lied to the FBI, and admitted to it in his plea agreement. Petraeus's biographer was not charged with anything despite her having unlawfully possessed classified information. DOJ summarized Petraeus's misdemeanor in just over one page, with an uncharacteristically thorough fifteen-page statement of facts.

Hillary Clinton purposefully established a home-based computer server to store her official emails when serving as secretary of state. Those servers contained at least over a hundred classified emails (slightly more than was seized in the Trump raid) and likely thousands more. Clinton's emails included classified documents that were TOP SECRET SCI, and all the emails contained classified information when they were sent. Clinton, her aides, and lawyers, all destroyed evidence. DOJ did not charge Clinton, her aides, or her lawyers, with anything.

All four of the precedents involved senior members of the Democratic party. Two of the four, Deutch and Clinton, unlawfully possessed over a hundred classified documents. The other two, Berger and Petraeus, made false statements to the FBI to cover up their crimes. None of the four senior Democrats were presidents, so they all lacked the level of authority a president possesses over classified information, and they were required to follow the same rules as every other member of the executive branch (except the Big Guy himself). All four of the senior Democrats were treated with incredible leniency either in the way DOJ charged them or by DOJ not charging them at all.

Now contrast these precedents to the case of Donald Trump, who, as president, had greater autonomy over classified information than anyone involved in the precedential cases.

In Trump's case, the FBI raided Trump's home and seized approximately 13,000 documents, only about 100 of which were classified. About the same number of classified documents that the FBI claimed Hillary Clinton had on her unsecured home server (with the actual count being likely much higher, in the thousands) and much less than John Deutch had on his unsecured home computers. Former President Trump had paper copies in his home that was guarded by the Secret Service, not in a maybe-locked closet in an unsecured building, or in a garage next to a Corvette, or on computers with internet capability.

Significantly, DOJ's Trump indictment establishes a new paradigm for charging Espionage Act cases by charging a specific felony for each classified document at issue. Thirty-two specific documents are individually charged in the indictment, listed with their levels of classification and descriptions of their contents. In all the precedents—all senior Democrats—DOJ did not provide an itemized list of the classified documents at issue or break them down to file *a separate felony count for each document.* In stark contrast to the Trump indictment, in all the precedents, DOJ took the exact opposite approach, condensing the violations to one charge, then either selecting one document with a lower-level classification or lumping all the documents into a catchphrase like "documents and material containing classified information." This one fact, standing alone, shows the extent to which the Biden administration went to persecute Biden's turbulent political rival. Not even in the classic espionage cases I worked on did DOJ charge the foreign spies for each individual classified document they stole.

Trump's indictment contains forty felony counts against him. Conversely, in all the precedents, the senior Democrats involved were either charged with one single misdemeanor (even when they possessed over a hundred classified documents, destroyed evidence, and lied to the FBI) or they were not charged at all. Trump is facing life in prison. The one-count misdemeanors DOJ permitted for Deutch, Berger, and Petraeus resulted in no jail time. Just fines and probation.

DOJ also piled on multiple charges against Trump for related offenses, which you don't see in any of the precedents: "Withholding a Document of Record," "Corruptly Concealing a Document of Record," "Concealing a Document in a Federal Investigation," "Scheme to Conceal," "False Statements and Representations," "Altering, Destroying, Mutilating, or Concealing an Object," and "Corruptly Altering, Destroying, Mutilating, or Concealing an Object." Again, contrast these charges to the precedents. John Deutch was, with near certainty, guilty of every one of the additional crimes listed in the Trump indictment, but Deutch was not charged with any of them. Sandy Berger was also, with near certainty, guilty of all the same crimes, but he was not charged with any of them. Hillary Clinton was also, with near certainty, guilty of every one of the same crimes, but was not charged with, well, anything at all. David Petraeus admitted to conduct that supported charges for "False Statements and Representations" and maybe "Scheme to Conceal," but DOJ did not charge Petraeus with these crimes.

In Trump's case, two of Trump's employees, Walt Nauta and Carlos De Oliveira, have also been indicted. The charges against the Trump employees all emanate from allegations that they assisted Trump by moving boxes and deleting security camera footage and then lying to the FBI about their actions. Nauta is facing a maximum jail sentence of 130 years and a maximum fine of $2 million. Carlos De Oliveira is facing a maximum jail sentence of sixty-five years and a maximum fine of $1 million.

Recall that in the Deutch and Clinton cases, aides and lawyers for Deutch and Clinton destroyed evidence, but they were never charged with anything. Also, Petraeus's biographer and mistress had knowingly possessed classified documents but was never charged with any crimes. In all four of the precedents, no one in the inner circles around the high-ranking Democrats was charged with any crimes, even though many of them could have been charged with every crime DOJ charged Nauta and De Oliveira. With near certainty, the reason for the disparity is that in the Trump prosecution, DOJ wants leverage over the two Trump employees to force them to provide testimony against Trump. It is equally clear that this is why DOJ never bothered to charge anyone surrounding Deutch or Clinton, and why DOJ never charged Biden's ghostwriter with obstruction of justice. DOJ was treading as lightly as possible around these high-ranking Democrats, and not seeking testimony, or any other evidence, to strengthen those cases.

More glaring inequity is obvious when comparing the basic facts of Biden's case to Trump's case. Biden possessed a large volume of classified documents in his home and D.C. office (and likely many more than have been publicly accounted for). Some were decades old, but most were from his vice presidency, which means he had retained them in unsecured locations for four years while he was a private citizen. None of the documents were dated from Biden's presidency. Trump may have possessed a higher total, but totals cannot be compared because Biden's total classified document count has not been publicly released. We do know that Trump's possession was for a much shorter time span, and the documents were in a much more secure location. Also, Trump was a president, and not a vice president, giving Trump much greater authority to handle documents as he pleased. Lastly, there is no available evidence showing that Trump knew his boxes contained any classified documents, while there is a 2017 tape recording of Biden acknowledging that he possessed classified documents in his home. Biden faces no criminal charges. Trump—again—faces forty felonies and what practically amounts to a life sentence.

Perhaps the greatest disparity between the two cases is that DOJ treated Biden as being inoculated from the laws for mishandling classified information by claiming that Biden could not be charged under the Espionage Act as it would raise "significant separation of powers concerns" and because the act does not expressly apply to a vice president. Now, those are good arguments and amply supported not charging Biden. But those same concerns apply, even more forcefully, to a former president, yet they were completely ignored when DOJ pursued a selective prosecution against former President Trump. The disparity is striking.

Comparing Trump's case to cases involving classic spying also clearly shows gross inequities. Theresa Squillacote was sentenced to twenty-two years in prison for spying; Kevin Mallory twenty years. Katrina Leung, who spied on the United States for China for twenty years, received no jail time, three years' probation, and a $10,000 fine. J.J. Smith, who provided a Chinese spy with highly classified information (at least some of it knowingly), received three months of home confinement, three years of probation, one hundred hours of community service, a $5,000 fine, and was permitted to keep his FBI pension.

Trump was president, with greater autonomy over classified information than anyone in the world. Yet, Trump has been charged by Biden's

DOJ with exponentially greater severity than in any of the precedents, even though none of the precedents involved presidents. While, because of my background, I can see things that most could not and can engage in a deeper examination than most, even a superficial analysis comparing Trump's case to Biden's case shows clearly that Biden's DOJ went out of its way to clear Biden, while doing everything possible to find ways to prosecute Trump. Even a casual comparison lays bare severe injustice, political persecution, and prosecutorial abuse. The available evidence on this is dispositive. And the Bard's eloquence particularly apt: "Something is rotten in the state of Denmark."[15]

CHAPTER 11

Kidney Punches & Low Blows

In addition to the baseless indictment and severe overcharging of Trump, I was particularly disappointed to see the DOJ Trump indictment infused with self-serving mischaracterizations, significant omissions, biased language, and irrelevant details, all obviously intended to bolster charges and unfairly prejudice public opinion. Reading the indictment was like watching a rigged boxing match where DOJ weighted both gloves, tied the opponent's shoestrings together, and then relentlessly pummeled a defenseless adversary.

Having spent decades as a lawyer in the executive branch, I hold government lawyers to a higher standard, especially prosecutors. Prosecutors have vast, nearly unchecked power to destroy lives. Therefore, they should be holier-than-thou in sticking to the relevant facts and law, not perverting them to gain unfair advantages. Maybe I am just too squeamish after having transitioned from cornerman to spectator, but I will relate what I viewed as the lowest blows in the indictment, and you decide if I am holding DOJ to too high a standard for fair fighting.

Misrepresentation of Presidential Authority

One of the most incredulous statements in the indictment is DOJ's characterization of a president's relationship with classified information as one of mere "lawful access." Like the FBI warrant affidavit, the DOJ indictment downplays a president's unique authority over classified information. Diminishing a president's authority over classified information to mere "lawful access" is like saying that parents have "lawful access" to their children. After denigrating a president's authority over classified information, the indictment then misleadingly describes classified information as being "owned by the United States government." The description is not wrong, mind you. The president is part of the government, so classified information, *being owned by the president*, is, in a broader, less precise sense, owned by the government. But similar to the "lawful access" description, DOJ obscures the truth using language that diminishes it to the point of obscurity. This is no accident.

An entire section of the indictment, titled "Classified Information," is just as misleading. Expanding on the inaccurate concept of classified information simply belonging to all of government, this section describes classified information as "owned by, produced by, produced for, and under the control of the United States government." In the precedential cases, this distinction—between a president and the government—would have no import because the defendants were not presidents. But when you are charging a former president, the distinction carries great weight. For presidents, whose power creates and controls classified information for "the government," stand in a category all by themselves. Similarly, the indictment, like the FBI affidavit, only briefly mentions that classification occurs pursuant to executive orders, making that critical fact seem like an inconsequential ministerial matter. It is not.

The indictment's diminution of presidential power over classified information does highlight the versatility of Special Counsel Smith. Smith's previous crusade to prosecute a high-ranking Republican showcased his ability to advocate for a novel, "breathtaking expansion" of federal law, whereas the Trump crusade has now showcased Smith's ability to advocate a novel, breathtaking *constriction* of federal law. The man is nothing if not versatile.

Despite Biden's DOJ stacking the Trump indictment with every conceivable charge, the indictment left something out that was supposed to be important. I have not seen anyone focus on this, but can you guess what's missing? The Presidential Records Act (PRA). Reading the indictment, you would not even know that this federal statute exists. Recall that PRA violations were one of the primary battering rams the Biden administration used to force entry into Trump's home. What happened to the PRA charges? Apparently, not even Special Counsel Smith—the "breathtaking expansionist" himself—could stretch the PRA to support a criminal charge. For none of the forty nails Smith fashioned for Trump's cross were forged from the PRA.

On the topic of missing laws, guess what else is missing from the indictment? The Atomic Energy Act (AEA). Which means no restricted data was at issue. The indictment lists one document as being classified formerly restricted date (FRD), but FRD is treated as information classified pursuant to executive order. Biden had two FRD documents—twice as many as Trump. Do you recall any media outlet clutching pearls over "nuclear information" in Biden's case?

Mischaracterization of the Document Custodian

One of the most shameful aspects of DOJ's Trump indictment was the treatment of Trump's document custodian. As noted earlier, the certification DOJ requested with the first subpoena invited Trump's lawyers to commit malpractice, and arguably perjury. Trump's lawyers ducked the right hook, but DOJ responded with a blow below the waist. Recall that Trump's lawyers added caveats to the custodian's certification so that, as a whole, it represented that all documents located after a diligent search were produced. Such caveats are common, given an affiant attesting to a search could never know if every document was located. DOJ knows all this, yet DOJ could not resist shamefully perverting Trump's custodian's certification as "representing that all documents with classification markings had been produced, when in fact they had not." DOJ's description is a material misrepresentation, and it must have been reviewed by dozens of lawyers in the Biden administration. This was not mere sloppiness: the indictment quotes the pertinent caveats from the custodian's declaration and then just ignores them when repeatedly mischaracterizing the certification.

DOJ made another hit below the waist by implying that the document custodian was negligent by signing a certification when he or she had not personally performed the searches or analyzed the subpoena. (The custodian "had no role in the review of **TRUMP**'s boxes" and "performed no search of **TRUMP**'s boxes, had not reviewed the May 11 Subpoena, and had not reviewed the contents of the Redweld folder.") Contrary to DOJ's misleading portrayal, the document custodian did nothing wrong, and in fact, the custodian performed in the same manner as government officials attesting to government searches in federal litigations.

Government affiants who attest to conducting reasonable searches rarely perform all searches or related tasks themselves. Certifications for government searches, which I have personally drafted hundreds of and supervised the drafting of thousands, typically state that their contents rely on information provided to the affiants in their official capacities and on legal counsel's advice. DOJ knows all this. Trump's document custodian expressly stated that the certification was "based upon the information that has been provided to me," yet DOJ portrayed the document custodian as being negligent for using the same approach that government affiants follow, and which DOJ routinely defends. Even the FBI affidavit supporting the Trump raid contained similar language: "The facts set forth in this affidavit are based on my personal knowledge, knowledge obtained during my participation in this investigation, and information obtained from other FBI and U.S. government personnel."

Lastly on this point, the indictment also completely ignores an important caveat in Trump's custodian's search certification: "I swear or affirm that the above statements are true and correct to the best of my knowledge." DOJ apparently accepted this as true. For if DOJ thought otherwise, the document custodian would have been indicted. But DOJ never mentions this important caveat and repeatedly describes the certification as a "false certification." The supposed falsity is based on the allegation that Trump moved boxes so they would not be searched and the FBI raid finding classified documents that Trump's lawyer did not. Even if true, however, it would not mean that the document custodian signed a "false certification." That characterization—"false certification"—carries legal weight.

If the certification was false, that implies the custodian knew it was inaccurate in some way. If there was no knowledge on the custodian's behalf that the certification contained an inaccuracy, then the certification would be inaccurate or incorrect. Not false. It was particularly shameful for DOJ to attack this person for simply doing his or her job. I have worked on Freedom of Information Act (FOIA) cases where agency affidavits had errors or courts deemed agency searches to be inadequate despite sworn statement to the contrary. DOJ would never—ever—describe those government affidavits as "false" just because they had errors or inaccuracies or a court ruled them to be deficient in some manner.

Analyzing the FBI raid affidavit, I highlighted numerous mistakes and misrepresentations in the sworn statements, but I have no evidence the FBI affiant knew of the errors, so I would simply call them errors, inaccuracies, mistakes, or misrepresentations. Absent evidence that the affiant knew something in the affidavit was false, I would not impugn the character of the affiant by calling the document a "false affidavit." And neither should a prosecutor.

Compare this approach to how DOJ handled Biden's case. Even though Biden's private lawyers had conducted numerous searches for evidence in Biden's D.C. office and private homes and found evidence of crime, DOJ never asked those lawyers to sign any certifications to attest to the diligence of their searches. And when the FBI finally searched Biden's Wilmington home, it discovered classified documents that Biden's lawyers had missed, repeatedly, in their earlier searches. Yet nowhere will you find Biden's DOJ criticizing the searches conducted by Biden's private lawyers as being deficient in any way.

Deceptive Handling of the FBI Raid

DOJ's indictment also hides the massive scope of the FBI raid on Trump's home. Recall that the raid warrant authorized the FBI to seize every single document from Trump's presidency. You would never know this from reading the indictment, however, which characterizes the raid warrant as authorizing "the FBI to search for and seize, among other things, all documents with classification markings." It is a completely true statement, but akin to describing a coordinated mass murder event by a group of psychotic terrorists as "some people did some things." The raid warrant authorized the FBI to seize "any government and/or presidential records created between January 20, 2017, and January 20, 2021," drawing no distinction between personal and presidential or government records. That is how the FBI seized 13,000 documents when only about 100 contained classification markings. By describing the FBI search as being for "among other things, all documents with classification markings," DOJ gives the misimpression that the search was focused on the 100 or so documents with classification markings. That is not true, and it cleverly hides that the "other things"—approximately 12,900 other things—were a considerably disproportionate amount.

Special Counsel Jack Smith was appointed to investigate two separate potential crimes: unlawful retention of classified information and election interference. The disproportionate number of documents seized in the raid—and the breathtaking scope of the warrant (*all documents* dated within Trump's presidency)—raises the possibility and maybe even a likelihood that the primary purpose of the raid was not to support the unlawful retention case. Perhaps it was a fishing expedition to find evidence for the election interference case. This is speculation, but it would explain why DOJ was downplaying the bulk of the seizure and conveniently hiding 12,900 documents behind the curtain of "among other things."

While hiding the scope and perhaps the true purpose of the FBI raid of Trump's home, DOJ's indictment goes to the extreme to highlight the irrelevant fact that Trump retained boxes of material from his presidency. As noted earlier, the classified documents Trump retained could likely have fit in one box. So why does the indictment contain six photographs of stacks of boxes? We all understand the power of a photograph ("a picture is worth a thousand words") and so does DOJ. That is why the indictment includes irrelevant photos of boxes stacked up to a ceiling in a storage room, boxes stacked around a toilet in a bathroom, and boxes stored on a stage in a ballroom. Boxes upon boxes upon boxes. Have you ever seen a photo of Biden's 2,000 boxes at the University of Delaware? No, you have not. And you never will.

Selective Emphasis on Trump's Residence

Amongst other irrelevant details in the indictment, DOJ unfairly portrays Trump's home as something between an open-air bizarre and the infield at the Preakness: "an active social club" that "between January 2021 and August 2022 . . . hosted more than 150 social events, including weddings, movie premieres, and fundraisers that together drew tens of thousands of guests" with "hundreds of members and . . . staffed by more than 150 full-time, part-time, and temporary employees." Only twice that I saw does the indictment use the term "residence." It never uses "home." But it does use "Mar-a-Lago Club" at least fifty-four times.

If the number of social events at Mar-a-Lago was relevant, then the security measures are also relevant, yet they were not described even generally. Compare DOJ's approach to the security measures at Trump's home (i.e., to ignore them) to the approach taken in the Hur report, and yet again you find stark disparity. For Trump, DOJ details social events and visitors at Trump's home to imply that the home was unsecure. For Biden, Biden's possession of classified documents in his home is used as an excuse not to prosecute Biden: "a reasonable juror could conclude that this is not where a person intentionally stores what he supposedly considers to be important classified documents." And just for fun, go through the Hur report and count how many times the word "home" is used to describe Biden's Wilmington and Rehoboth Beach residences, and then compare that number to the number of times "home" is used in DOJ's Trump indictment.

Facts in the Trump indictment concerning the number of guests, visitors, and employees around Trump's living quarters would be relevant to a charge of gross negligence, but Trump was not charged with gross negligence. Trump is charged with unlawful possession of national defense information (NDI) and not returning it when demanded. Given the charges, it would not matter if Trump had kept his boxes in, say, an unguarded garage next to his Corvette. So why has DOJ included these details? Maybe the indictment needed more seasoning, given DOJ ran out of PRA. DOJ's descriptions of Trump's home also leave the impression that the Secret Service could not have protected Trump in his own home, which simply cannot be true. And the Secret Service is only mentioned in one paragraph, where the indictment concedes that, after Trump's presidency, the Secret Service was still protecting Trump at the "Mar-a-Lago Club." Of course, DOJ immediately adds that the Secret Service mission did not include protecting Trump's boxes. Not that anyone claimed the Secret Service was protecting the boxes. The fact is that the Secret Service was guarding the home where the boxes were stored. Period.

Contrast these details in the DOJ Trump indictment to the precedents, and, again, we find gaping disparity. DOJ never mentioned how many visitors, guests, or employees were at the homes of Deutch, Berger, Petraeus, or Clinton. Granted, Clinton's home would have been guarded by the Secret Service, but given Clinton had her classified documents stored on unsecured computer servers, the danger was not so much from surreptitious entry of the home, but of the servers being hacked by a nerdy twelve-year-old. Or a foreign intelligence service.

Irrelevant Conversations & Private Exchanges

Rabbit punching away, DOJ also details in the Trump indictment conversations Trump had with friends and associates wherein Trump mentioned apparently classified information. These statements are unflattering for the former president, but even if true, are completely irrelevant, as DOJ has not charged Trump with unauthorized sharing. Compare this to Biden's case, where Biden was caught on tape telling his ghostwriter he had "just found all the classified stuff downstairs," but DOJ dismissed the statement as mere "loose talk." With Trump, DOJ does not even attempt to tie the conversations to any of the formal charges, apparently adding them to spice up the indictment to make it more digestible for the public to hate Trump. Or at least to not vote for him.

Along the same lines, the indictment alleges that Trump *suggested* to his private attorney that the attorney "falsely represent" to DOJ that no classified documents were found from the attorney's search pursuant to the subpoena, and that the attorney "hide or destroy" responsive documents. I found this portion of the indictment to be particularly ludicrous. DOJ forced Trump's attorney to divulge attorney–client privileged communications. Trump—who is not known for precision in choosing his words in the first place—would likely have been even more casual (as would anyone) about expressing thoughts in protected conversations. The indictment even tries to hide the context of the discussion it attempts to criminalize. The dialogue, as related in the indictment, involved Trump comparing his situation to that of Hillary Clinton's. DOJ, of course, excised any direct reference to Clinton, but it is certain that Trump is comparing himself to Clinton because of a reference to deleting "30,000 emails." It is in this context that Trump is asking his lawyer how it could be that Clinton's attorneys found a way to delete over 30,000 emails and yet he must provide DOJ with everything DOJ is demanding. It's reasonable for Trump to ask his lawyer this question, and his frustration is understandable given the clear disparity in how DOJ handled his case compared to the Clinton "matter."

Reading this section of the indictment, I was laughing out loud, envisioning Trump lambasting his attorney. "Let me get this straight, Hillary got to decide what she was going to provide to the government? And her lawyers deleted thousands of emails without even reading them? But I have to bend the knee? Why can't we just do this? Why can't we just do that?" What Trump could never have imagined—and no reasonable person could—was that DOJ would find a way to criminalize the mere fact that Trump even asked these questions, in private, of his private attorney. Ask yourself this: Have you ever heard of anyone being criminally charged for discussing with their private attorney how and whether to comply with a subpoena? Anyone? And this was not just any old subpoena—it was a political instrument issued by his political rival targeting him in a politically motivated action. Contrast this approach to how Biden's case was handled. When Biden was caught on tape admitting to a crime, DOJ dismissed the admission as mere "loose talk."

Imagine you have an attorney preparing your taxes and you throw out a couple of ideas for aggressive tax deductions. Your attorney tells you they are bad ideas because they are illegal, so you don't do them. You are frustrated because you know that Hunter Biden never even paid taxes some years, and you read that he owed millions of dollars in back taxes that DOJ did not even pursue because Hunter's father was a powerful politician. So, you say to your attorney, "Why should I even pay taxes at all? Why don't you find a way for me to pay nothing like Hunter Biden?" And your attorney tells you that you must pay your taxes because your father is not a powerful politician and, unlike Hunter Biden, DOJ will not permit the statute of limitations to expire against you. You will go to jail. You decide to follow the guidance, and you pay your damn taxes. DOJ then subpoenas your tax attorney for testimony, and based on the compelled testimony, DOJ indicts you for *conspiring to not pay taxes*. Crazy right? Well, that is about what DOJ did to Trump.

Attorney–client privilege typically protects communications about legal advice or services between an attorney and a client. While the privilege is near absolute, the law has recognized circumstances when the privilege can be overcome. One of those circumstances is the "crime fraud exception," whereby the government can defeat the privilege if an attorney–client communication furthered a crime or fraud that the client subsequently committed.

The presiding judge who determined that the crime fraud exception applied to some of Trump's attorney–client communications was Judge Beryl Howell. A frequent engineer on the Get Trump Train, Howell is an Obama appointee who had served ten years as a senior advisor to the Democratic chairman of the Senate Judiciary Committee. Howell was the supervising judge for Special Counsel Mueller's Trump investigation, which involved 2,800 subpoenas, 500 search warrants, and 230 orders for communications records. Howell also presided over, and approved, the House Democrat's request for access to Mueller's grand jury records, which was part of a Democratic party impeachment inquiry of Trump. In late 2023, Howell received a "Champions Award" from the Women's White Collar Defense Association, and in her acceptance speech, Howell commented that because of her work presiding over the sentencing of January 6th defendants, "I regularly see the impact of big lies." Howell also remarked about the United States "teetering on the brink of authoritarianism," a common theme of the Democratic party and the Biden administration.

As an interesting sidenote (and good example of the D.C. swamp), the master of ceremonies for the awards gala where Howell received her award was none other than Loretta Lynch, the former U.S. attorney general (AG) who had asked FBI Director Comey to publicly describe the criminal investigation of Hillary Clinton's classified emails as a mere "matter," and who had clandestinely met with former President Clinton during that criminal investigation of his wife. And one of the program speakers at the awards gala was Kathryn Ruemmler, who had previously worked for the Clinton Foundation and had also served as President Obama's White House counsel, where she replaced her mentor and former White House Counsel Bob Bauer. The same Bob Bauer who served as Biden's private counsel throughout Biden's classified documents fiasco, and who is reportedly the first person who was called when one of Biden's other personal attorneys discovered the classified documents in Biden's Penn Biden Center office. The swamp is not a myth. And it runs deep and wide. Given the dense fog and murky water, the average citizen cannot see its depth or breadth, or the gators thriving within, but this gives you a glimpse.

In granting the crime fraud exception against Trump, Judge Howell issued a ruling that was eighty-seven pages long. Now, admittedly, a lengthy judicial opinion often reflects thoughtful, thorough analysis. But sometimes it signals a desperate attempt to justify the unjustifiable. Take a guess as to which category Howell's opus falls into.

Tellingly, at every pressure point in her analysis, Howell adopted the Biden administration's mischaracterizations of facts and law. For instance, this is how Howell described the circumstances surrounding the raid of Trump's home: "The government's investigation revealed a need to search Mar-a-Lago for any retained documents with classification markings." Presumably, the judge could read a warrant, the plain language of which showed that the raid's scope was far beyond "retained documents with classification markings." The warrant sought every single document dated within Trump's presidency, regardless of classification markings. That is how the FBI hoovered up 13,000 documents from Trump's home when only about 100 contained classification markings. Also, in describing the probable cause justifying the raid, Howell omitted any reference to the

PRA, even though the PRA was one of the primary battering rams the Biden administration used to gain forced entry into Trump's home. Very convenient. No need to explain how a civil law was used to justify a criminal search warrant, if you just ignore the history.

Howell also dutifully marched to the Biden administration's drum by repeatedly mischaracterizing the search certification from Trump's document custodian as being "false." That is the same erroneous description Special Counsel Smith used throughout the Trump indictment, and Howell even went a step further by blatantly misrepresenting the legal import of the certification as being "that all responsive records were being turned over." That language is indeed in the certification, along with caveats attesting that a diligent search had been conducted, and that what was being produced was all the responsive records from the search, not all responsive records. As explained earlier, no search certification could legitimately claim that a search discovered every responsive document, and it is shameful for a federal judge, who knows better, to adopt and amplify such a mischaracterization.

As for the law, Howell of course adopted the special counsel's erroneous interpretation of Executive Order 13526, which twisted that order to a point that it would purportedly require Trump to seek access permission from Biden for documents Trump already possessed from his own presidency. Again, this is not a minor legal issue—it is a lynchpin in the faulty logic behind the entire indictment and in Howell's ruling, because the lack of an access approval from Biden is how the special counsel determined that Trump's possession was "unauthorized" and hence a crime under the Espionage Act. No unauthorized possession, no crime. Here is the relevant language from Howell's opinion where she adopted the special counsel's erroneous interpretation of the executive order: "The former president would have been authorized to possess classified information only upon the current administration's waiver of the need-to-know requirement." That "need-to-know requirement" is for granting access to classified information. Granting access. No one seeks access to something they already possess, and the section of the executive order upon which so much weight has been placed was clearly designed to permit former presidents and vice presidents to seek access to classified information that they did not possess. Period.

Recall that in trying to justify this clearly erroneous interpretation of the executive order, Special Counsel Hur admitted that it was only by "implication" that the access provisions at issue could "appear" to govern a situation where a former vice president or president had retained classified documents from their time in service. An unbelievably weak basis for thirty-two felonies, and an equally weak basis upon which to impugn the attorney–client privilege of a former president.

When litigating before Judge Howell the scope of one of Special Counsel Smith's subpoenas, Trump's lawyers sought an eleven-day extension of a court-imposed deadline that implicated the Thanksgiving holiday. Special Counsel Smith's office opposed the extension (perhaps because every day matters when you have limited time to interfere with an upcoming election). Judge Howell ruled that Trump's request for eleven more days was "grossly excessive." Not just "excessive" mind you. "Grossly excessive." Howell based her ruling in part on the "risk to national security of storing classified documents outside of appropriately secured conditions." Recall that in Biden's case, when the FBI recovered classified documents found in Biden's garage, a month went by before the FBI returned to search the garage. One has to wonder, where was the grave concern for the "risk to national security of storing classified documents outside of appropriately secured conditions" for the month the FBI waited to go back to search Biden's garage?

In her defense, although Howell denied the request for a "grossly excessive" eleven-day extension, she did find it within her heart to magnanimously grant an extension of five days. Five full days. Happy Thanksgiving, MAGA scum.

When the parties were fighting over the scope of a post-raid subpoena, Howell actually suggested—all on her own—that the Trump team search Mar-a-Lago again, "just to make sure." Not even the special counsel had requested another search of Trump's home, presumably because thirty FBI special agents had already raided the premises. Judge Howell might as well have been sitting at the special counsel's table instead of up on the bench, pretending to be a neutral and detached magistrate.

Before Howell issued her ruling on the crime fraud exception, Trump's team highlighted the apparent reality that the entire investigation was a politically driven attack against Biden's most turbulent political rival. Judge Howell quickly dismissed that conspicuous reality as a mere allegation "long on theatrics and short on substance." She then provided a lecture on the American justice system, which was itself long on theatrics:

> The former president expresses concern about being personally targeted by the executive branch in the course of this investigation, but the design of the criminal justice system sets out checks and balances, including the roles of the grand jury and this Court, two institutions that sit outside of the executive branch.

Long on theatrics, as the core issue was not separation of powers or the general "design of the criminal justice system." The core issue was, and remains, politics. Politics, politically driven bias, and political party animus that infects every aspect of all the Trump prosecutions. As with all of the cases involving the mishandling of classified information by senior political figures, you cannot honestly analyze the cases without analyzing the politics. And despite Judge Howell's theatrics and misdirection, the Biden administration's prosecutions of Trump represent the most political prosecutions in U.S. history. A former Republican president and challenger to the incumbent Democrat being prosecuted by the incumbent administration; a Democratically appointed special counsel with a history of overzealously prosecuting a high-ranking Republican; a grand jury in

Washington, D.C., a Democratic party stronghold, where the voting population voted over 92 percent for Biden in the 2020 presidential election; and an investigation supervised by a Democratically appointed federal judge with a long history within the Democratic party and a recent history of assisting the Democratic party to get Trump. That is reality. Not theatrics. And the reality is most assuredly not, as Judge Howell would have you believe, a just system of unbiased checks and balances. It is a firing squad.

Howell's eighty-seven-page pretense of a fair ruling was long on, well, everything, except unbiased analysis. Perhaps the date she signed it—March 17, 2023—explains a lot. Maybe she had too many Irish coffees at breakfast. And maybe she is a mean drunk.

Again, contrast this approach to how Biden's case was handled. Biden's private attorneys were not compelled to testify even though they gathered evidence and rummaged through the crime scenes. Special Counsel Hur even acknowledged that he might have obtained relevant evidence from interviewing Biden's personal attorneys, but he did not attempt to do so because the conversations were protected by the attorney–client privilege:

> We considered the possibility that Mr. Biden alerted his counsel that classified documents were in the garage, but our investigation revealed no evidence of such a discussion because, it if [sic] happened, it would be protected by the attorney–client privilege.

DOJ treated Biden's conversations with his private attorneys as inviolate, while aggressively piercing Trump's attorney–client privilege, and then criminalizing Trump discussing options for a subpoena response with his private attorney. It is as if the two special counsels occupied alternate universes, despite both being bound by DOJ policies and procedures and both reporting to Biden's AG. Another interesting aspect of the attorney–client privilege issue is that Richard Sauber, who walks and talks like Biden's private attorney, was actually in the White House Counsel's Office, which means he was a government attorney, and had no attorney–client privilege to claim against a federal investigation. Sauber could have easily been interviewed by Hur's team with no privilege protection to stop them.

Distorted Concept of Causation

And the hits kept coming, as DOJ repeatedly jabbed to the kidneys with a unique and novel concept of criminal "causation." According to Special Counsel Smith, you see, the chaotic pack out of the White House was *all Trump's fault*, because Trump "*caused*" it all [emphasis added]:

- "As he departed the White House, **TRUMP** caused scores of boxes, many of which contained classified documents, to be transported to The Mar-a-Lago Club."
- "**TRUMP** caused his boxes, containing hundreds of classified documents, to be transported from the White House to The Mar-a-Lago Club."

As a practical matter, of course Trump directed that his papers and personal effects be sent to his home, and Trump is ultimately responsible (practically, if not legally) for the pack out even if he delegated the authority. But the language DOJ uses implies that all mistakes were, as a legal matter, Trump's fault because Trump "*caused*" them. As ludicrous as this concept is, I saw no commentary in the media on this simply incredible expansion of the concept of causation flagrantly designed to get Trump. This also struck me as somewhat humorous, as DOJ makes it seem like Trump was running around the White House knowing the pedigree of every single document aides were throwing into boxes, barking orders to everyone, "causing" everything, while simultaneously planning and executing a coup d'état. Quite the multitasker.

Now let's compare DOJ's novel concept of causation supporting Trump's prosecution with DOJ's more restrictive approach to causation that was used to excuse Biden's retention:

- "Mr. Biden did not move the files himself at the end of the Obama administration."
- "Biden depended on staffers to maintain his Senate files, organize and pack them, transport them to the proper place of storage, and review them before they were sent."

Contrasting DOJ's novel and expansive concept of Trump's "causation" to Biden's case is like comparing night to day. Neither individual packed their own boxes, yet DOJ claims that Trump *caused* everything while Biden was just the victim of sloppy packing by everyone around him. Even worse, in Biden's case, DOJ made Biden's departure from the White House appear chaotic, highlighting testimony that "packing the office was a challenge"; everything had to be packed up in "maybe a couple of days"; and the exercise was "somewhat 'random.'" But Biden had four year's notice that he would be leaving the vice presidency, and he even knew the exact date of departure. Trump's situation was truly chaotic, as even the National Archives and Records Administration (NARA) acknowledged ("We know things were very chaotic, as they always are in the course of a one-term transition."), yet in Trump's case, DOJ ignores—and for the first time ever, criminalizes—the acknowledged chaos that "always" characterizes a one-term president's White House exit. The dichotomy between the approaches to "causation" in the two cases is astonishing.

Manipulating Document Classification Details

One last example of a DOJ cheap shot before ending my critique of the DOJ Trump indictment. Most people would probably think this a small and relatively harmless spin, and maybe it is, but I view it differently. See what you think.

DOJ described the classified documents in the fifteen boxes of presidential records Trump provided to NARA as follows: "the boxes contained 197 documents with classification markings, of which 98 were marked 'SECRET,' 30 were marked 'TOP SECRET,' and the remainder were marked 'CONFIDENTIAL.'" Factually, I would accept all that as true and most people would see no issues here. But I am not most people. This is what I saw.

First, DOJ included CONFIDENTIAL documents in the total count (197). As I have mentioned, prosecutors do not care about CONFIDENTIAL documents. Yet DOJ includes them in the total because it provides a much bigger number. Maximum impact.

Second, normally classified documents are listed in ascending or descending order of damage: CONFIDENTIAL (if you are bothering with it), SECRET, then TOP SECRET, or vice versa. But that's not what DOJ did in the indictment. DOJ wants the public to see high numbers, so after providing the total (197), DOJ jumps right to the middle classification level, SECRET, because that is the next highest number (98). Then DOJ goes up to TOP SECRET, which is 30, and then leaps over SECRET to go all the way down to CONFIDENTIAL. This is unusual, and erratic, but permits DOJ to provide the public with two successive high numbers (197 and 98).

Third, after DOJ jumps from TOP SECRET to CONFIDENTIAL, it omits providing the number of CONFIDENTIAL documents by just stating, "the remainder were marked CONFIDENTIAL." Why would DOJ not provide the actual number of CONFIDENTIAL documents even though it included that number in the total count? Because it did not want the public to see that a high number of the documents (69) were only classified CONFIDENTIAL. I spotted this right away but dismissed it as not worth pointing out. But it kept gnawing at me, and I finally realized why: it showed how far DOJ would go to manipulate even the most basic facts.

Every word in the first-ever indictment of a former president was undoubtedly checked, double-checked, and finely tuned by a phalanx of offices in Biden's DOJ. Nothing in the indictment is happenstance. Every point has a purpose. Even if that purpose was just to make Trump look as bad as possible in the court of public opinion. Or in the voting booth.

Defending the Don

The massive scope of the Trump indictment opens itself to numerous potential defenses for the former president. Currently the case has been dismissed by the district court judge, but that ruling will be appealed to the circuit court, and maybe to the Supreme Court. Given there is a chance the dismissal will be reversed, it is worth exploring the dismissal and some of the other interesting defenses.

Violation of the Appointments Clause

As of this writing, the district court judge handling the case, Judge Aileen Cannon, has dismissed the indictment against all the defendants on the grounds that AG Garland's appointment of Special Counsel Smith violated the Appointments clause of the U.S. Constitution.[16] Under the Appointments clause, presidential appointment and senate confirmation is the primary means for appointment of principal and inferior officers, but Congress also has the power to pass laws permitting inferior officers to be appointed by the president alone, the courts, or department heads within the executive branch. Judge Cannon determined that even if a special counsel was an inferior officer, there was still no law that permitted AG Garland to appoint a special counsel who was from outside the executive branch and lacked an existing appointment. Under Cannon's ruling, Garland could appoint an existing U.S. attorney as a special counsel, as U.S. attorneys already possess formal appointments, but someone like Smith, who is from outside government and lacks an appointment, cannot lawfully be appointed by the AG as a special counsel. There are many complexities to Cannon's ruling, but that is the essence of it.

As with every aspect of the cases we have been exploring, the politics cannot be ignored. Cannon's ruling was issued soon after U.S. Supreme Court Justice Clarence Thomas commented, in another recent case we will cover presently, that lower courts should be focused on this issue, as he did not see how Attorney General Garland had the authority to appoint special counsels who did not already possess a constitutional appointment. Justice Thomas is one of the leading conservatives on the Supreme Court, and he has been a favorite target of the Democratic party, which desperately wants Thomas off the court. And you have probably already figured out who appointed Aileen Cannon to the bench: President Donald Trump. In Cannon's defense, she had other opportunities to dismiss the indictment against Trump, and she declined, but every ruling from Cannon that permitted even a slight delay in the case has resulted in the Democratic party, and the majority of mainstream media that it controls, criticizing Cannon for being biased in favor of Trump.

AG Garland has already publicly attacked Cannon's ruling. After citing his two decades of experience as a federal judge, which is admittedly substantial, Garland proclaimed that he was incapable of making such a basic mistake about the law concerning appointments. Garland may ultimately be right about the legal issue and DOJ may win the appeal, but I personally was shocked by Garland's hubris and arrogance in claiming that he was infallible. It will be very interesting to see how Cannon's ruling stands on appeal, but even the appeal will be similarly infused with politics.

Presidential Immunity

The Supreme Court has recently ruled that a former president has immunity from criminal prosecution for official acts that occurred during his presidency, but not for non-official acts.[17] This Supreme Court opinion overruled decisions from the D.C. district court presiding over the prosecution of Trump for election interference and the D.C. Circuit, both of which firmly rejected any criminal immunity for a former president. Do I even need to tell you the political background of the district court judge presiding over that case? Judge Tanya Chutkan. An Obama appointee.

There are many subtleties to the Supreme Court's decision, which we don't need to delve into, but much is left to the lower court's to determine what acts are official versus non-official. So, the case will now return to Judge Chutkan for her to decide which of Trump's acts were official, and cannot be prosecuted, and which were non-official, for which Trump can be prosecuted. How Chutkan will rule is anyone's guess. Not. Even though the ruling leaves district court judges with a lot of leeway, the political result is a net benefit to Trump, as the lower courts had refused to recognize any presidential immunity from criminal prosecution. This has generated even more political intrigue, as President Biden—who routinely chides the Republican party for not respecting the Supreme Court whenever the Republicans so much as criticize a court ruling they did not like—is now advocating for term limits on Supreme Court judges and for an amendment to the U.S. Constitution to eliminate presidential immunity. So much for respecting the court.

As for the prosecution over Trump's retention of classified documents from his presidency, the immunity ruling could prove devastating to the prosecution if the case is returned to the district court after the pending appeal on the Appointments clause. In the indictment, Special Counsel Smith fuzzed up the timing of Trump's documents leaving the White House. There is no doubt that this was purposeful, as the specific timing is favorable to Trump given he was still wielding full presidential power when he "caused" the documents to leave the White House. With the new ruling on presidential immunity, the timing is even more critical, as Trump's document removal was likely an official act, and official acts likely carry immunity. As a result of this official act immunity, even if the current dismissal is reversed, thirty-two felonies may well drop out of the indictment because of presidential immunity. Special Counsel Smith will then be left to prosecute the former president for obstructing an investigation that should have never occurred in the first place. Isn't that rich.

The Espionage Act's Inapplicability to Presidents

Another broad defense for Trump is one I have previously mentioned and that Special Counsel Hur used to defend not charging Biden: the Espionage Act does not apply to a president, because it does not state that it applies to a president. As the Hur report highlighted, there are Supreme Court cases holding that certain laws do not apply to a president unless they expressly state that they apply to a president. If this was a good enough reason to not prosecute Vice President Biden—and it was—it should apply even more forcefully to President Trump. A simple, straightforward solution to a big challenging problem. Like when David took a stone from the bag and slung it at the philistine and struck him in the head.

As Trump was a president when he retained the documents at issue, he could also claim that, as president, he could do whatever he wanted with classified documents, to include taking them home and keeping them. DOJ does its best to hide a president's authority over classified information, by, among other things, denigrating a president's relationship to classified information as one of mere "lawful access." However, clever wording cannot change that information is classified under executive power, and a president personifies executive power in pure form. DOJ knows all this but tries very hard to hide it, because this truth destroys its case.

To work around this weakness, DOJ blurs the timing of the movement of Trump's boxes, leaving the impression that Trump might not have been president at the time. "As he departed the White House, **TRUMP** caused scores of boxes" containing classified documents to be sent to his home, the indictment claims. As soon as I read this muddy description I wondered: *Before he left office or after?* If the transfer was *after* Trump left office, DOJ would have highlighted that fact, as it would have been very beneficial to the prosecution given Trump would no longer have been president. Since DOJ does not provide the specific timing, and has chosen language to blur it, it is a near certainty that the documents were removed from the White House while Trump was still president, which places Trump at the apex of presidential power when the boxes were moved from the White House. No wonder DOJ wants people to believe otherwise.

Recall also that the PRA leaves it completely up to a president to determine what is a "presidential record" and what is a "personal record." One possible and obvious outcome of that regulatory scheme is that a president may decide that a classified document is a "personal record." I don't like that, but it is a viable interpretation. That is what President Reagan did, and DOJ knew it and took no action against Reagan.

There are even facts in the DOJ indictment supporting that Trump designated the documents he retained from his presidency as "personal records," as the indictment quotes text messages from Trump's employees referring to the contents of the boxes as "his papers." DOJ's indictment repeatedly states, as I suppose it must, that Trump "was not authorized to possess or retain classified documents." DOJ's indictment speaks with such certitude that you would never know that the allegation that Trump's possession was "not authorized" was not only unprecedented, but it was also contrary to the closest existing precedent. Reagan's diaries were the closest precedent, and they contained classified information. So if Reagan was authorized to keep classified documents from his presidency, why couldn't Trump?

One has to wonder: *Where is James Comey? Should Comey not be publicly denouncing the Trump indictment as anti-American?* Given Comey's strong opinion that "American tradition" dictates "that before you're going to lock somebody up, you prove they knew they were doing something wrong," why is Comey not defending Trump, who had no notice that a president could be prosecuted for keeping documents from his own presidency?

The core charges against Trump are Espionage Act violations. Specifically, a section of 793 that begins with this clause: "Whoever having *unauthorized* possession of, access to, and control over any document . . . relating to the national defense," [emphasis added]. Right from the first clause of this 793 section, we are confronted with the unprecedented legal issue of whether Trump's possession was "unauthorized." If the possession was authorized—and I would say it was—thirty-two felony counts disappear because this law is then inapplicable. To put it another way, where is it written that a president can't take classified documents home, and having taken them home, keep them? Nowhere. Nowhere. This is why it was critical for Special Counsel Smith—the Great Expansionist—to extend the executive order post-presidency access provisions to cover retention of documents from a president's term in office. Smith needed to make the retention unlawful under the executive order, so he could describe the retention as "unauthorized" and make it a crime under the Espionage Act. As discussed earlier, the order has no such requirement, which is why DOJ had to speculate as to what the order "appears" to govern by "implication." Very clever. And absolutely shameless.

Another element of the 793 charges against Trump is that the defendant failed to deliver the documents on demand to an officer or employee of the United States *entitled to receive them*. Here again, the PRA could be a viable defense, for given the PRA does not state that a president cannot designate classified documents as "personal records," Trump could claim that all the documents he kept were "personal records" and *no one in the government was entitled to receive them*. This may strike non-lawyers as too clever a distinction, and maybe it is, but I think this is a strong defense. In Biden's case, Biden's private lawyers—and the White House counsel—argued that Biden's highly classified notebooks were personal records. This argument should have been accepted, and maybe the only reason it wasn't was because DOJ did not want to undermine the Trump prosecution.

Obstruction Charges

If any part of the indictment might have traction, it is the obstruction charges related to hiding boxes and deleting videotapes. The indictment appears to tell a convincing story surrounding these events, which ironically sounds a lot like what Biden's White House counsel, other aides, and Biden's private counsel did when they secretly took a large volume of Biden's documents from the Penn Biden Center before Biden's private attorneys formally informed the White House about classified documents being found in the maybe-locked closet. Putting those similarities aside, the indictment has what appears to be a compelling story of evading subpoena compliance, but the indictment has so many misleading characterizations, one is left to wonder if this is the only section where DOJ did not play fast and loose with the facts.

Declassification of Documents

While this would be a stretch, another potential defense is that Trump declassified the documents that were taken to his home. Under DOJ policy (which binds the special counsel), information is not NDI if it is not classified. Given that a president can declassify for any reason and in any way he chooses—Trump could have waived a wand over the boxes and chanted "*Spectro declassiarmus!*"—the burden of proof for the special counsel could get rather interesting. If Trump decided to take the stand, it could literally come down to a he-said, she-said moment: "I declassified it!" "No, you didn't!" "Did so!" "Did not!" "Prove it!" "There is no memo!" "I didn't need no stinking memo!" Sad, surreal, and unlikely, but possible.

Selective Prosecution

One final defense, which by this point should be obvious: selective prosecution. All the precedents—all of which involved high-ranking Democrats—involved the gentlest of criminal processes, wherein typical investigative strategies were not followed, and great deference was given to the subjects. Either no charges were brought, or the defendants were treated to single-count misdemeanors with only fines and probation. This was the case even when one high-ranking Democrat purposefully brought home more classified information than Trump and had stored the classified information in a manner that made it much more vulnerable to unauthorized disclosure.

President Biden's case presents a particularly good example, as Biden had classified documents all over his house and in his downtown D.C. office; had apparently been hoarding classified information for over four decades; was aware that he had classified information in his house, which he never reported; shared classified information with his ghostwriter; possessed a high volume of classified documents; and was *not a president* for much of the time he possessed the classified information.

Biden is not charged with any crime. Trump is facing forty felonies and life in jail.

CHAPTER 12

Context & Continuum

Viewed in isolation, the Biden administration's abuse of the criminal justice system to persecute a political rival is bad enough. Firsts in American history, the raid of Trump's home and subsequent forty-felony-count indictment of Trump were based on novel legal interpretations and broke starkly from what few precedents existed. Historically bad when viewed in isolation, the Biden administration's conduct becomes historically horrific when viewed in context.

During Trump's 2016 presidential candidacy, the FBI and DOJ knowingly relied on salacious, fabricated intelligence reporting, purchased and provided by the Clinton campaign (the infamous "Steele dossier"), as a pretext to target Trump's campaign. Purporting to show that Trump was colluding with Russia to get elected, the false reports were used by federal law enforcement to obtain electronic surveillance warrants targeting a Trump campaign staffer, and in doing so, concealed the true origins of the false reports from the Foreign Intelligence Surveillance Act (FISA) court that granted the warrants. An FBI lawyer even falsified a record to corroborate the fabricated intelligence. That FBI lawyer was subsequently prosecuted but only received probation and a fine.

While the FBI and DOJ were unlawfully targeting the 2016 Trump campaign, they were simultaneously paving the way for the Democratic party candidate, Hillary Clinton, to be cleared of obvious crimes for unauthorized retention of classified information. Despite these efforts, Donald Trump still managed to pull off one of the greatest upsets in political history and was elected president. Clinton then claimed that Trump stole the election from her by colluding with Russia, and the Democratic party smeared Trump as an "illegitimate" president based on the party's fabricated intelligence.

The Russia collusion hoax blossomed into the biggest soft coup attempt our nation has ever seen, and it even included FBI Director Comey unlawfully leaking classified memos that memorialized his official meetings with President Trump. Trump eventually fired Comey for conduct the DOJ inspector general (IG) described as "extraordinary and insubordinate." Instead of Comey being investigated for leaking classified memos, the FBI counterintelligence section used Trump's entirely justified firing of Comey to open an obstruction of justice investigation targeting . . . President Trump.

Comey's unlawful leak, combined with the salacious and fabricated intelligence (the "Steele dossier") that the Clinton campaign purchased, from Russians, led to the appointment of a special counsel to investigate the bogus allegation of Trump colluding with Russia. Special Counsel Mueller hand-picked a team of Trump-hating DOJ prosecutors and FBI agents, and then targeted Trump with a massive $32,000,000 investigation. Think about that for a moment: $32,000,000 for a fraudulent investigation, the goal of which was to politically assassinate a sitting president. A soft coup, based on a hoax, or what I like to call a "HoaxCoup."

There are many bizarre stories surrounding the Russia Collusion HoaxCoup, but the strangest may be the story of Bruce and Nellie Ohr. Bruce Ohr served as the associate deputy attorney general (AG)—one of the highest-ranking DOJ officials during the DOJ investigation of the Trump campaign. His wife, Nellie Ohr, was a Russian analyst who, from October 2015 to September 2016, worked for an entity called Fusion GPS. Fusion hired Nellie Ohr as a research analyst one week after it was hired by the *Washington Free Beacon* to obtain derogatory information on Trump. After the Fusion–*Free Beacon* relationship ended, Fusion continued the same work for the Clinton campaign and the Democratic National Committee (DNC).

To hide the relationship, Fusion was technically hired by a law firm, Perkins Coie, which hired Fusion on behalf of the Clinton campaign and the DNC. Hard to follow, right? That was the idea. And it shows the extraordinary lengths to which the Clinton campaign and the DNC went to hide their tracks: The Clinton campaign paid Perkins Coie, which in turn paid Fusion GPS. Fusion GPS then paid Nellie Ohr and former British spy Christopher Steele, who paid Russian sources to gather sensational stories about Trump being a Russian agent. Fusion even signed a nondisclosure agreement preventing it from admitting the relationship with Perkins Coie, and the Clinton campaign hid the payments to Fusion by labeling them "legal services," which was a violation of campaign laws for which the Clinton campaign and the DNC were subsequently fined $113,000. If you needed more evidence that the Swamp is real, one of the senior partners at Perkins Coie was none other than Bob Bauer, Biden's private attorney, who had also served as President Obama's private attorney, general counsel of Obama's 2008 presidential campaign, and the general counsel to the Democratic National Committee (DNC).

The layer upon layer of obfuscation to hide the dossier's funding probably would have worked if it were not for Congressman Devin Nunes. Nunes followed the advice that Deep Throat gave to Woodward and Bernstein: *follow the money.* Nunes issued congressional subpoenas for relevant bank records, and the money trail eventually pierced the carefully constructed layers of secrecy the Clinton campaign and the DNC had created to hide that they had paid for the infamous dossier.

Bruce Ohr and his wife Nellie met with Steele in July 2016, while Nellie and Steele were working for Fusion, and after that meeting, Bruce Ohr—again, one of the highest-ranking attorneys at DOJ—brokered an introduction between Steele and the FBI. Steele was subsequently hired by the FBI as a paid FBI informant to provide intelligence on then-candidate Donald Trump. That is how things get done in the Swamp. In November 2016, the FBI learned that Steele was a source for a media article entitled "A Veteran Spy Has Given the FBI Information Alleging a Russian Operation to Cultivate Donald Trump." The FBI then fired Steele and warned Bruce Ohr that Steele could not be trusted. As difficult as this may be to believe, Bruce Ohr continued meeting with Steele (thirteen more times, to be exact) to obtain Steele's reporting and . . . peddle it back to the FBI, who had already fired Steele as an asset because Steele was untrustworthy. Again, I emphasize that I am not making any of this up—it is all documented in DOJ IG reports. Meanwhile, as Bruce Ohr's wife Nellie was also working for Fusion to dig up dirt on Trump, Bruce Ohr was also passing his wife's research directly to the FBI. Basically, a top DOJ official was laundering fabricated intelligence coming from his wife, his wife's employer, the Clinton campaign, the DNC, and . . . Russians.

And the story gets weirder. In May 2016, while she was working for Fusion, Nellie Ohr applied for a ham radio license and purchased a ham radio shortly thereafter. In later sworn congressional testimony, Nellie Ohr was evasive and claimed that she had obtained her license "well before" working for Fusion. That was a lie, as she had not applied for the license until after she started working for Fusion. When portions of her congressional testimony became public, there was speculation that Nellie Ohr was using the ham radio to communicate with sources in Russia, which may be true, but it seems more likely to me that she was using the ham radio to communicate with Steele. A ham radio would permit someone to talk to another person (even across continents) without generating a call data record, without cell tower data being collected, and without an email trail. That is why spies were historically trained to use shortwave radio (synonymous with ham radio)—their communications were more likely to go undetected and leave no trace. Theresa Squillacote, for instance, used shortwave radio to communicate with her handlers. The timing could be just a coincidence, but Steele was a trained spy and Nellie Ohr obtained a ham radio while she was working with Steele. Also, the record reflects that Steele was trying to hide his communications. For instance, in 2017, at Steele's request, Bruce Ohr stopped communicating with Steele through his email and changed to commercially encrypted communication. Things that make you go, *Hmmm*.

In sworn testimony, Nellie Ohr claimed that she had obtained her ham radio license (call sign KM4UDZ) because there was a local program for ham radio operators to help "with community response in case of an emergency." I suppose that is possible. But it looks suspicious that the highly educated wife of one of DOJ's most senior attorneys—a Harvard graduate who studied in the Soviet Union and also holds a degree in Russian literature and a PhD in Russian history from Stanford—suddenly became some sort of doomsday survivalist. It made me wonder what other hobbies Nellie might have acquired to prepare for the apocalypse. Archery? Snare building? Butter churning? Nellie was never prosecuted for lying to Congress, but her husband was demoted and resigned from DOJ just before his likely termination. What got Bruce Ohr into trouble, ironically, was not all the shady shenanigans with his wife, Fusion, and Steele. What got Bruce into trouble was that he had never *informed his superiors* at DOJ about all his shady shenanigans with his wife, Fusion, and Steele, and his superiors were upset that Ohr had not informed them of his clandestine involvement in a counterintelligence investigation, given that Ohr's responsibilities were in organized crime and drug enforcement.

Despite the special counsel's extensive Russian HoaxCoup investigation, which probably cost more than the combined GDPs of many third-world countries, the special counsel found no evidence of the Trump campaign colluding with Russia (and, in fact, he disproved all the dossier reporting that could be investigated). Even though his investigation neglected to find anything supporting the "collusion" allegations, the special counsel, evidencing his own bias, formally concluded that he "could not exonerate" Trump because the investigation had not found sufficient evidence to rule out that Trump might be guilty of . . . the unproven allegations against him. In an emperor-has-no-clothes moment, one observer noted how strange that conclusion was, given that there is no DOJ Office of Exoneration. Prosecutors typically either find evidence to support charging a crime, or they don't. Prosecutors do not "exonerate." The special counsel just made that "exoneration" stuff up. *Prosecutors are not supposed to make stuff up.*

While the Russia Collusion HoaxCoup ultimately failed, senior FBI agents and DOJ officials succeeded in publicly debasing themselves and damaging federal law enforcement's reputation. Among other things, DOJ and the FBI criminally prosecuted Trump's incoming National Security Advisor General Michael Flynn. What was Flynn's alleged crime? Did he steal TOP SECRET documents? No. Did he destroy evidence and knowingly lie to federal investigators? No. That was President Clinton's national security advisor. What did Flynn do? Well, nothing. He got framed by Democratic party loyalists working in the FBI and DOJ because Flynn committed the mortal sin of working for Trump. Let me quickly cover how this all went down.

Ambushing Flynn by going to see him on a ruse and not telling him the interview was part of a criminal investigation, the FBI asked Flynn questions about a phone conversation Flynn had with a foreign counterpart, for which the FBI already had a recording. Flynn was a three-star general and the former head of the Defense Intelligence Agency and well aware of U.S. electronic surveillance capabilities. Flynn's first response to the FBI was along the lines of, "You tell me, you must have a recording." But when Flynn misremembered details, the FBI did not say, "Are you sure? Because we have the recording, and it sounds like you said something different," and the FBI did not excuse Flynn for being a likable old man with a poor memory. Instead, the FBI agents shook Flynn's hand

and left the office, because they had what they came for: a bogus basis to charge Flynn for making a false statement. Felony. Five years.

Senior FBI agents and lawyers then doctored the interview record (the FBI lawyer who edited the interview record had not even participated in the interview) to make it incriminating, then they lost the original record. This may seem like a wild conspiracy theory, but it is not, and we know this because the AG appointed a neutral prosecutor to review the case. Among other things, the review discovered notes from a senior FBI agent who pondered this question:

> **"What's our goal? Truth/admission or to get him to lie, so we can prosecute him or get him fired?"**

That note has been attributed to the chief of FBI counterintelligence. Another FBI email discovered in the neutral case review discussed the possibility of trying to get the national security advisor to admit to violating the Logan Act. Few have ever heard of the Logan Act, and for good reason, since no one has ever been convicted of violating it. The statute is from the late 1700s and makes it illegal for a U.S. citizen to undermine the U.S. government in negotiations with foreign governments. What was Flynn's alleged nefarious conduct? The incoming national security advisor was calling his foreign counterparts to establish relationships, and one of those counterparts was . . . wait for it . . . Russian.

Step back from this for a moment and contemplate the entrapment of a high-ranking, and innocent, federal official who was one of President Trump's most senior advisors. Federal law enforcement—senior FBI agents, lawyers, and DOJ attorneys—created and steered a bogus investigation, falsified evidence, and suppressed evidence. All to frame the president's national security advisor and coerce him to testify against a lawfully elected president. What do you call that? Treason? Coup? Insurrection? Political assassination? Regicide?

They called it saving the world.

This is a shameful low point in the history of U.S. law enforcement. And unfortunately, they kept digging, to include raiding the home of an old friend and advisor to President Trump, Roger Stone, an elderly man with no prior convictions and no history of violence. The early morning raid involved over two dozen heavily armed agents, some carrying M4 rifles, who looked like infantrymen storming Omaha Beach. CNN somehow knew of the raid and was present with cameras rolling before it even started. Which makes you wonder, if the element of surprise was so important—which is what the FBI must have sworn to, under oath, to get the raid warrant—how was it okay to leak it to CNN so they could have a film crew waiting?

Even though the Russia Collusion HoaxCoup failed, some justice did come from it. The FBI deputy assistant director assigned to HoaxCoup, who really hated Trump, got caught sending text messages (on his government-issued phone) describing his deep hatred of Trump. This, by the way, is the same senior FBI officer who worked on the Clinton "matter" and who the DOJ IG determined had expressed political opinions that tainted and biased that investigation. Here are some examples of his texts:

> **"Trump is a disaster. I have no idea how destabilizing his presidency would be."**
>
> **"Just went to a southern Virginia Walmart. I could SMELL the Trump support."**
>
> **"I am riled up. Trump is a fucking idiot . . . I CAN'T PULL AWAY. WHAT THE FUCK HAPPENED TO OUR COUNTRY, LIS?!??!?!"**
>
> **"God Hillary should win 100,000,000–0."**

When those texts came to light, the FBI deputy assistant director assigned to Russia Collusion HoaxCoup was removed from HoaxCoup for being so careless as to say the quiet part out loud. Again, the sarcastic side of me could not help but observe that the first rule of HoaxCoup is that you don't talk about HoaxCoup. The firing was formally described as being necessary to "protect the integrity of the investigation." Isn't that special?

In a closely related matter, a senior FBI lawyer who served as the FBI special counsel to the deputy director, who strongly disliked Trump, and who had worked on both the Clinton investigation and the Russia Collusion HoaxCoup, was also caught in compromising acts, some of which were documented on her government-issued phone. Here are a few examples of her texts:

> **"Trump . . . has no dignity or class. He simply can not [sic] be president."**
>
> **"God trump [sic] is a loathsome human."**
>
> **"Seriously, how are people [Trump supporters] so incredibly ignorant?"**
>
> **"I can not [sic] believe Donald Trump is likely to be an actual, serious candidate for president."**
>
> **"Trump should go f himself."**

The FBI special counsel to the deputy director who sent those texts was also removed from Russia Collusion HoaxCoup for talking about HoaxCoup (integrity and stuff) and left the FBI in shame. She was hired by MSNBC and NBC as a national security legal analyst. In addition to all the texts between the FBI deputy assistant director and the FBI special counsel to the deputy director, both of whom really hated Trump, were these:

FBI special counsel to the deputy director: "And maybe you're meant to stay where you are because you're meant to protect the country from that menace."

FBI deputy assistant director: "I want to believe the path you threw out for consideration in Andy's office—that there's no way he gets elected—but I'm afraid we can't take that risk. It's like an insurance policy in the unlikely event that you die before you're 40 . . ."

Let that sink in for a moment. These are two senior FBI officers, both Democrats, assigned to investigate Clinton (whom they loved) and Trump (whom they viewed as the devil incarnate). Make of it what you will, but be forewarned that if you interpret any of their language as nefarious, you will be labeled a violent right-wing extremist. And if you share your violent right-wing extremist thoughts, you might be banned from social media for spreading disinformation. And rightfully so. There are so many innocent explanations for those statements. So many it could be a board game. Colonel Mustard. In Andy's office. With a subpoena.

One last thing about that obviously innocent text from the FBI deputy assistant director assigned to Russia Collusion HoaxCoup: the "Andy" whose office in which "the path" was being thrown out "for consideration" and which would mean "no way Trump gets elected" was the deputy director of the FBI. Second in charge of the FBI. Ponder that. Amongst his many duties, Andy was involved in an investigation of . . . himself. As it turned out, Andy was the leaker whom the FBI was looking for as part of an FBI leak investigation. That sordid tale—another excursion into the Swamp—involved Andy's wife, a Democrat running for office, who had accepted around $650,000 from the Democratic party. Anyway, Andy lied, repeatedly, under oath, to his own FBI investigators to cover up his unlawful leak, until call records identified him as the leaker and he confessed to the crime.

Andy left the FBI in shame but was never prosecuted for false official statements or obstruction of justice. You see, the criminal referral from the DOJ IG had gone to the Fraud & Public Corruption Section of the D.C. U.S. Attorney's Office, where it sat for years until the chief of that office sent a letter to Andy's defense counsel, dated February 14, 2020, informing them that "the Government has decided not to pursue criminal charges against your client." Guess who signed the DOJ letter formally declining to pursue criminal charges against Andy? That would be none other than J. P. Cooney, loyal squire to the Great Expansionist, the Maker of Chains, the Slayer of Conservatives—Special Counsel Jack Smith.

After his unceremonious departure from the FBI, Andy—big surprise here—was hired by CNN. In case you wondered about his biases (and no reason you should), Andy published a book: *The Threat: How the FBI Protects America in the Age of Terror and Trump.* The only surprise is that Andy put "Terror" before "Trump."

If you or I lied to the FBI under oath, like Andy, DOJ would call it a "false statement" and prosecute us for a felony with a penalty of up to five years in jail. That is the law the FBI used to frame General Flynn (after they doctored the interview record to manufacture evidence he had lied). Andy purposefully lied, repeatedly, under oath, when he knew he was being interviewed as part of a criminal investigation. Flynn misremembered details, was purposefully not informed by the FBI that he was being questioned as part of a formal FBI investigation, was not under oath, and the interviewing FBI agent believed Flynn was doing his best to remember the details. Flynn was prosecuted for a felony. Andy was never prosecuted at all.

So, the Russia Collusion HoaxCoup failed, but ironically it ended up taking down some of the HoaxCoup conspirators who forgot the first rule of HoaxCoup is you don't talk about HoaxCoup. Other conspirators got caught breaking the law by leaking stuff and generally being their unethical egomaniacal selves. So, a bit of justice came out of the whole mess.

On a side note, the special counsel to the deputy director of the FBI and the FBI deputy assistant director both filed lawsuits against the government based on alleged violations of the Privacy Act. The claims were based on the public release of their text messages, which were all on government-issued phones.

Now, the Privacy Act is a very complicated federal statute that only a couple dozen people in the world really understand. While I would not call myself an expert on the Privacy Act, I am a veteran of many Privacy Act litigations, and I know the statute fairly well—well enough to recognize that those two miscreants had no valid cause of action under the Privacy Act. Their Privacy Act claims are what lawyers call "frivolous." Yet, as this book was going to print, DOJ settled those Privacy Act claims for . . . wait for it . . . two million dollars. Which looks a lot like Biden's DOJ rewarding two veterans injured while waging the Democratic party's holy war against Trump. Two million dollars for frivolous claims. And that is taxpayer money.

AG Garland publicly insisted that the settlement was "not a question of reward" but was only "a question of the government paying for violating the law." Garland avoided providing particulars as to how the law was violated, which was probably wise, given that there were no violations. It is possible that the claims were settled for other reasons. After all, Merrick Garland officiated at the wedding of the lawyer representing one of the miscreants—another swamp creature with deep ties to the Democratic party. But again, I digress.

Meanwhile, given the floundering Russia Collusion HoaxCoup, elected Democrats in Congress, lacking the most obvious tools of today for tyranny (badges, guns, subpoenas, and search warrants), planned a different type of HoaxCoup: Impeachment HoaxCoup. Democrats were calling for Trump's impeachment before he even took office, but they still needed to find an excuse.

Enter a Trump-hating U.S. Army colonel who forgot about this thing army folks call "chain of command." Colonel Trumphater hears a classified phone call between Trump—whom he really, really hated—and another head of state, and relates the call to a friend who probably had no need-to-know but also really, really hated Trump, and then the friend filed a "whistleblower complaint" about the call he had never actually even heard. You follow? Try and keep up. If you want to see a document that was finely word-smithed by numerous lawyers (I have been around long enough to detect a change of tone, writing style, and expertise in a legal document), check out the complaint allegedly written by the "whistleblower." Very well written. But completely wrong on the legalities of classification, among other pesky details. No wonder that failed too.

Endeavoring to persevere, the haters and hoaxers without badges, guns, and search warrants but with congressional subpoena power, instituted another HoaxCoup: J6 HoaxCoup. This was a forward-thinking group, whose goal was to prevent the need to conduct a future HoaxCoup by making Trump ineligible to run for office again—like a sci-fi time-travel movie but without special effects. Well, I take that back: they actually hired a former TV producer to assist with special effects. For the first time in history, the speaker of the house refused to let the minority party, the Republicans, pick their own committee members. This permitted Speaker Pelosi to handpick and pack a J6 kangaroo court with Trump haters and simultaneously avoid any examination of her own conduct (the speaker was technically in the chain of command for little things like physical security of the Capitol building). Among other things, Speaker Pelosi buried evidence that could exonerate Trump, including a recently surfaced video of the speaker herself admitting, on January 6, that *she was responsible* for the lack of security around the Capitol that permitted the riot to occur.

The narrative for the J6 HoaxCoup is that when Trump told a group of people to protest peacefully, the Orange Devil was actually sending subliminal messages to the Basket of Deplorables to protest *not so peacefully*. Now, you can call the J6 riot a riot (not the other riots—those must be called "mostly peaceful protests"), but the preferred narrative is "Insurrection!" If you want to see what a real "Insurrection!" looks like, gather a group of Democrats and recount to them everything that has been done to baselessly target Trump, but substitute the name "Obama." Before you even finish, they will be throwing tea in the harbor, tarring and feathering bureaucrats, and raiding federal arsenals to get some of those black plasticky rifles they try so darn hard to make illegal. It will make Shay's Rebellion look like a glamping trip. Imagine one of those horrific zombie mob scenes from *World War Z*, but with a CNN commentator standing in front blathering about a mostly peaceful parade that is important for the health of the country.

And while we are talking Insurrection!, let us not forget the ten 2016 Electoral College electors, led by Nancy Pelosi's daughter, who, after Clinton lost the presidential election, wrote an "Open Letter to Director of National Intelligence James Clapper." The "Open Letter" demanded that intelligence briefings be provided to the electors—*before they voted*—concerning any investigations, ongoing or closed, of Trump and his aides' alleged connections with the Russian government. The ten electors who signed the "Open Letter" unequivocally stated that they would vote their conscience and vote for the candidate whom they viewed as most fit for office, regardless of which candidate won the majority of votes in the districts they represented. They even claimed that their role was to "investigate" the candidates, and they chastised Trump for declaring victory in the election "despite the Electoral College not yet casting its votes." The nerve of the guy. Making such a scandalous claim.

Immediately after the "Open Letter" was published—maybe this was coordinated?—Clinton's campaign chairman, John Podesta, made a public statement saying that the letter raised "very grave issues involving our national security," emphasizing that the Clinton campaign fully supported the request for intelligence briefings for the electors *before they voted*. Of course, the only purpose for this was to justify the electors being "faithless" and voting for Clinton even though she lost the election. That sounds awwwwfuly insurrectiony. And particularly devious, given the Clinton campaign, and a small circle of Democrats around them, were the only ones (at the time) who knew that the intelligence briefing they were "fully supporting" would have consisted of fabricated intelligence that the Clinton campaign had purchased. From Russians. You literally could not make this stuff up. My favorite quote from this affair was from Clinton's campaign chairman, John Podesta: "Never before in the history of our Republic have we seen such an effort to undermine the bedrock of our democracy." At least he got that right.

The Faithless Electors Gambit HoaxCoup was real: much more than a riot, it was an actual attempt to overthrow the results of a presidential election. I wonder if the D.C. U.S. Attorney's Office is investigating this attempted Insurrection!, because this was not just a plan: the Clinton camp was executing the plan. When DOJ does not like you, they call this type of thing "overt acts in furtherance of a criminal conspiracy," or something like that. Although a lot of time has passed since the Faithless Electors Gambit HoaxCoup, Clinton keeps claiming the election was stolen from her. When DOJ does not like you, it calls such statements "overt acts" and uses them to toll the statute of limitations.

Democratic party hoaxers and persecutors, determined to undermine their greatest political rival, have not confined their efforts to the federal arena. The New York State AG Letitia James—who really, really hates her some Trump—campaigned on a promise to prosecute Trump, who she repeatedly described as an "illegitimate president" (which, if she were Republican, would have her denounced as a heretic and an "election denialist"). While campaigning to be the top law enforcement officer for the State of New York, James stated that Trump's "days are numbered!" and that New Yorkers would "rise up and defeat this man" and "bring him down."

Enter Alvin Bragg, the Democratic Manhattan district attorney, who campaigned on being an experienced anti-Trump prosecutor. Bragg lived up to his campaign promise and prosecuted Trump on a criminal charge that even previous Trump-hating prosecutors declined to pursue, because there is no actual crime. Judy Sheindlin, of the iconic television show *Judge Judy* (who is not a Trump fan), even described Bragg's prosecution of Trump as "nonsense" and quipped that "you gotta twist yourself into a pretzel to figure out what the crime was." According to Bragg, the crime was that Trump falsified a business record to hide a payment to a woman with whom he allegedly had an affair. Democrats typically excuse such conduct as "just lying about sex," which they claim everyone does, even when under oath.

Bragg's prosecution advanced an unprecedented and highly dubious legal theory linking the alleged false business record to a federal campaign law violation, despite the federal government having determined *that there was no federal violation*. This resulted in Trump being found guilty of thirty-four felonies. Recall that when Hillary Clinton and the DNC paid for fake Russian intelligence they wrote off the payments as "legal services." For which they received a fine. Trump was prosecuted. For thirty-four felonies. In a city controlled by the Democratic party, by a prosecutor who belongs to the Democratic party, where the AG is a Democrat, the mayor is a Democrat, the judge is a Democrat (who violated New York State judicial ethics rules by making political donations to Democratic party fundraisers during the 2020 presidential race), and the governor is a Democrat. That governor, by the way, had previously told Trump supporters that they were not welcome in her state because they did not represent New York State values. New York State values apparently include vilifying those who have political opinions you don't like, and abusing the criminal justice system to go after political opponents.

Meanwhile, the district attorney (DA) for Fulton County, Georgia, Fani Willis, is pursuing a massive criminal indictment against Trump that is so complicated no one really understands it, and no reasonable person even believes her office drafted the monstrosity of an indictment that is almost one hundred pages long. As it turned out, the Fulton County DA hired her married lover to prosecute the Trump crusade and paid her lover a lot of money, which her lover-turned-prosecutor then used to fund expensive vacations for the two of them (without his wife). The Fulton

County DA and her lover–prosecutor, as of this writing, have both obviously perjured themselves in court testimony, lying about when they began their sexual relationship, which is relevant to their mutually profitable professional relationship to prosecute a former president of the United States. You really could not make this stuff up. Unfortunately, you don't need to.

If you think the Democratic party has only weaponized the American justice system, think again. As the Democrats novel and unprecedented New York prosecution of Trump was ongoing, Democrats in the U.S. House of Representatives introduced legislation to remove Secret Service protection from Trump once they achieved the nearly guaranteed guilty verdict they had orchestrated in New York. Secret Service protection is to protect the life of the former president. Period. That is how low the Democratic party has stooped. They would pass a federal law to make it easy to murder Donald Trump. The Democratic party legislation was proposed by Congressman Bennie Thompson, the ranking member of the House Committee on Homeland Security, who also chaired the J6 HoaxCoup Committee. Having failed in the J6 political assassination, Thompson and the Democratic party focused on facilitating more extreme means of removing the turbulent threat to democracy. Had the Democratic party succeeded in stripping Trump of his Secret Service protection, Trump might not have survived the recent assassination attempt in Butler, Pennsylvania.

Can you imagine the Republican party trying to remove Secret Service protection from former President Obama? The Democratic party would be describing the act as attempted murder, even without an actual assassination attempt. Democratic prosecutors across the country would be empaneling grand juries, issuing subpoenas, raiding the homes of congressional Republicans, rounding them up and herding them into internment camps to protect the national security pending their trials—before juries of rage-filled Democrats—for some kind of novel criminal conspiracy involving hundreds of felonies. That is where were we are at, God help us.

Two weeks before the Trump assassination attempt, President Biden made this posting on his social media account:

> Donald Trump is a genuine threat to this nation.
>
> He's a threat to our freedom. He's a threat to our democracy. He's literally a threat to everything America stands for.

Days before Trump was shot, President Biden told supporters "it's time to put Trump in a bullseye." And yet, after an assassin's bullet grazed Trump's head, the bulk of the mainstream media were criticizing the *Republican party* for heated rhetoric. The hypocrisy knows no bounds.

After Trump was shot, most mainstream media downplayed the heinous act, even to the point of ignoring that a shooting had even occurred.

Almost an hour after the assassination attempt, a CNN headline read "Biden departs church and is asked about Trump rally." From the headline, a reader would not know that Biden was being asked about "the rally" because that is where an assassin had just, one hour ago, fired on the Republican party's presidential nominee, grazing his head with a bullet and leaving one rallygoer dead and two critically injured—all as a result of a colossal security failure by Biden's own administration.

Here is an example of the journalistic creativity that was deployed, with some blow-by-blow commentary:

> After the bangs [not shots, mind you, just bangs], Trump fell to the ground [depicting him as weak, feeble, and cowardly] and was covered by Secret Service agents. He was stood back up [again, making him appear weak] by security personnel and had blood on his face [leaving the impression he might have been injured when he "fell"]. He was yelling back to the crowd and raising his fist [feeding the Democratic narrative that Trump is angry and deranged, as opposed to the reality that

> Trump had instinctively responded with courage and resolve] before being whisked away by security personnel.

More than *five hours* after the shooting, the media was still refusing to describe the shooting as an assassination attempt. NBC political reporter Kelly O'Donnell took to the internet—over five hours after a bullet passed through Trump's ear—to stress the need for a "measured approach" "for accuracy" and to explain that "media guidelines" prevented reporters from using the "A" word until law enforcement formally described the event using the "A" word. So the media was waiting on the Biden administration's approval before they would describe water as wet or the sky as blue.

A full day after the assassination attempt—even after the Biden administration had finally approved using the "A" word—major media outlets still shunned it in their headlines. The *Washington Post* headline: "Trump injured in rally shooting"; the *New York Times*: "Trump hurt, but safe, after a shooting"; the *Boston Globe*: "Trump survives shots at rally"; and the *Los Angeles Times*: "Trump is rushed off stage in rally shooting."

Echoing O'Donnell's dutiful defense of the necessity for a "measured approach," the *Washington Post* published an article defending the "early reporting" as necessarily "cautious," given that "the full dimensions of the tragedy were not yet clear." According to the *Post*, even though journalists "suspected" the noises they heard were gunfire (you know, what with the blood, death, critical injuries, ambulances, and bystanders screaming about the guy on the roof with a rifle), they could only describe the sound of what they witnessed because doing anything more would be reckless. "If you heard 'loud pops,' that's all you can say," the *Post* quoted a journalist as proclaiming, as it would be "incredibly irresponsible" to report anything more.

One is left to wonder what happened to caution and a measured approach when the same media outlets were breathlessly reporting all the baseless fabrications concerning the Russia Collusion HoaxCoup—reporting for which journalists were awarded Pulitzer Prizes. Of course, given that this was the *Post*, the article found a way to blame Trump for the "impatience" of some readers who expected a shooting to be described as, well, *a shooting*. This impatience was Trump's fault, you see, as Trump has "ritualized hostility toward the media."

Now we are admittedly left to speculate as to why the media consistently downplayed an assassination attempt against Donald Trump and distorted the instinctive strength and courage with which Trump responded. Perhaps the motive was captured by Democratic Colorado state Rep. Steven Woodrow, who publicly proclaimed after the assassination attempt that "the last thing America needed was sympathy for the devil, but here we are."

While Woodrow bluntly said the quiet part out loud, Democratic party leaders made the obligatory condemnation of violence while psychotically continuing to encourage it through more of the same hate-filled histrionics and dangerous rhetoric. President Biden's public statement, days after the assassination attempt, is a good example: Trump was "still a danger to the community, to the nation." What class.

To further illustrate the completeness of the media's corruption, compare the reporting on July 13, 2024, to the reporting on March 31, 1981, the day President Reagan was shot. Initial reports of the 1981 assassination attempt against Reagan—which began *mere minutes* after Reagan was shot in the chest—described the incident as "a shooting." Words like "shooting," "assailant," and "victims" defined the initial reports, which also admittedly included descriptions such as "popping noises" and fire-crackers," but only to relate what *the shooting* sounded like. And within a few hours of Reagan being shot, the shooting was described as an assassination attempt.

Not so with Trump. In Trump's case, the headlines—and not just minutes, but *hours* after the shooting—purposefully avoided even mentioning that *a shooting* had occurred: "Trump speech interrupted by

Secret Service"; "Secret Service rushes Trump offstage at rally"; "Trump taken away after loud noises at rally"; "Trump removed from stage by Secret Service after loud noises startle former president, crowd." Imagine headlines after the Kennedy assassination being along the lines of "Loud Noises at Dealey Plaza Interrupt Presidential Motorcade"; "Kennedy Falls from Convertible After Popping Noises Along Parade Route"; "Secret Service Interrupts JFK Motorcade." It is unthinkable. Yet those were the types of headlines the mainstream media was carrying hours after a bullet quite obviously grazed Trump's head.

Journalists were *at* the rally where Trump was shot. So it was not like reporters had to struggle to piece together a complicated story through painstaking investigative work. This was not Watergate. Or Russia Collusion HoaxCoup. Reporters had witnessed the shooting. Videos were all over the internet showing clearly what had transpired. Shots rang out. Trump flinched, winced, and grabbed his ear. Blood flowed down his face. One man in the crowd was killed. Others were critically wounded. Bystanders had been shouting about the man on the roof with a rifle, who now lay dead. Ambulances were carting away dead and wounded. Despite all this, two-and-a-half hours later, this was a headline: "What pool reporters saw and heard at the rally where Trump was rushed off stage."

In 1981, as surgeons were preparing to remove the bullet lodged an inch from President Reagan's heart, Reagan pulled down his oxygen mask and quipped, "I hope you are all Republicans." The lead surgeon—who was a registered Democrat—replied, "Today, Mr. President, we're all Republicans."

My, how American politics has changed. Not too long ago, the assassination attempt of a president quieted the political rhetoric, at least for a while, and reminded the nation that despite party affiliation, we were all Americans. Amidst that dark moment, the just pride of patriotism exalted over the jealousies and heartburnings of party politics. Today's political climate is so poisoned that, in a similar circumstance, the media downplayed the assassination attempt and Democrats lamented any "sympathy for the devil." Right after Trump was shot, a staffer for Democratic Congressman Bennie Thompson—the same congressman who was sponsoring legislation to *forcibly remove* Trump's Secret Service protection—publicly proclaimed "I don't condone violence but please get you some shooting lessons so you don't miss next time ooops that wasn't me talking." That is the world we live in today, Mr. President.

Soon after the assassination attempt, FBI Deputy Director Paul Abbate was testifying before Congress when he revealed that the FBI had "just very recently uncovered" a social media account likely belonging to the shooter, on which some comments were "anti-Semitic and anti-immigration" and called for "political violence." Abbate dated the social media account to four or five years prior.

Abbate did not disclose—until he was questioned by a Republican congresswoman—that the FBI had also uncovered a more recent social media account likely belonging to the shooter. And that more recent account espoused views that the account provider described as belonging to a "pro-lockdown, pro-immigration, left-wing Joe Biden supporter."

Now, this is all preliminary, and it may turn out that neither account belonged to the shooter. But what is clear is that the FBI deputy director cherry-picked for his public testimony the account that espoused "anti-immigration" views and called for "political violence," which just so happens to feed the liberal narrative of evil Trump supporters. Meanwhile, the FBI deputy director conveniently omitted the more recent, and ostensibly more relevant, social media account associated with the shooter, in which the commentary supported left-wing, pro-Biden views. Do you think that is a coincidence? This was the FBI deputy director almost certainly skewing, for political purposes, facts pertaining to the attempted assassination of a former president and current presidential candidate.

This is just a summary of *some* of the illicit activity the Democratic party and the governmental institutions it controls have orchestrated against Trump since his 2016 campaign. As is evident from this parade of historic horribles, the FBI raid of Trump's home and the DOJ indictments of Trump were not isolated events. Just some of the latest actions along a continuum, spanning years, of blatantly political acts to destroy a political opponent of the Democratic party.

You really must ask yourself, first, how these injustices could happen in America, and second, having happened, how is it that half the country not only supports the injustices, but applauds them, and craves more? Well, I have a theory.

[redacted]M

UBJECT: [redacted]

PART IV

I. [redacted] [redacted]wor

f [redacted] [redacted]

[redacted]and [redacted]

A Uniform Vigilance

ntil [redacted]

[redacted]

[redacted] [redacted]doa

nto will

ntinue to be D[redacted], [redacted] and [redacted]

CHAPTER 13

The Taste of Tyranny

During the Obama administration, when the Democratic party controlled the White House and Congress, the party smugly convinced itself of moral and intellectual superiority over the other half of the country, who it viewed as knuckle-draggers clinging to their Bibles and their guns. Platitudes like, "When they go low, we go high," are easy when you hold all the power. But when their party lost the White House in 2016, and Democrats no longer enjoyed complete power, they acted like a contumacious child throwing a hissy fit over having to share a toy. Overnight, they went from, "They go low, we go high," to "Democracy sucks; we must undermine it." The Russia HoaxCoup; the impeachment farces; framing the president's national security advisor; and a litany of smaller acts of vindictive churlishness, such as the Democratic party speaker of the house tearing up the president's State of the Union address on live television. Any means necessary to seek vengeance and regain the power that, in their minds, rightfully belonged to them and them alone. Democracy was on the ballot. But only one choice.

An avid moviegoer, I have always enjoyed the James Bond films. Aside from the glitz, glamour, and action, at which the franchise always excels, another highlight is the superlative villainy. Good stories need good villains. And the Bond films have some of the best. In *Skyfall*, Javier Bardem masterfully portrays the chilling antagonist Raoul Silva. In one scene, Silva describes to Bond how Silva's grandmother handled a rodent problem on her small island. Rats were gorging themselves on coconuts, so the grandmother and Silva used coconut to lure the rats into a pit. Trapped in the pit, the rats began to eat their only food source: each other. When only two rats were left, Silva's grandmother freed them, solving her rodent problem forever, because now, Silva tells Bond, "they only eat rat . . . You have changed their nature."[18]

This is analogous to what happened to the Democratic party after Trump won the 2016 election, and I witnessed it, firsthand. Washington, D.C., where I live, is *the biggest* Democratic party stronghold in America (in 2020, for instance, Biden won D.C. with 92 percent of the vote). After the 2016 election, I saw my loving, good-natured neighbors, trapped in rage-filled despair, turn. Stunned and trapped in a Trump presidency, the Democrats fed on unhinged hatred and vengeance. And it changed their nature, infecting them with a rageful psychosis. Hooked on the hate, they craved it, became addicted to it, and you could not talk to them about it. Like addicts, they would deny they had a problem, deflect, and project their sickness onto you. Question the blind hatred, and you were reflexively tossed into the Basket of Deplorables. Once in the basket, they could justify hating you, persecuting you, prosecuting you, and silencing you.

Early in the Trump administration, a neighbor's child was walking by when I was out working in the yard. He looked sad and I asked, "Hey buddy, why you looking so glum?" He shrugged his shoulders, shook his head, and dejectedly chortled, "*Trump.*" This was a child, mind you. So complete was his parents' psychosis that they infected their own child with their hatred. During Trump's presidency, a seven-year-old in my area, for her birthday, wanted to have an *impeachment party*. A seven-year-old. Her parents were so proud. The *Washington Post* of course ran a story on what ended up being a birthday party positive protest with a march around the White House. You see, the child's "dream protest" was to be able to chant things like "Ho, ho! Donald Trump has got to go!" but her mother was a federal worker and feared she would be fired if her child's birthday party was impeachment themed. A justifiable fear. *Munch munch munch.* So, the mother "begged" the child "to change her mind." There are so many things wrong with that story I don't know where to start. *That child*, I thought unkindly, *might be better off being raised by raccoons.* Not the rabid ones. She already had that.

My neighbors still believe in Russia Collusion HoaxCoup, even though a team of experienced crusaders with warrants, subpoena power, and a blank check could not prove any of it and disproved any part of it that could be investigated. After the Mueller report was released and it turned out that the Russia collusion story was indeed just a hoax, a neighbor, who was a lawyer, told me that even though Mueller's team could not find any evidence of collusion he just knew—*he just knew*—that Trump had colluded with Russia. I asked him, jokingly, where the "I just know" standard fell on the burden of proof scale. Below preponderance of the evidence or somewhere between preponderance and reasonable doubt? He did not appreciate my humor, and from that day forward, cowered from the topic.

Shocked and angry were my neighbors, before the 2020 presidential election, because Trump was *stealing mailboxes* so voters could not mail in ballots. Oh yes, they ate it up. *Chomp chomp.* Because it came from their party and their hate-filled propaganda outlets. No matter that mailboxes were simply being refurbished. No matter the refurbishing was under an Obama-era program. No matter truth. They had the sustenance needed to fill their bellies.

The hatred had no bounds. "Can you believe he is keeping kids in cages?" "Well, actually, no, Karen, I can't: that photograph is from the

Obama administration." "Oh, really? Not according to *The View*. You're just a MAGA Trumpkin!"

Having subscribed to the *Washington Post* for many years, I canceled the paper when I noticed the Food section was running articles criticizing Trump. "For some people, what's coming out of Donald Trump's mouth is downright scary. Almost as frightening, at least to those of us who see the stomach as a window to the soul, is what is going in." "Flavor and nutrition appear to be afterthoughts," wrote the *Post* food critic, Tom Sietsema, who added that if Trump "eats anything cruciferous, it's a mystery, right up there with how he combs that hair." Pandering to the elitist progressive base, Sietsema added that Trump's "eating habits, no doubt, are bound to endear him to certain voters." You know the ones, *wink wink*. This, I remind you, is the *Food section*. How appropriate. *Munch munch munch*. The hatred had no bounds, but at least I was no longer subsidizing it.

Throughout Trump's presidency, my neighbors whined about political discourse degrading across the country, blaming Trump and anyone who would not, while psychotically unaware that they were the ones frothing at the mouth with unhinged rage. My neighbors were adamant that Trump was unfit for office because he walked slowly down a wet metal ramp with no guardrails. "Did you see it!?! *How can he be president!?*" Conversely, they saw no problems with President Biden (at least not until the first 2024 presidential debate) when he could not remember the names of his own cabinet members, needed a three-by-five card to tell him to sit in *his* chair, and was shuffling around the White House like Tim Conway's character Mr. Toddleberry from *The Carol Burnett Show*.

When I asked one of my neighbors what he thought about the Biden administration's disastrous withdrawal from Afghanistan, he told me that he considered it unpatriotic to criticize the president at a time of crises. "I am surprised to hear you say that," I chided. "You never ran out of criticism for the previous president, which you claimed was four years of crisis." He didn't talk to me anymore. Another neighbor stopped me one day as I was walking to my car, as he was anxious to discuss the weighty topic of Trump appearing at a golf course without golf clubs. It was some kind of sign, he was certain, like the seas boiling, or a locust plague. CNN told him so. *Munch munch.* All they eat is hate.

Special Counsel Smith's forty-felony-count indictment against Trump had my neighbors quite excited. For the few who were willing to discuss it with me, I approached it like a chess game, and it was always the same game.

First, I'd push a few pawns: "Do you see any problems with DOJ's stark departure from how similar cases have been handled?" The response would always be the dreaded Ostrich Defense: "Well, I don't know about those cases, so I can't comment on them." So I would penetrate the defense with a knight: "Let me give you the relevant facts from the precedents, which coincidentally all involved high-ranking Democrats." Having told them what they didn't want to hear, I would ask again for their opinion. (As you can imagine, this made me very popular in the neighborhood.) Then they would deploy more firepower and bust out a rook: "Well, maybe those historical cases were not handled correctly, but that doesn't mean the law should not be applied to Trump. This is America, and in America . . .". Snatching the rook, I would threaten their king: "If precedents don't matter and the law is to be applied blindly, what about Biden's case?" Then I would lay out the relevant facts of Biden's case. Their faces would contort like they just smelled a fart. Backs to the wall, they'd be forced to break out the queen: "But Biden did the right thing and *cooperated with the process*."

Then I would trap the queen: "But *the process* was biased and not even close to normal. Also, do you think if a murderer cooperates with a murder investigation, it exonerates the murderer?" They really wouldn't be prepared for that move. Which surprises me. It is an obvious move, and obvious moves have known counters. But when you only play in a friendly echo chamber you don't need to worry about defending your positions. Well, meet Big Blue. At this point, the psychosis they'd be trying to hide behind a veneer of faux logic could no longer be contained, and they'd scatter the pieces across the board: "Well, maybe it's not completely fair, *but this is Trump!* You don't get it because you are an Ultra MAGA Trumpkin! Haha! We should change the topic. I hear it's going to rain tomorrow."

"Yes, storm coming." Checkmate, by the way.

Not long ago, I ran into a former DOJ lawyer, whom I had worked with quite a bit when I was practicing. A great lawyer and wonderful person, and we chatted for a long time about our lives in retirement. When the topic turned to the Trump prosecution, I got the "no one is above the law" speech. So, I pointed to all the facts that showed Biden's far worse malfeasance in mishandling classified information, at which point I got a shoulder shrug and an unexpected response: "Yeah, but don't you think they all do it?" Within seconds we went from "no one is above the law" to justify prosecuting Trump, to "no one should be prosecuted for it because they all do it" to justify *not prosecuting* Biden. I gave up.

Some of my neighbors not long ago were out on their front lawns, banging pots and pans with wooden spoons. Out on my porch, enjoying a coffee, I immediately knew that the verdict had been announced in the trumped-up New York Trump prosecution, and I knew the verdict was guilty, as I had not been treated to the wood on pan cacophony since the results of the 2020 election were announced.

My neighbors are of course ecstatic over the verdict—because, you know, the law in America should be applied equally and all—but they become very uneasy when I ask them about the sentencing. Every Democrat I have spoken to about the sentence gets very uneasy and quickly emphasizes that there should not be jail time. Oh no—no jail time. Just heavy fines and probation. So, I ask them how they could justify not wanting jail time for someone who has been found guilty of thirty-four felonies, in response to which they hem and haw, because they realize they have been exposed: not wanting jail time for someone convicted of thirty-four felonies shows the political motivation behind the whole farce. For they needed to label Trump a felon to influence the election, but jail time would risk turning him into a martyr.

There are a few moderate Democrats I know, and some will still talk politics with me. When I engage with them on any one of the litany of examples showing the Democratic party's weaponization of America's justice system, they won't deny it, but will immediately give me the exasperated, "Yeah, unfortunately there is a lot of that going around on both sides of the aisle" deflection. I used to just let it go. Now I provide them with specific examples from their side of the aisle, and I ask them for what commensurate examples they have from the conservative side. They uncomfortably hem and haw, and then quickly change the topic. This, as you can imagine, makes me very popular. No wonder I drink alone.

Every presidential election, I hang the stars and stripes from my porch. Regardless of the election's outcome, I celebrate living in a nation where the citizenry selects who will govern. It took quite a bit of research, but I found a flag that was not made in China and not made of nylon. My flag is made in America. From cotton. Having gone to all that trouble, I was not going to hang my flag on any old pole, but a suitable pole was not to be found. So, I bought a sturdy piece of wood, sanded, stained, polyeurathaned, and attached brass hardware. On a side note, burn my flag, and you will learn that there really is a difference between speech and conduct. Anyway, on the morning of the 2020 presidential election, one of my neighbors was walking by as I was hanging my flag. Loudly, and proudly, she proclaimed that she was not going to hang her flag unless Joe Biden won the election. Welcome to my neighborhood. It is like *Mr. Rogers' Neighborhood*, except instead of a sweater and slippers, you put on hatred and hubris.

And that is how a former president can be targeted with blatantly political persecutions, thinly veiled as prosecutions, while half the country supports the injustices and hungers for more. Good people, overcome with hatred, compounded by hubris, and made to believe absurdities, are driven to crave the taste of tyranny.

CHAPTER 14

American Values to Venerate

American history has many examples of times when raging political passions were building to an all-consuming wildfire that could have permanently scorched the nation, but principled citizens intervened, at great personal risk, to tamp the rage back down to a warming fire. For guidance and inspiration, let us examine a few of these events.

In 1770, the entire city of Boston consisted of only about 16,000 British colonists. That number did not include the 2,000 British soldiers garrisoned in the city, whose mission was to ensure that those 16,000 increasingly unruly colonists paid their taxes.

Boston's atmosphere was becoming increasingly tense, as colonists loyal to the British monarch clashed with a growing number who were considerably less so. Altercations between the different minded were becoming more frequent and more violent. Those generally opposed to British rule—and specifically opposed to paying British taxes—were acting out in various ways, including vandalizing loyalist shops selling British goods. One incident resulted in a child being shot and killed by a British customs officer. The rising tensions came to a crescendo on a cold snowy night in March 1770, when a lone British sentry at a Customs House was assaulted by a rowdy mob of colonists. British reinforcements arrived, but it was only a small squad and the violence escalated as the mob pelted the soldiers with snowballs, ice chunks, and oyster shells and assaulted the soldiers with clubs. Amid the malaise, the British troops panicked and opened fire. Five of the rioters were killed.

Prominent patriots like John Hancock and Samuel Adams used the tragedy to foment greater anti-British sentiment through their writings. Paul Revere published an infamous engraving depicting the British soldiers as crazed murderers and the rioters as mostly peaceful protesters. Good examples of successful early American propaganda.

Arrested on murder charges, the British soldiers were facing the death penalty in a colonial Boston courtroom. Local opinion was so poisoned against the soldiers that the lead defense attorney convinced the trial judge to seat jurors from outside Boston. That defense attorney was John Adams, one of the Founding Fathers of our country and a future president. Adams was a patriot and was just as opposed to tyranny as men like John Hancock and Paul Revere, but despite his political leanings, Adams was more concerned with justice. Fearing that the anti-British fervor in Boston would lead to the criminal justice system being used to mete out vengeance, causing irrevocable damage to the colonial justice system, Adams and his co-counsels risked their livelihoods and reputations to defend the most hated men in all of Boston.

At trial, Adams and the defense team showed that chaos and confusion reigned during the riot, and that the British soldiers, fearing for their lives, had panicked. All the soldiers were found not guilty of murder. Two were convicted of manslaughter, and, in an odd custom of the time, were branded on the thumbs! It speaks well for the colonists of Boston that they begrudgingly accepted the unpopular verdicts and, in time, came to hold no lasting ambivalence against the defense lawyers. But it took time. On the three-year anniversary of the riot, Adams wrote in his diary that representing the British soldiers was "the most exhausting and fatiguing Causes I ever tried: for hazarding a Popularity very generally and very hardly earned: and for incurring a Clamour and popular Suspicions and prejudices that are not yet worn out." Adams added that the representation was "one of the best Pieces of Service I ever rendered my Country."

Perhaps the most historic riot in U.S. history, "the Boston Massacre" is remembered as a catalyst for anti-British sentiment and a notable steppingstone on the path to Revolutionary War. It should also be remembered for the courage of the principled individuals who risked their reputations and livelihoods to defend the despised targets of political rage, out of commitment to a higher cause: fairness and justice.

In the late 1970s, when I was just a child, the National Socialist Party of America (a neo-Nazi group) applied for a permit to demonstrate in a Skokie, Illinois, public park. A particularly devious request, by some very evil people, as Skokie did not just have a large Jewish population: it reportedly had the highest number of Holocaust survivors outside of Israel. Although just a child, I remember this historic event not because Nazi's wanted to parade, and not because the local council predictably denied the permit. I remember this incident because of the lawyer who zealously represented the Nazis and took their case all the way to the Supreme Court. That lawyer was David Goldberger, regional director for the American Civil Liberties Union (ACLU) and a member of the very race the Nazi's were advocating to eradicate.

Even as a child, I understood the importance of Goldberger's actions, and it made me proud to be American. It made me proud to be in a country where the constitutional right to free speech was so valued that a Jewish lawyer would defend the right to express anti-Jewish bigotry and hatred. Goldberger was denounced by many in his community and repeatedly attacked for being a traitorous jew. Even a rabbi at his parent's synagogue excoriated him during a service at a local synagogue. ACLU board members resigned, as did many members (some estimates were up to 50,000). Through it all, Goldberger remained true to his moral compass, which pointed him directly at any government attempting to decide what speech was acceptable. He had the foresight to see through the justifiable rage gripping the community; to see that Nazi's were not the real issue; to see that, no matter the cost, his role was to prevent "the erosion of the First Amendment as a bulwark against rule by tyrants." For a government that could censor Nazi's could also censor "the press from publishing embarrassing facts and criticism." I honored David Goldberger for his sacrifice and dedication, which were intuitively obvious to me, even as a child.

Fifty years later, reflecting on the Skokie case, Goldberger noted that after the "pain and anger" had subsided, the residents of Skokie channeled their energy into positive action: they built the Illinois Holocaust Museum, "to ensure that the damage done by the Holocaust will never be forgotten." Three seconds into checking out the website for this museum, I broke down crying. And I am a hard-ass former infantry officer.

One last example, which is particularly apt as it involved the Espionage Act, is the prosecution of the Soviet spy Rudolf Abel. Abel was a colonel in Soviet intelligence who was sent to the United States in 1948 to run a network of Soviet spies. Julius and Ethel Rosenberg, the American citizens caught stealing nuclear secrets for Russia and executed in 1953, were among the spies reporting to Abel. Abel's alias was Emil Goldfus, and his cover was that of an artist in Brooklyn who specialized in painting and photography. Goldfus was also an amateur shortwave radio operator (and may have also dabbled in butter churning). The cover was smartly designed, as it gave Abel plausible explanations for possessing spy equipment. Abel was reported to federal authorities in 1957 by a Soviet defector and was arrested soon after.

Abel's arrest was at an especially contentious time in U.S.–Soviet relations. The Cold War was not just chilly, it had dropped well below freezing. Given the unpopularity of the Soviet Union—America's greatest adversary and viewed as animated by world conquest—finding a suitable defense counsel was proving difficult, and the Brooklyn Bar Association became involved in the search. Eventually a bar committee decided to ask

James B. Donovan to represent Abel. Donovan was a senior partner in a New York law firm and had served as a navy lawyer in World War II, during which time he was the general counsel for the Office of Strategic Services (OSS). The OSS was America's spy agency during WWII, and the predecessor to the CIA. So, Donovan knew the spy business. On a side note, James Donovan was not related to the U.S. Army general who ran the OSS, William "Wild Bill" Donovan, who, after the war, also became the first director of the CIA.

Upon agreeing to represent Abel, and with Abel's permission, Donovan started a diary that, years later, became a book detailing Donovan's experiences representing Abel. Which means we have a unique historical account—a detailed firsthand account—of a lawyer who went from being the top lawyer for America's spies to being the defense attorney for the top spy of America's greatest adversary. Donovan's book recounted some of the harassment he and his family endured due to his representation, including "everything from open hostility to so-called banter, some good-natured and the rest not so well intentioned." Particularly poignant, for me, was Donovan's telling of how the Brooklyn Bar had framed its request for him to represent Abel: "Jim, our committee feels very strongly that American justice, along with the Soviet colonel, will be on trial."

Despite Donovan's zealous defense of Abel, the strong evidence of Abel's guilt prevailed, and Abel was found guilty and sentenced to thirty years in prison. Abel could have received the death penalty under the Espionage Act, but Donovan made a persuasive argument to the judge that Abel's life could be useful if an American spy was ever captured by the Soviets, given that Abel, if alive, could be traded. That argument was prophetic. For three years into Abel's sentence, the pilot of an American spy plane, Francis Gary Powers, was shot down over Russia and captured. Abel was subsequently traded for Powers and another American, in what I believe was the first spy swap in U.S. history. The swap was orchestrated by Donovan, who had been authorized to represent the United States in the negotiations. Donovan's book, *Strangers on a Bridge: The Case of*

Colonel Abel and Francis Gary Powers, chronicled details of the swap along with Donovan's representation of Abel. Donovan dedicated his book to "those among the American bar who defend the weak, the poor, and the unpopular."

In 2015, Steven Spielberg directed a movie, *Bridge of Spies*, apparently based on Donovan's book. Tom Hanks played Donovan and Mark Rylance (who won an Academy Award for Best Supporting Actor) played Abel. The movie is wonderful, but for one major flaw: it never provides the audience with Donovan's highly relevant background as the general counsel for the OSS. If you only watched the movie, you would think Donovan was just a high-priced insurance lawyer from New York. After the movie's success, Donovan's book was re-released and in the forward by Jason Matthews (a former covert CIA operations officer who became a renowned spy novelist), Matthews succinctly summed up Donovan's conduct as "the ultimate act of patriotism" and "an affirmation of the American rule of law, and fairness, and justice."

American history has many such examples, where brave citizens assumed substantial risk to defend unpopular people and views, out of commitment to fairness and justice and to prevent lasting damage to their communities and country. History has not given them their due. And sadly, the heroic actions of men like John Adams, David Goldberger, and James Donovan could not likely happen today. Our current political climate would not tolerate it, and that is a sign that we are not healthy. Can you imagine the ACLU representing Donald Trump, no matter how grievous the constitutional deprivation?

CHAPTER 15

Reinforcing Our Edifice

Our national unity—"the main pillar of our independence"—has been steadily eroding from the "baneful effects" of political party passions. The Biden administration's unprecedented use of force and novel indictments against its greatest political rival are just the latest and greatest fractures in a steadily decaying foundation. While not beyond repair, the growing cracks in our national unity are not going to fix themselves. We need to roll up our sleeves, mix some mortar, and get busy patching.

For starters, we can all temper our own rhetoric (I am just as guilty at times, try as I may), and we can stop mindlessly ingesting and regurgitating whatever talking points are slopped onto our plates. And lay off the rat. Disagreement is healthy; hatred is not.

Five days before the assassination attempt against Trump, President Biden told a group of supporters that it was "time to put Trump in a bull's-eye." Most media outlets either ignored the statement or mentioned it in the context of those angry violent Republicans "pouncing" on harmless campaign rhetoric. It is true that, when fighting rageful rhetoric, one must be careful not to respond in kind. Do I think Biden intended a sniper to put an actual bull's-eye on Trump? No. But I also consider it completely inappropriate for the leader of the free world to be using such extreme symbolism. The bulk of the media and Biden's party (not that there is a difference anymore) ignored Biden's comments or just turned them around to criticize the Republican party for reacting to them, but such language needs to be denounced. Calmly, and dispassionately, but firmly denounced, as unhealthy, unwise, and *unpresidential.*

At most, if you must, view the un-like-minded as misguided children. As an infantry officer, a leadership tactic I used when a soldier was not getting along well in the unit was to catch them doing something well and praise them in front of the platoon. This often boosted morale and built positive common bonds. Maybe we could all try that. Find a topic on which you can agree with someone you would normally not and would normally criticize. Find common ground—somewhere, anywhere—even if not political. Tell them their dog is cute. Work out from there.

If we are going to vilify anyone, it should be those who attempt to silence our voices or censor our speech. Those are the voices we should identify and revile—regardless of party affiliation or ideology—for they are the true threat to liberty. My experience is that censoring speech and silencing opposing views is almost exclusively the domain of the Left, but depending on where you live, your experiences may be different. No matter the source, the remedy for bad ideas must be more speech, not less. Sounds like something we could all agree on, but college polls show a significant percentage of students are in favor of the government censoring speech they don't like. If that does not scare you, you are part of the problem. If that does not scare you, go have a debate with a free-speech advocate. See who wins.

Back when Benjamin Franklin was a printer in Pennsylvania, he was criticized at times for publishing unpopular views or printing items for unpopular people. In defense of his unrestricted printing policies,

Franklin offered some timely wisdom. "If what is thus publish'd be good, Mankind has the Benefit of it. If it be bad . . . the more 'tis made publick, the more its Weakness is expos'd, and the greater Disgrace falls upon the Author." On one occasion, after publishing an unpopular advertisement, local clergy threatened to boycott Franklin's print shop (colonial-era cancel culture). Franklin, however, owned a printing press, had courage and wit, and was unwavering in his dedication to free speech. Instead of bowing to pressure to censor unpopular views, Franklin published a humorous and thoughtful "standing Apology" to "all who are angry with me on the Account of printing things they don't like." Franklin's standing apology contained a list of particulars, including that it was "unreasonable in any one Man or Set of Men to expect to be pleas'd with everything that is printed, as to think that nobody ought to be pleas'd but themselves" and included that "if all Printers were determin'd not to print anything till they were sure it would offend nobody, there would be very little printed." Universities should consider adding some modern-day Benjamin Franklins to their faculties.

Last year, I was enjoying a drink at the Old Ebbitt Grill, chatting with a vacationing pharmacist from Wyoming. His family had just visited Congress and the National Archives, and he related to me what impressed him the most from the recent trek through our founding era: how much the architects of our political system valued debate. Open, vigorous, respectful debate. We both lamented that our electorate and our representatives in Congress rarely engage in civil debate or discourse anymore. To maturely discuss issues facing our country, we need to talk to each other, to listen, to be open to modifying even the most strongly held positions. We need to debate with open minds instead of just hurling talking points at each other like primates. So, debate. Debate openly and forcefully. And be leery of anyone who expresses strong opinions but won't debate or defend them. Attack opinions you don't agree with, but not the person voicing them, unless that person is trying to stifle free speech. That form of villainy, no matter the motivation or source, should be given no quarter.

Besides tempering our rhetoric, challenging our party histrionics, calling out those who would censor speech, and encouraging debate, there are important structural changes our government can implement to shore up our foundation. Specifically, the government can install safeguards to prevent any ruling party from ever again appropriating law enforcement and intelligence-gathering mechanisms to seek political vengeance or retain power.

After the terrorist attacks of 9/11, there was much debate as to whether and how the U.S. government should reform its approach to domestic intelligence gathering. Various options were considered, from maintaining the status quo to creating an entirely new organization for domestic intelligence gathering (which is the model followed in the United Kingdom). After much deliberation, the FBI was given the domestic intelligence mission. While the FBI already had a counterintelligence mission, it focused on surveilling and building criminal cases against foreign spies. Giving the FBI the entire domestic intelligence mission was a massive increase in power, and history has now shown that it was a mistake: combining domestic law enforcement and domestic intelligence puts too much power in one place, and the result, inevitably, is tyranny. Basically, we created our own Stasi. For proof, one need look no further than the FBI's and DOJ's unlawful targeting of the 2016 Trump campaign, Trump's national security advisor, and Donald Trump himself—before, during, and after his presidency.

I want to reiterate that the FBI has many good people. But they are human, and humans, when given the chance, will abuse power. Especially in pursuit of ends they deem virtuous. President Washington, in his Farewell Address, presciently commented on the "love of power and proneness to abuse it which predominates in the human heart." He emphasized that "the exercise of political power" should be checked by "dividing and distributing it into different depositories." We failed to follow his wise counsel when we merged law enforcement with domestic intelligence. This error needs to be fixed.

In *Strangers on a Bridge*, James Donovan related that toward the end of World War II, President Roosevelt tasked the OSS Commander General "Wild Bill" Donovan to draft a plan for a post-war central intelligence agency, given that the OSS would be disbanded after the war. General Donovan turned to his top lawyer, James Donovan, for assistance, and in doing so, provided some insightful policy guidance:

> When General Donovan directed me, as his general counsel, to draft such a plan, he repeatedly stressed the necessary differences between secret intelligence and counterintelligence on an international level and the constitutional bounds of domestic law enforcement within the United States. He believed that any attempted unification of such powers in a single government agency would be dangerous in a democracy, since the temptation to "efficient" methods of investigation inevitably leads to creating a Gestapo.

Expanding the FBI's authority to include domestic intelligence is the exact kind of "unification" that General Donovan wisely counseled against. It is not too late to undo our error. Splitting federal law enforcement and domestic intelligence-gathering will also increase the efficiency of these two distinctly different missions. Intelligence gathering and law enforcement rely on different legal authorities and require different skill sets, mindsets, training, and tools. Given the disparate disciplines, bifurcating those missions would enable both to function more efficiently. It will take time, effort, resources, and strong leadership, but a separate domestic intelligence agency should be created, and it should report to the director of national intelligence, not the FBI director or the attorney general (AG).

If the FBI's focus is redirected to where it should be—exclusively to law enforcement—that focus should include reform within the FBI's law enforcement culture. Changing culture within any organization is a very difficult task, but history has now proven that reform is necessary, and we must meet the challenge. Reform is best when driven by those who have risen through the ranks, understand the strengths and weaknesses of the organization, and are committed to bringing about necessary changes. Whoever accepts this challenge will need the authority and support to eliminate those aspects of the culture that permit, up to the highest levels, political bias, self-serving leaks, and ends-justifies-the-means conduct. We don't need to throw the baby out with the bathwater, but the water has sufficient contaminants that it merits changing, and we cannot shy away from the difficult task.

During Jim Comey's tenure as FBI director, he was a guest speaker at a function I attended. He was charismatic and a wonderful speaker. The thing I remember most about his lecture was how he described culture within an organization. Comey compared the driving habits of people in a small town, where everyone is polite and respectful because everyone knows each other, to the driving habits of people living in a large city like Boston, where he had lived. "The technical rules of the road are the same," he said, "but the culture is different—if you use a blinker before you change lanes in Boston, it will be immediately perceived as a sign of weakness, not courtesy, and if you keep a respectful distance from the car in front of you in Boston, the driver behind you has already claimed ownership of that space and will soon take it from you." I wonder if Comey has ever thought about the impact his actions, and the actions of many senior FBI officers during his tenure, had on the culture of the FBI. Because, as has now been thoroughly documented, it was not positive.

Strong law enforcement is necessary. Cops must have the appropriate training, equipment, and community support to effectively police our streets in a manner that protects law abiding citizens and themselves. But we must recognize the concomitant threat strong law enforcement poses to liberty and institute commensurate oversight mechanisms.

In the colonial era and the early days of our Republic, the greatest threat to liberty was the blunt force of musket and bayonet from a king's standing army. Washington noted this in his Farewell Address and warned that "overgrown military establishments" were generally "inauspicious to liberty" and "particularly hostile to republican liberty." Our nation's historical fear of a standing army led to passage of the Posse Comitatus Act in 1878, which generally banned using the military for domestic law enforcement. However, that law does not prevent law enforcement from adopting military tactics and equipment, which is what has happened. Modern American law enforcement has become so militarized that police raiding the home of an elderly man with no priors are nearly indistinguishable from the SEALs who took out Osama bin Laden in Pakistan. I am not advocating against the police being properly equipped or trained. Cops sometimes go up against heavily armed criminals, and they should never be at a tactical disadvantage. I am, however, advocating for greater oversight of law enforcement—because the greatest domestic threat to liberty today carries a badge, not a bayonet.

Lest you think I'm exaggerating the need for oversight of domestic law enforcement, read the DOJ IG reports that reviewed FBI conduct in relatively recent major FBI investigations. The 2019 DOJ IG report criticizing FBI FISA abuses and DOJ's unlawful targeting of Trump's 2016 presidential campaign would be a good start. Among other things, it discovered seventeen significant mistakes in the FBI's FISA applications targeting the Trump campaign:

> That so many basic and fundamental errors were made on four FISA applications by three separate, hand-picked teams, on one of the most sensitive FBI investigations that was briefed to the highest levels within the FBI, and that FBI officials expected would eventually be subjected to close scrutiny, raised significant questions regarding the FBI chain of command's management and supervision of the FISA process.

Another good example of the need for greater law enforcement oversight is DOJ's targeting of House and Senate Oversight Committee staffers. Yes, that really happened. Recently. When Congress was investigating DOJ and the FBI for their participation in Russia Collusion HoaxCoup (i.e., exercising legitimate oversight authorities), DOJ and the FBI did not take kindly to being investigated. As unbelievable as this may be, federal law enforcement struck back by subpoenaing phone and email logs of the congressional staffers supporting the oversight investigation. Beyond mere poor judgement, this type of conduct shows how far the law enforcement train has careened off the rails. And into the abyss.

Recent history has shown that the existing oversight mechanisms for the FBI and DOJ are insufficient. Oversight is not an area where I have much experience, having never worked in an IG office or served on a congressional oversight committee, so determining how to institute more effective oversight is beyond my expertise. But I know enough about bureaucracies to know how to spot a good oversight scheme when it is proposed: the FBI will fight it. Any oversight proposals that the FBI readily agrees to will share one commonality: fecklessness. As for DOJ, current events have shown that political bias saturates DOJ's decision-making in highly political cases. DOJ's recent targeting of Donald Trump is the perfect example, as Biden's DOJ has acted like the medieval knights of King Henry II, ridding the king of his turbulent rival. The only difference is that DOJ used subpoenas instead of swords. If you need further proof, examine again the DOJ's conduct in the most political cases, including completely different approaches in the appointment of special counsel, stark disparities in charging decisions, significant deviations from typical investigative strategies, and the biased use and structuring of plea agreements.

Decisions concerning whether to appoint a special counsel need to remain with the AG, but the AG does not need to select who will be appointed special counsel. That decision carries the greatest risk of political bias, and there are viable solutions to minimize that risk. A bipartisan panel or commission could be established to pick special counsels, or there could be a pre-selected list of potential special counsels, agreed on through a process involving both political parties, and then when the need arises a special counsel could be chosen at random from that list. Whether any of these ideas are viable will depend on how the higher courts rule in the ongoing litigation over the lawfulness of the AG appointing special counsel from outside government without express statutory authority. But regardless of the outcome of the litigation, a new process should be instituted for the selection of special counsel.

Eliminating all bias from DOJ charging decisions in cases involving senior government officials is likely an unattainable goal. However, comparing the cases of Deutch, Berger, Petraeus, Clinton, Biden, and Trump shows clearly that political bias exists, which means that possible remedies—imperfect though they may be—must be explored. A president could adopt, through executive order or DOJ regulations, a bipartisan approval process that a federal prosecutor would be required to follow before being permitted to indict officials in specific high-ranking positions. A special grand jury process could also be adopted for such senior elected officials. If the president fails to reform this area through executive action, Congress could explore legislative measures to mandate additional procedural safeguards before DOJ may indict such officials, current or former.

Plea bargaining has become the defining fixture of America's criminal justice system. Over 98 percent of federal criminal convictions are obtained through guilty pleas. Think about that. Though nowhere mentioned in the Constitution, plea bargaining has almost entirely supplanted constitutionally prescribed jury trials, along with the accompanying checks on prosecutorial abuse inherent in a transparent adjudicative process that culminates before a jury of your peers. To see the inequities, you need look no further than the cases we have discussed, but if you need more convincing, look at the novel and shameless plea agreement offered to President Biden's son Hunter by the Delaware U.S. Attorney's Office. Although plea bargaining has come to dominate the criminal justice system, no systemic oversight mechanism has evolved alongside it to regulate it and ensure unbiased implementation. To address bias and ensure consistency in federal plea bargaining, a new independent office should be created, with reporting responsibilities to both Congress and the AG and supervisory responsibility over all federal plea deals. Ensuring government-wide consistency, identifying cases of first impression, eliminating bias, and preventing coercion would be the core mission of such an office. As with any meaningful law enforcement reform, I guarantee you this: DOJ will hate this idea. A lot.

The Supreme Court's recent decision on presidential immunity will hopefully diminish politically driven prosecutions of former presidents, but that decision leaves much for the lower courts to decide and plenty of room for future political shenanigans. That being the case, Congress should consider legislation granting a form of immunity that will insulate former presidents and vice presidents from political persecutions masquerading as criminal prosecutions. Newton's Third Law is that every action has an equal and opposite reaction. In the army, we reduced this law of physics down to a base level: "payback is a medevac," and I believe both can be extended to American politics. Politically persecuting a former president will lead, inevitably, to the political persecution of the incumbent, or his successor, and so on. This cycle is not in anyone's interest. Except our enemies.

Reforming our institutions, laws, and practices will be futile if we do not start by reforming ourselves. Because our institutions reflect the body politic, they reflect us. If our Congress is dysfunctional, it is because we are dysfunctional. We elect those who reflect and effectuate our dysfunction. If our justice system is broken—and in highly politicized cases, it most assuredly is—it is because We the People are broken. If a fair and impartial jury cannot be found, then even the purest of justice systems will yield a corrupt outcome. In defending and downplaying his role as defense counsel for Rudolf Abel, James Donovan stated that "we advocates fight hard for our clients' causes but should have the humility to believe that it is our system of jurisprudence which produces just determinations," because "our common law system of justice provides an impartial judge and jury." But what if, because of our current political climate, an impartial judge and jury cannot be found? Whose fault is that but ours?

As a nation, we have come a long way and endured much. Our edifice has been badly shaken before, from without and from within, but always, eventually, we came together and continued building toward a better future. To fix the current damage, we must acknowledge the inherent weaknesses encoded into our DNA. We must practice the uniform vigilance George Washington implored us to adopt, so many years ago, to protect us from ourselves and to ensure that no reigning political party can ever again abuse our justice system to seek political vengeance or retain power. For starters, we need to address our own mental, emotional, and spiritual states and wean ourselves off the hatred and derision of our fellow citizens, which tends "to render alien to each other those who ought to be bound together by fraternal affection."

On the morning after her husband was shot, Melania Trump released a statement asking for Americans "to look beyond the left and the right, beyond the red and the blue" and expressing her hopes for a more peaceful future: "America, the fabric of our gentle nation is tattered, but our courage and common sense must ascend and bring us back together as one." The former first lady expressed no hatred, no anger, no violent rhetoric, no division. To the contrary, she asked her fellow citizens to "ascend above the hate, the vitriol, and the simple-minded ideas that ignite violence." With an open heart, she spoke directly and eloquently:

> We all want a world where respect is paramount, family is first, and love transcends. We can realize this world again. Each of us must demand to get it back. We must insist that respect fills the cornerstone of our relationships, again.

If we can achieve that first step—rejecting rageful rhetoric and political party histrionics and replacing them with mutual respect—the other steps will follow, naturally, as we work together toward achieving what we need to remain a great nation: an imperfect but universally acceptable path to a common and more prosperous future. One where the American justice system gets out of politics, stops acting as an enforcement arm of the Democratic party, and gets back into the business of fairness and justice.

Notes

1 *Department of the Navy v. Egan*, 484 U.S. 518 (1988) at 527.

2 *U.S. v. Snepp*, 444 U.S. 507 (1980).

3 *Free Enterprise Fund v. Public Company Accounting Oversight Bd.*, 561 U.S. 477 (2010) at 497, 498.

4 Prior to 9/11, the head of the CIA was also the head of the intelligence community, hence the title "director of central intelligence." After 9/11, the director of national intelligence (DNI) position was created. The head of the CIA was no longer the head of the intelligence community, and the title thus became "director of the CIA."

5 The only reason I can publicly acknowledge this group even existed is because the fact was declassified to support the prosecution of a CIA hacker who leaked classified information.

6 Shakespeare, William; *Measure for Measure*, Act 3, Scene 2, lines 261–262.

7 U.S. Constitution, Article III, Section 3.

8 *Armstrong v. Bush*, 924 F.2d 282 (D.C. Cir. 1991).

9 *Armstrong v. Bush*, 1 F.3d 1274 (D.C. Cir. 1993).

10 *Judicial Watch v. NARA*, 845 F.Supp.2d 288 (D.D.C. 2012).

11 To justify his retaining highly classified information, President Biden similarly blurred the distinction between a president and a vice president. Discussing his notebooks, Biden told Hur that "every president before me has done the same exact thing." But Biden was not a president. He was a vice president. And they are not the same.

12 Shakespeare, William; *Hamlet*, Act III, Scene II, line 253.

13 *Star Wars, Episode IV—A New Hope*, directed by George Lucas, Lucas Films, 1977, performance by Sir Alec Guinness.

14 *McDonnell v. U.S.*, 579 U.S. 550 (2016)

15 Shakespeare, William; *Hamlet*, Act I, Scene IV, line 90.

16 U.S. Constitution, Article II, Section 2, Clause 2.

17 *Trump v. United States*, 603 U.S. ____ (2024).

18 *Skyfall*, directed by Sam Mendes, Eon Productions, 2012, performance by Javier Bardem.

About the Author

Joseph B. Sweeney served in the CIA Office of General Counsel for twenty-five years in support of a broad spectrum of intelligence operations all over the world, including espionage and terrorism investigations and prosecutions.

His work has been recognized with a 1999 Public Service Award from the Eastern District of Virginia for his support of an espionage prosecution, a 2002 Attorney General's Award for his support of the Southern District of New York's prosecution of Osama bin Laden and others for bombing U.S. embassies in East Africa, a 2011 Intelligence Community Legal Award for his support of a spy swap, and a 2018 Assistant Attorney General Award for his support of the DOJ National Security Division.

He is a 1987 graduate of the United States Military Academy and served as an Airborne Ranger-qualified infantry officer for six years. After graduating law school in 1996, he was accepted into the CIA National Security Law Honors Program, and in 2012, he earned an LLM in national security law from Georgetown Law School.

Made in the USA
Las Vegas, NV
04 October 2024

bea481ea-affe-4194-ab56-629259a191d0R02